ROYAL PAPERS

ROYAL PAPERS

The Reign of Her Majesty Queen Elizabeth II Told through Newspaper Front Pages

INTRODUCTION BY NIGEL DEMPSTER

FRONT PAGES REPRODUCED FROM THE JOHN FROST HISTORIC NEWSPAPER SERVICE

Fontana

An Imprint of HarperCollinsPublishers

FONTANA
An Imprint of HarperCollins*Publishers*
77-85 FULHAM PALACE ROAD,
HAMMERSMITH, LONDON W6 8JB

A FONTANA ORIGINAL 1992
9 8 7 6 5 4 3 2 1

A CATALOGUE RECORD FOR THIS BOOK IS
AVAILABLE FROM THE BRITISH LIBRARY

ISBN 0 00 637763 7

PRINTED IN GREAT BRITAIN BY
THE BATH PRESS, AVON

PRODUCED FOR FONTANA BY
GLAZER AND POMFRET

COMPILED AND DESIGNED BY
STANLEY GLAZER

ROYAL PAPERS

TUESDAY February 5, 1952 was a crisp, sunny day, and King George VI, who had been with his family at Sandringham since Christmas, led a shooting party over the estate, bagging 280 hares. After dinner his younger daughter Princess Margaret played the piano for him while he struggled with a crossword. It was a comforting tableau after months of worry over the Monarch's health.

The previous year, on September 1, the royal physicians examined the King at Balmoral – being summoned from London by the Queen who was concerned that his condition showed no improvement after a summer dogged by illness, first diagnosed as flu and treated with penicillin. Two weeks after the examination he underwent a bronchoscopy and was informed that he was suffering from a bronchial tube blockage that would necessitate the removal of his left lung and certain nerves in his larynx, which might permanently affect his speech. On September 23, Clement Price Thomas, the leading chest surgeon, performed the operation in the Buhl Room at Buckingham Palace and discovered that the King's other lung was also affected. In fact he had cancer, and his doctors doubted he would live more than two years, but he was never told.

After losing 21lbs, he surprised his family by a quick recovery which allowed his heir, Princess Elizabeth, and the Duke of Edinburgh to make a thirty-five day tour of North America that had been temporarily postponed. The King's apparent return to health was celebrated in churches all over the country, with a day of National Thanksgiving on Sunday December 2, and the King spent his fifty-sixth birthday, on December 14, with his family at Buckingham Palace, travelling down with them to Sandringham a week later for Christmas 1951.

He had been invited by the Prime Minister of South Africa, Dr Malan, to recuperate at his official residence near Durban in Natal in warm sunshine, rather than suffer the British winter and it was arranged that the King and Queen would leave England on March 10. A tour of East Africa, Australia and New Zealand would be carried out on their behalf by Princess Elizabeth and the Duke.

On January 30, the eve of their departure, they went with the King and Queen to see *South Pacific* at the Drury Lane Theatre, with Princess Margaret and the King's Equerry and Deputy Master of the Royal Household Group Captain Peter Townsend making up the party. Next day, hatless in a chilling wind, the King waved goodbye forever at London airport to his elder daughter and returned to Sandringham for a week's rough shooting.

At the Royal Lodge at Nyeri, near Nairobi. Princess Elizabeth, reported *The Star* (price Three Halfpence) on Wednesday February 6, was given the news that her father had died quietly early that morning in his sleep 'Then she broke down and wept'.

This collection of front pages from a wide selection of newspapers ranging from Britain to Canada, North America and Australia, begins with Princess Elizabeth's accession (biographers tell us that she became The Monarch while watching animals from the vantage point of a hide above the ground. 'I went up a tree a Princess and came down a Queen!'). Now she celebrates forty years which have seen the Monarchy never more popular, with Britain the envy of the world. For that we owe the Queen heartfelt gratitude

ROYAL PAPERS

and admiration for four decades of selfless devotion to a daunting task.

It was not always thus: when the Duke of York (Bertie) took over the throne abdicated by his brother David, briefly King Edward VIII, the Monarchy had lost much of its popularity and was tainted with scandal. As Defender of the Faith and head of the Church of England, Edward had shown a sorry example to his future subjects by his infatuation with a divorcee; and his other weaknesses bode ill for the future. Surrounding the coronation of George VI in May 1937 was an underlying unease at the long-term future of the Monarchy.

But, thanks to the example of the King and Queen during the war when they refused to leave London, and their home, Buckingham Palace, was bombed by the Luftwaffe, this uncertainty had been largely dispelled. By the time Elizabeth became Queen (almost 350 years after the death of her namesake, and a half century after the death of Victoria) the *Yorkshire Herald* greeted the accession with the headline: A Queen Rules Again.

No front page photograph captured the funeral better than the *Daily Mirror*'s of February 12 with three Queens – Elizabeth II, the Queen Mother and Queen Mary – veiled in black standing at the entrance to Westminster Hall as the King's coffin was carried past.

But what kind of Monarch was Elizabeth going to be? The early years of her reign were celebrated by headlines and photographs of the set pieces of the pageant of being Head of State: Trooping the Colour (waving from the Buckingham Palace balcony, accompanied by Charles and Anne and the Duke) after opening Parliament and, a first,

seated in front of a microphone to broadcast her first Christmas message.

Her Coronation, in June 1953, was treated in time-honoured style with the *Daily Sketch* splashing a drawing of her dress, designed by Norman Hartnell (allowing only the headline EVEREST! to reveal, on the back page, the first news of the conquest of the world's highest mountain), and the *Evening Standard* bringing the first published photographs of the Queen in King Edward's Chair, faced by the Archbishop of Canterbury a moment after he placed the crown on her head and flanked by the Bishop of Durham and the Bishop of Bath and Wells.

The front pages did not neglect Princess Margaret and her tortuous romance with Group Captain Townsend. It had begun after the death of her father, and was reaching a climax that prompted the famous *Daily Mirror* headline of August 19, 1955: 'Come On Margaret!', with the plea at the bottom of the front page 'Please make up your mind!'. On November 1 the *Mirror* told the nation: 'Margaret decides: Duty Before Love' above the dramatic announcement that she had renounced Townsend.

As the Monarchy became ever more popular, a jarring note of Republicanism crept into the headlines. The *Daily Mirror*, on August 21 1957, splashed: 'Lord A Attacks Again', referring to Lord Altrincham (later to renounce his title to become plain Mr John Grigg). He had earlier that month hit the headlines when he criticised the Monarchy for: 'failing to move with the times', and called the Monarch 'priggish' and described her speaking voice as 'a pain in the neck'.

Family matters received equal prominence – a beaming Queen and Duke of Edinburgh graced the *Mirror* again under the headline:

ROYAL PAPERS

Only They Knew (with They underlined) after carrying the announcement that she had cancelled all engagements and was pregnant again (with the future Duke of York), nine years after the birth of Princess Anne.

Nor was there any shortage of visits – either to the Continent or the New World, or greeting President Eisenhower who came to lunch at Balmoral. In February 1957 the *Daily Mirror* captured the reunion of the Queen and Philip in Portugal at the end of his solo, four-month world tour, pointing out the heart motif on his tie. Two months later the Royal Couple were feted in Paris when a visit to a ballet in the Opera House drew a crowd of 50,000 chanting: 'We want the Queen.'

In October 1957 it was the turn of the United States with the *Mirror* proclaiming: 'Belle of New York', as 600,000 Americans gave her and the Duke a tickertape parade through Manhattan. It was the climax of their visit, and was not to be reciprocated until 1961 when Jackie Kennedy, whose husband John had been elected President the previous November, was welcomed to Buckingham Palace.

The start of the Sixties saw more family occasions and a heightening of intimacy in the Press treatment of the Royal Family. Gone was the deference which surrounded royal stories at the time of her accession and, while familiarity was not quite beginning to breed contempt, it was certainly producing a new critical slant. On February 9, 1960 the *Daily Mirror* devoted its front page to the decision by the Queen to change her surname.. It trumpeted: 'The Queen: A Curious Decision', adding 'Some of her descendants will be called Mountbatten-Windsor', adding in a front page Comment: 'The *Daily Mirror*

considers the Queen's decision will NOT be applauded by the British public'.

Only eleven days later the *Mirror*'s headline 'Oh Boy!' greeted the birth of Prince Andrew, but it was not until a month later that the first mother and baby pictures were released. Then it was the turn of Princess Margaret who had become engaged to slightly raffish Old Etonian photographer, Antony Armstrong-Jones. He was to be ennobled as the Earl of Snowdon after the May 6, 1960 marriage which was captured by that day's *Evening Standard*.

In February 1963, the Queen and Philip undertook a two-week tour of New Zealand followed by 37 days in Australia, with an estimated 3 million seeing her on television as she was greeted by Prime Minister, Bob Menzies, in Canberra. The royal couple were treated to an extensive itinerary, including barbecues in Alice Springs, racing in Melbourne, three days in remote Darwin, pearl fishing in Broome, a regatta in Hobart, Tasmania, and a grand finale in Perth.

The following year, in October 1964, it was the turn of Canada where signs of future problems were evident. *The Windsor Star* reported on its front page: 'Police Grab Agitators, Separatists Demonstrate as Queen Tours'. The French-speaking Quebec Libre (Free Quebec) faction was determined to get their message across although the Queen addressed the Quebec Legislature, outside which the scuffles took place, in fluent French.

Back on the family front, the Duke of Windsor was not neglected. In inimitable style the *New York Daily News* of March 16, 1965, captures the first meeting of the Queen with the Duchess of Windsor, headlined: 'Queen Meets Wally – At Last'. The

The sixties saw a heightening of intimacy in the Press treatment of the Royal Family

600,000 Americans gave the Queen and the Duke a tickertape parade through Manhattan

ROYAL PAPERS

two women were introduced at the bedside of the ailing former King Edward at the London Clinic.

On the political front, the Queen, states the *Evening Standard* of November 11, 1965, suspends rebel Rhodesian premier Ian Smith when he declares UDI, four years after neighbouring South Africa left the Commonwealth. On a State Visit to Germany in the same year, the Queen was photographed at the Berlin Wall after telling 58 million Germans that they and Britons now had a common cause after two world wars.

The first twenty years end with a problem that is to become a recurring theme in the second two decades of the Queen's reign: her money. On June 4, 1971 the *Daily Mirror*, in a Page One comment, says that four out of five readers believe she is being paid enough. Later in the year, it gives equal prominence to attacks on Princess Margaret and her Civil List payments by left wing MP, Willie Hamilton, who had called her: 'This expensive kept woman.'

Now the familiarity that had been spawned a decade earlier was breeding contempt. Much of it was aimed at the unfortunate Princess Margaret, whose marriage had been unconventional and was already in difficulties and, curiously, the Queen Mother – both soft targets as newspaper editors (and proprietors) realised that any condemnation of the Queen would have been self-defeating.

Therefore the easiest way to attack the Monarchy was from the sides. On December 16, 1971 the *Daily Mirror* devoted its front page to a letter to the Monarchy, headlined: 'Dear Queen . . .' counselling her not to be upset at the continued attacks on her sister and mother by Willie Hamilton (who represented a dour Scottish mining constituency with rising unemployment). In fact their front

page served only to repeat Mr Hamilton's jibes – an old journalistic device.

The Seventies and Eighties are more familiar territory for our memories: Princess Anne's wedding to Captain Mark Phillips: the Queen and Philip's 25th wedding anniversary (captured by a new royal photographer, the Earl of Lichfield) and the Queen Mother's 75th birthday when, arm in arm with the Prince of Wales, she is photographed by another new royal snapper, the late Peter Sellers!

The Queen's 50th birthday was celebrated in typically ebullient style by the *Daily Mirror* with a front page greeting: 'From the Mirror's 12,500,000 readers' above pictures of her taken in 1947 and shortly before her half century.

For the first time she herself became embroiled in controversy when, in September 1976, she joined the protest over plans to make a film about the sex life of Jesus Christ. *The Mirror* summed it up in a one word headline attributed to her: OBNOXIOUS! As head of the Church of England and Defender of the Faith, it was a relevant comment.

The Queen's peripheral involvement in politics occupied headlines in March 1977 when *The Sun*, owned by Australian-born, Oxford-educated Rupert Murdoch, reported that she was publicly insulted by former Premier Gough Whitlam (who had been ousted by the Governor-General) after she opened Parliament. The headline was: 'Queen of Sheba Jibe – Sacked Australian Premier in shock at Royal party'. Whitlam, now the smarting Leader of the Opposition, told her and 1,200 guests that it had been proposed that she would become Queen of the Solomon Islands in a new constitutional move and: 'What next, Queen of Sheba?'

ROYAL PAPERS

The following month royal finances were again the order of the day. The *Evening Standard* reported: 'The Royal Shares Start Row', a reference to the continuing 'controversy' that the Queen's personal investments in British companies should not be open to scrutiny.

And in May 1977 the *Daily Express* headlined: 'The Queen's amazing plea' with MY UNITED KINGDOM reporting how she had revealed her long-held anxiety that her Kingdom may have been splitting up through devolution. Later that year there were more joyous times, with her Jubilee in June – an occasion rejoiced in by the *Daily Mail* with a smiling Monarch outside St Paul's Cathedral and the headline: 'Is Everybody Happy? I am!'

Much of her happiness centres on her private relaxation of racing, both as a bloodstock breeder and successful owner, and the *Mirror* front page, following Derby Day at Epsom in June 1978, says it all. The picture has the Queen, binoculars in left hand, thumping the air with her other arm, watched by her racing manager Lord Porchester, as they witness a nail-biting finish (in which none of her horses was involved). But there were less happy memories of 1979, with the murder of Earl Mountbatten on August Bank Holiday.

The Eighties began with more joy: the celebrations for the Queen Mother's 80th birthday were all but eclipsed the following month, September, when Lady Diana Spencer was revealed as the new girl in the life of the Prince of Wales in a front page photograph, showing the future Princess in a see-through skirt. In October 1980, the Queen's own fashion sense occupied the front page of *The Sun* as, dressed in black velvet from head to toe, she met the head of the Church of

Rome, Pope John-Paul II. The headline: 'Black Magic'.

And weeks before the July 1981 wedding of Charles to Lady Diana, the *Sunday Mirror* captures 'the awful moment' when six shots rang out as the Queen was in The Mall on horseback en route to the start of Trooping the Colour (the shots turned out to be blanks and a 17-year-old was arrested).

The most dramatic story of the '80s concerned the intruder who made his way into the Queen's private apartments at Buckingham Palace. *The Sun*, on July 12 1982, put the incident in focus with the headline: 'Queen Spoke To Prowler At Her Bedside: Ten-minute chat . . . then she escaped from room.' Less than two weeks later it was revealed that Commander Michael Trestrail, the 51-year-old Head of the Royal Protection Squad, had admitted to a lengthy affair with a male prostitute. The *Daily Mirror*: 'Shame of the Queen's Police Chief'. Only three years earlier Professor Sir Anthony Blunt, the homosexual Surveyor of the Queens art collection, had been exposed as a Russian spy and the 'fourth man' in the Burgess and Maclean spy scandal.

Now 65 and possibly the most photographed woman in the world over the last four decades (although the Princess of Wales must be catching up rapidly), the Queen was unfamiliar to at least one of her loyal subjects. *The Sun* revealed him on May 13, 1991, with the headline above a smiling snap of the Monarch: 'Dear Carl, You refused to allow The Queen into Royal Windsor Horse Show thinking she was an "old dear who'd get lost". Keep this photo handy, you might bump into her again.' But perhaps Carl Bhimmin, the security guard in question, does not read newspapers. For him, in particular, this book will be required reading!

Much of her happiness centres on her private relaxation of racing, as a bloodstock breeder and successful owner

The Queen is possibly the most photographed woman in the world over the past four decades

Wednesday, February 6, 1952

THE STAR

No 19,835   Three Halfpence

New Queen Flies Home

THE KING DIES IN HIS SLEEP

PRINCESS ELIZABETH, the new Queen, was given the news of her father's death at the Royal lodge at Nyeri, near Nairobi, today. She heard it quietly. Then she broke down and wept.

The Story of King George—by Colin Frame: Pages 5, 6, 7, 8 and 9.

WEATHER

Weather forecast for London and SE England until noon tomorrow :

Cloudy. Some bright periods. Milder.

Further Outlook : Bright periods. Occasional rain or showers. Rather cold.

The first news to reach the lodge came from a Nairobi newspaper. It was decided to withhold the news from the Princess until direct confirmation was obtained by radio-telephone from the Royal Family in London.

The radio-telephone call was routed to the Princess through a little Kenya country post office.

It took nearly 30 minutes for the call to be properly connected and established from London so that the Princess could receive it.

The new Queen and the Duke
CONTINUED ON PAGE TWO

First picture of the King after his illness at the birthday party for Prince Charles at Buckingham Palace.

WITH most profound grief the nation learned today that His Majesty The King died peacefully in his sleep early this morning at Sandringham.

The announcement was made from Sandringham at 10.45 a.m.

CONTINUED ON BACK PAGE

DAILY HERALD

No. 11204 (A)   PRICE 1½d

FUNERAL A WEEK TODAY
The Queen, home, makes her first decision

Arrangements for the funeral of King George were approved by the Queen last night and later announced by the Earl Marshal, the Duke of Norfolk. They are—

THE FUNERAL: At St. George's Chapel, Windsor, on Friday, February 15.

On Friday morning there will be a State funeral procession from Westminster Hall to Paddington station.

LYING-IN-STATE: At Westminster Hall.

The Royal coffin will be brought by train from Sandringham on Monday. Westminster Hall will be open to the public on Tuesday, Wednesday and Thursday between 8 a.m. and 10 p.m.

QUEEN MARY GREETED HER

AT four minutes past five last night the royal standard was broken for the first time over Clarence House. Queen Elizabeth had come home.

Her aircraft, the Atalanta, had arrived to the minute at 4.30 p.m. at London Airport, having flown 4,444 miles from Entebbe in Uganda in 18 hours 37 minutes.

In the almost deserted airport 30 people—relatives, Ministers of State—waited to welcome the arriving Queen.

As the plane taxied to a stop the Duke of Gloucester led the waiting party across the tarmac. There was only one woman, the Countess Mountbatten.

The Duke went aboard. Then the Queen, alone, appeared at the door of the plane. She stood for a moment looking down on Mr. Churchill, Mr. Attlee and the others waiting bareheaded to meet her.

Then she stepped down and shook hands with the waiting Ministers. The Queen and the Duke of Edinburgh, who had followed her, said good-bye to the airliner's crew of eight and drove off to Clarence House.

It was there that she heard Mr. Churchill broadcasting at 9 o'clock last night. He said:

"In the last few months the King walked with death as if death were a companion. In the end death came as a friend."—*The broadcast is on Page Three.*

The Queen's homecoming had been watched by thousands. For two hours and more crowds gathered on the Mall. By five o'clock they exceeded 2,000.

The roar of a police patrolman's motor-bike—typical

★ CONTINUED ON PAGE THREE

This historic picture shows her as she stepped down to English soil for the first time as Queen.

Waiting to greet her are *(from right to left)*, Mr. Churchill, Mr. Attlee, Mr. Eden and Lord Woolton.

★

On the left, the Queen, pale-faced but composed and the Duke of Edinburgh talk to Earl and Countess Mountbatten.

Queen Elizabeth arrives home.

Nations in sympathy

When the House of Commons met yesterday for Members to continue taking the Oath of Allegiance to Queen Elizabeth, the Speaker, Mr. W. S. Morrison, read messages of sympathy from the Parliaments of France, Belgium, Luxembourg, Italy, Iceland and Japan.

Work on place of homage begins

ERECTION of the catafalque on which the coffin will be placed for the Lying-in-State was begun in historic Westminster Hall yesterday afternoon.

Van-loads of timber arrived, and by last night the foundations of the structure were laid.

Rolls of felt carpeting were wheeled in to cover the stone floor and silence the slow footsteps of the thousands who will come to pay homage.

GUN CARRIAGE

A DETACHMENT from Portsmouth Naval Gunnery School will take charge of the gun-carriage on which the coffin is borne in the funeral procession through London.

The carriage will be the one used at the funerals of Queen Victoria, King Edward VII, and King George V.

Rugby off

THE Scottish Rugby Union has advised clubs to cancel tomorrow's matches. Welsh and English fixtures have already been postponed.

Wales FA has asked for a one-minute silence before all week-end games.

ALL L C C schools will be closed on the day of burial.

The Yorkshire Herald

NORTH

Incorporating the WEEKLY TELEGRAPH

No. 2,855 FRIDAY, FEBRUARY 8, 1952.   A KEMSLEY NEWSPAPER. 2d.

A QUEEN RULES AGAIN

WE have known her as a radiant Princess who has walked among her people — here in Yorkshire, as elsewhere — clad in her own particular charm.   Our Sovereign Lady, now the Queen of England — our first since Queen Victoria — she reigns not only in our Law but in our hearts. To her we owe as duties, but shower as gifts, our allegiance, our love, our respect. May she live long to receive them.

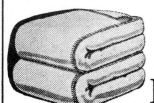

Daily Mirror

FRI
FEB. 8
1952

1½d

No. 15,004

Registered at G.P.O. as a Newspaper.

FORWARD
WITH THE
PEOPLE

THIS IS A VERY TRAGIC HOMECOMING

SAID QUEEN ELIZABETH

This was our girl Queen, Elizabeth, as she drove home to Clarence House yesterday—pale, wearing black, wistful but calm. There were no tears. Indeed, there had been a smile when she stepped from her plane. She told Mr. Churchill: "This is a very tragic homecoming." The bravery behind that smile can be guessed at. She is only twenty-five; she has lost a beloved father.—Other pictures in Centre Pages.

FUNERAL IS ON FRIDAY

Three-day public Lying-in-State

THE King will be buried at St. George's Chapel, Windsor, on Friday, February 15—a week today.

The Earl Marshal, the Duke of Norfolk, announced that the Queen had approved the following arrangements:—

MONDAY, February 11.—The Royal coffin will be brought to London by train from Sandringham and will be taken to Westminster Hall for the Lying-in-State.

TUESDAY, WEDNESDAY AND THURSDAY, February 12-14.—Westminster Hall will be open to the public between the hours of 8 a.m. and 10 p.m.

FRIDAY, February 15.—There will be a State funeral procession from Westminster Hall to Paddington Station. From there the coffin will be taken by train to Windsor.

FIRST . . . A CALL TO HER MOTHER

"DAILY MIRROR" REPORTERS

THE Royal Standard flew from the top of Clarence House last night. The Queen was in her own home.

As the flag was broken just after five o'clock, the slightly built Queen, followed by her husband, hurried from her car into the brightly lit hall.

There she embraced her waiting grandmother, Queen Mary. The next minute the staff telephone operator was calling Sandringham.

A few quiet words with Sir Alan Lascelles, her father's Private Secretary—and then the Queen went to the telephone and spoke to her mother.

That was the moment for which she had been rushed by cars and planes through a whole night and a day.

All through the long dash from Africa she looked the same . . . a slender, straight-shouldered figure, a little pale, though sometimes gravely smiling.

The smile she gave at London Airport yesterday was not so different from the one she gave her

Continued on Back Page

Evening Standard

39,735   FRIDAY, FEBRUARY 8, 1952   ● Three-halfpence

The people watch in silence, they hear the sound of guns, and then the words of the Proclamation—

GOD SAVE THE QUEEN

QUEEN MARY WATCHES FROM A WINDOW

Evening Standard Reporter

Queen Elizabeth II was to-day proclaimed Queen from the balcony of St. James's Palace in a ceremony that lasted little more than two minutes.

THE QUEEN SPEAKS

A time of deep sorrow

The Accession declaration made by the Queen to the Council at St. James's Palace was:

"Your Royal Highnesses, My Lords, Ladies and Gentlemen :—

"By the sudden death of my dear father I am called to assume the duties and responsibility of Sovereignty.

"At this time of deep sorrow it is a profound consolation to me to be assured of the sympathy which you and all my peoples feel towards me, to my mother, and my sister, and to the other members of my family.

'Loss is shared'

"My father was our revered and beloved head as he was of the wider family of his subjects : the grief which his loss brings is shared among us all.

"My heart is too full for me to say more to you to-day than that I shall always work, as my father did throughout his reign, to uphold the constitutional government and to advance the hapiness and prosperity of my peoples, spread as they are all the world over.

His example

"I know that in my resolve to follow his shining example of service and devotion, I shall be inspired by the loyalty and affection of those whose Queen I have been called to be, and by the counsel of their elected Parliaments.

"I pray that God will help me to discharge worthily this heavy task that has been laid upon me so early in my life."

EXPLOSION TRAPS GIRLS

Two girls were trapped and injured in an explosion to-day which wrecked part of the ground floor of the J. Lyons laboratory in Hammersmith Road, Hammersmith, opposite Cadby Hall.

They were taken to the West London Hospital, Hammersmith.

Five fire appliances fought the blaze. A call was made for police reinforcements.

"A sheet of fire seemed to sweep part of the laboratories," said one of the assistants. "I don't know how we managed to get the second girl out."

This was the first and principal of a series of proclamations in London and at Windsor. Thousands of people had gathered in the area of the Palace, but only a few hundreds saw the scarlet and gold proclamation party in their brief appearance on the balcony.

Fewer still saw the Queen. She took no part in the public ceremony, but attended a meeting of the Privy Council—her first—in the white and gold Throne Room of the Palace to make her Declaration of Accession.

At twenty minutes to ten she came through the main doors of Clarence House, and received a salute from the Queen's Company of the Grenadier Guards, drawn up in the gardens of Clarence House with the Royal Standard.

IN THE THRONE ROOM

She wore the same black hat and coat in which she arrived at London Airport yesterday.

Then, as the Guards were dismissed, she walked along the garden path which links her home with St. James's. A few yards behind her walked Prince Philip, coatless and wearing dark glasses.

In the white and gold throne room of St. James's Palace her Counsellors were waiting. They bowed deeply as she entered.

In a clear voice, the Queen made her declaration of Accession, and then subscribed the oath. The proceedings of the Council lasted barely 10 minutes; and shortly before the Proclamation was due she came out from St. James's Palace into the garden with the Prince. Pointing to the snow lying thickly on the lawn, she walked back to Clarence House.

CRIMSON AND GOLD

Across the bare trees of St. James's came the chimes of Big Ben. A wintry sun appeared from behind the clouds, and the State trumpeters, in gold tabards, came on to the crimson-draped balcony of St. James's Palace.

They were followed by the Serjeants-at-Arms with maces. Then came Garter Principal King at Arms leading the procession of Kings at Arms.

Their tabards gold embroidered and emblazoned with the Royal arms, provided a note of colour against the sombre background.

Then came heralds and Pursuivants in cloth of gold tabards, carrying staffs of gold, silver gilt and ebony.

This was the Proclamation read by Garter King of Arms, Sir George Rothe Bellew:

"Whereas it has pleased Almighty God to call to His mercy our late Sovereign Lord King George VI of blessed and glorious memory by whose decease the Crown is solely and rightfully come to the high and mighty Princess Elizabeth Alexandra Mary :

"We therefore the Lords Spiritual and Temporal of the Realm being here assisted with these His Late Majesty's Privy Council with representatives of other members of the Commonwealth with other principal gentlemen of quality with the Lord Mayor aldermen and citizens of London do now hereby with one voice and consent of tongue and heart publish and proclaim that the high and mighty Princess Elizabeth Alexandra Mary is now by the death of our late Sovereign of happy memory become Queen of this realm and of her other realms and territories, Head of the Commonwealth Defender of the Faith to whom her lieges do acknowledge all faith and constant obedience with hearty and humble affection beseeching God by whom kings and queens do reign to bless the Royal Princess Elizabeth II. with long and happy years to reign over us.

"God save the Queen.

"Given at St. James's Palace this sixth day of February in the year of Our Lord nineteen hundred and fifty-two."

● Back Page, Col. One

The Proclamation is read at Temple Bar to-day by Norroy and Ulster King of Arms, Sir Gerald Wollaston.

More pictures on Page Four, on the Middle Pages, and on the Back Page.

Duke of Windsor sails for England

NEW YORK, Friday.—The Duke of Windsor sailed for home in the Queen Mary to-day to attend the funeral of his brother, King George.

"The voyage I am embarking on is indeed sad," he said. "And it is all the sadder because I am undertaking it alone. The Duchess is remaining here."

There were only a few people at the pier as the Duke and Duchess arrived about 90 minutes before sailing time.

The Duke was wearing a black Homburg, grey overcoat, black tie and black armband.

The Duchess wore a short black fur jacket, black dress, black hat, shoes and handbag.

Ship's welcome

Ship's officers welcomed them and they were led quickly up the gangplank.

On board, hundreds of passengers gathered. But the Duke and Duchess hardly glanced to left or right as they entered a waiting lift and were taken immediately to the Duke's stateroom.

Fifteen minutes later they appeared in the grillroom for the Duke's statement. Television networks recorded and photographed the scene for broadcasting later.

The Duke said : "I am sailing for Great Britain for the funeral of a dear brother and to comfort Her Majesty, my mother, in the overwhelming sorrow which has overtaken my family and the Commonwealth of British nations.

"This will be the fourth time that I have participated in the obsequies of a British monarch.

"Fifty-one years ago it was

▲ Back Page, Col Three

WEATHER—Cold

Forecast to noon to-morrow : Moderate to fresh N.W. to N. winds; bright periods; scattered showers, with snow or sleet in places; cold; night frost. Further Outlook : Continuing cold.
Lighting-up time (London) 5.30 p.m.

Daily Mirror

TUES FEB. 12 1952

FORWARD WITH THE PEOPLE

1½d

No. 15,007
Registered at G.P.O.
as a Newspaper.

A sorrowing family group of three Queens—Elizabeth the Second, Queen Mary and the Queen Mother—stand at the entrance to Westminster Hall as the King's coffin is carried past them for the Lying-in-State. On the right is Princess Margaret.

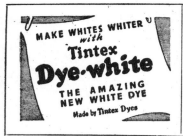
SUNDAY GRAPHIC

No. 1,923. February 17, 1952   (C)   A Kemsley Newspaper 2½d.

THE KING THE PEOPLE LOVED

THE QUEEN WHO IS OUR HOPE

We have said our last farewells to King George VI.   Let us remember him not in sadness, but in the spirit that he would himself have wished, putting grief behind us in the memory of his courage, his kindliness and his faith. Those virtues that we loved in him live on unconquerably in his daughter, our Queen.

DAILY GRAPHIC
DAILY & SKETCH

Friday, June 6, 1952   ★★★★★   A Kemsley Newspaper   2d.

The Queen waves from the Palace balcony after the Trooping

16 Pages

All the Royal Pictures

See pages 7, 8, 9 and 10, and read the brilliant account of the TROOPING THE COLOUR ceremony by PAUL GALLICO on Page 6

The "Daily Graphic" is Britain's picture newspaper — you can always SEE the news.

The Queen chooses her seal

This is the seal the Queen will use on State documents and which will also be the pattern for Coronation souvenirs.

★   ★

Haley quits the BBC

Story on Back Page

TIMELY WORDS OF FAITH
Who shall separate us from the love of Christ?
—Romans 8, 35.

THE STAR

No 20,067   Three Halfpence

LATE NIGHT
Queen Opens Her First Parliament

Prince Charles and Princess Anne—who stood on a chair—joined their parents when the Queen and the Duke of Edinburgh came out on the Palace balcony to wave to the crowds today.

With a smile whose sparkle matched her diamond necklace and tiara the Queen drove to Westminster for today's State Opening of Parliament. Report on Page Three. More pictures on Pages 3, 8 and 9.

THE TIMES

WEEKLY REVIEW

World affairs · Social life · Finance · The Arts · Sport · News & Comment from London

LONDON THURSDAY JANUARY 1 1953

NO. 53

The Postage for this Issue is: Inland and Abroad 1½d

PRICE 6ᴰ.

FIRST CHRISTMAS BROADCAST BY THE QUEEN

The Queen seated at the microphone at Sandringham House when she made the
first Christmas broadcast of her reign. Her message, addressed to the peoples of the
Commonwealth and Empire, was received in many parts of the world.

THE RECKONING

The Queen and the Duke see the damage—"hardly credible there could be so much..." (Flood Stories on Page 3)

DAILY SKETCH
2d

AND DAILY GRAPHIC
TUESDAY, FEBRUARY 3, 1953 ★★★★

1,300 DEAD AND MISSING

24,000 homeless

Churchill names Floods C-in-C

ALL-OUT BATTLE TO CLOSE THE GAPS

Cities—and Lynmouth—open funds

Daily Mirror

WED MAR. 25 1953

Three Half-pence   No. 15,353

Registered at G.P.O. as a Newspaper.

DEATH OF QUEEN MARY

This is one of the last pictures of Queen Mary. It was taken when she returned to London after her last holiday at Sandringham. A few weeks later Queen Mary was ill with gastric trouble.

SPECIAL QUEEN MARY FEATURES —Page Two and Centre Pages

IT IS WITH THE DEEPEST REGRET THAT THE "DAILY MIRROR" ANNOUNCES THE DEATH OF QUEEN MARY. SHE WAS EIGHTY-FIVE.

At 11.10 last night, Mr. Churchill rose in the House of Commons and, in sombre tones, said: "Mr. Speaker, I rise to move the adjournment of the House. I have with great regret to make the announcement that Queen Mary has died."

WITH A BREAK IN HIS VOICE, MR. CHURCHILL WENT ON: "TOMORROW, IMMEDIATELY AFTER PRAYERS, I WILL MOVE AN ADDRESS OF CONDOLENCE TO THE QUEEN AND PROPOSE THAT THE HOUSE SHOULD ADJOURN THEREAFTER UNTIL THURSDAY AS AN EXPRESSION OF OUR PROFOUND SORROW AND RESPECT."

Then Mr. Attlee, leader of the Opposition, said: "I am sure the whole House will join in that expression of sorrow."

Gasp of Dismay

Members of the House filed slowly out of the chamber, talking quietly amongst themselves, and Mr. Churchill moved past the Speaker and out of sight with his head bowed.

Mr. Churchill's announcement was received by the packed House in a silence broken only by exclamations of dismay which came from the public gallery.

Simultaneously, the fourth and last bulletin of the day was posted on the gates of Queen Mary's residence, Marlborough House.

It said: "While sleeping peacefully, Queen Mary died at twenty minutes past ten o'clock."

A silence fell on a crowd of 500 at the gates as the news was flashed from mouth to mouth.

The Duke of Windsor and the Princess Royal were at their mother's deathbed.

Her Greatest Wish

IT was Queen Mary's great wish that the Coronation of her granddaughter, Queen Elizabeth II, on June 2, should go on.

But last night there had been no official statement that the arrangements would go forward as planned.

This will not be known until the Queen announces what period of Court mourning she wishes to be observed for her grandmother.

Queen Mary had discussed with many members of her staff the possibility that she would not be alive at the time of the Coronation.

She knew of the plans to begin decorating Westminster Abbey in March. In view of that, she had no wish for a service to be held in the Abbey, where other Queen Mothers had been honoured in death.

The Queen's Visit

YESTERDAY afternoon, when the Queen visited Marlborough House, Queen Mary, her grandmother, was barely conscious.

The Queen was accompanied by her sister, Princess Margaret, and by her

The problem of the Coronation

Continued on Back Page

Daily Mirror

1½d

FORWARD WITH THE PEOPLE

THURS MAY 28 1953

No. 15,407

FIVE GOLDEN DAYS TO JUNE 2

THE TOAST IS —'THE QUEEN'

MR. HAROLD HOLT, AUSTRALIAN LABOUR MINISTER.

H.M. THE QUEEN.

SIR WINSTON CHURCHILL.

MRS. ST. LAURENT.

MR. R. G. MENZIES, AUSTRALIAN PREMIER.

Sir Winston Churchill leads the cheers for the Queen

THE historic scene in Westminster Hall yesterday when the Toast was "The Queen."

The Toast was proposed at a banquet given to the Queen by all the Parliaments of her Commonwealth. Australia's Minister of Labour, Mr. Harold E. Holt, who proposed it, called the Queen "the radiant embodiment of hope to millions."

The Queen was standing at the time the picture was taken because the National Anthem had just been played—and the Monarch always stands for the Anthem.

Sir Winston Churchill told the 750 guests at the banquet: "We feel that her Gracious Majesty here with us today has consecrated her life to all her peoples in all her realms. We are resolved to prove, on the pages of history, that this sacrifice shall not be in vain."

West End may be 'sealed off'

THOUSANDS of Coronation sightseers yesterday caused the most fantastic traffic chaos so far in London. Now Scotland Yard, fearing that Central London will be brought to a standstill, are considering banning all cars except buses and priority traffic, from the Coronation route area from tomorrow night until after June 2. (Story in Back Page.)

CORONATION LONDON— It's all in the 'Mirror'

Evening Standard

40,141   MONDAY, JUNE 1, 1953   ●● Three-halfpence

LONDON CAMPS OUT
On Coronation Eve

THE GREAT CRUSH in Trafalgar Square this afternoon. People squatting on the spots from which they hope to see to-morrow's procession block the pavements. Pedestrians and sightseers walk around them, or on the roadway. One woman sleeps, her head against the rail.

PRINCESS GOES TO THE ABBEY

Evening Standard Reporter

Great crowds piled up this afternoon along to-morrow's Coronation route, and brought traffic to a stop-go-stop crawl.

Outside Buckingham Palace there was a crowd of 50,000.

By Tube and bus thousands more arrived. At Trafalgar Square station there were long queues waiting to get out.

The second row

Thousands squatted on the pavement edge at the best viewpoints in Trafalgar Square, The Mall, Whitehall, and Parliament Square.

Nineteen hours before the Queen leaves Buckingham Palace for the Abbey, people ready to camp out all night were taking up "second row" positions.

The kerbside campers forced sightseers and newcomers into

● Page Two, Col. One

SHOWERS —SUNSHINE

Here is the Coronation Day forecast issued this afternoon:

London area, 6 a.m. to midnight—Winds northerly, fresh or strong and gusty. Some sunny intervals. Occasional showers, heavy at times, perhaps with hail and thunder here and there. Very cool. Mid-day temperature 50 to 55.

Further outlook—showers.

TELEPHONE: CENTRAL 3000
Amusements Guide—Page 12

Stabbed girl is found in the Thames

Evening Standard Reporter

A girl of 16 was found dead in the Thames at Richmond to-day.

She had four stab wounds in the back. There was a gash on her forehead.

The girl was found near the towpath at Water Lane. This part of the bank is frequented by courting couples.

The girl, 5ft. 6in. in height, was wearing a coat, slacks and white socks, but no shoes. The name Prendergast was found on some of her clothing.

Round her waist was a wide cloth belt with silver buckles.

The girl is believed to have been attacked, then pushed

▲ Back Page, Col. Four

DAILY SKETCH

AND DAILY GRAPHIC

Coronation Souvenir

TUESDAY, JUNE 2, 1953   2d.

EVEREST!!

—— SEE BACK PAGE

To-day

GODFREY WINN

who will be in the Abbey to describe the Coronation for the "Daily Sketch." —See Page 4.

NORMAN HARTNELL

who designed the Queen's Coronation dress, writes on "Behind the Scenes." — See Page 14.

JOHN PUDNEY

writes a Coronation poem.—See Page 4.

£1,000 PICTURE CONTEST

Choose the best Coronation picture. The prize — £1 a week for life or £1,000.—See Page 16.

"GLORIOUS" — that was the one word the Queen spoke when she saw her Coronation dress. It is in white satin and gold, embroidered with diamonds and pearls. More pictures of the Royal gowns— Pages 2 and 3.

The Dress

THE CROWNING GLORY: EVEREST IS CLIMBED

THE QUEEN'S DRESS TODAY *Back Page*

Tremendous news for the Queen

The new Elizabethan

HILLARY DOES IT

GLORIOUS Coronation Day news! Everest—Everest the unconquerable — has been conquered. And conquered by men of British blood and breed.

The news came late last night that Edmund Hillary and the Sherpa guide, Tensing, of Colonel Hunt's expedition had climbed to the summit of Earth's highest peak, 29,002 feet high.

Queen Elizabeth the Second, resting on the eve of her crowning, was immediately told that this brightest jewel of courage and endurance had been added to the Crown of British endeavour. It is understood that a message of royal congratulation was sent to the climbers.

Announcers broke into U.S. radio and television programmes last night to relay the news.

Hillary, a 34-year-old New Zealander, and Bhotia Tensing, 38-year-old leader of the Sherpa guides and bearers, are said to have made the final 1,000-foot ascent from Camp Eight on the upper slopes.

The feat was apparently accomplished on Monday. A year ago Bhotia Tensing climbed to within 800 feet of the summit with Raymond Lambert, of the unsuccessful Swiss expedition.

NEWS BY RUNNER

The latest news of the progress of the expedition hitherto—despatched by runner and received in London yesterday—was that the climbers were ready, as soon as the weather was suitable, to set out from Camp Seven, established high on the South Col at about 26,000 feet, to pitch Camp Eight high up near the summit.

David Walker, below, describes how the conquest is likely to have been accomplished:

The two figures are in wind-proof smocks of different colours, double-lined with nylon, and each wears two hoods. Beneath the visors the eyes peer out on the roof of the world from goggles greased against frosting.

Down to the right lies Tibet and to the left Nepal, while death is a height no man can survive without extra oxygen, involving 26lb. of dead weight, when every ounce can count; but at this stage science must supply what nature will not give. The endurance-time of this oxygen, carried on the back in cylinders, is estimated at five hours.

Hands are lumpy in three sets of gloves: outer gauntlets of windproof cotton enclose mittens made of down. Next to the skin, worn tight, are gloves of silk.

It may be necessary for one or other of the men to look at his watch. This is a major decision because of the intense effort of will that must be followed by the physical distraction. It can take a minute to carryout.

TEN STEPS A MINUTE

Step by step, in Martian clothing, the two figures move forward, pursuing their race against time and the mountain in the slowest of slow motion. Ten steps a minute, Eric Shenston tells me, could be considered "satisfactory"; five hundred feet an hour is what their leader, Colonel Hunt, was hoping for. The estimates roughly tally.

The boots used for so many weeks in the early stages have been discarded. The pairs now worn are not even waterproof —glacé leather over an inch of kapok with soles of microcellulose rubber—"looking rather like boxing gloves," says Mr. Shipton.

Before setting off from the final Assault Camp on the South

Turn Page Two, Col. 3

SMILING, mountain - wise Bhotia Tensing, is the leader of the Sherpa guides and porters who accompanied the expedition.

He is 38 and a veteran of four previous attempts on Everest by the northern route. His Sherpa comrades call him the Tiger.

On May 29 last year Tensing climbed to 28,215 feet with Raymond Lambert of the unsuccessful Swiss expedition before the failure of their oxygen apparatus forced them back.

Tensing's people are a caste of mountain dwellers whose "capital" is Namche Bazar, on the road to Everest. They live by trading with Tibet, Nepal and India.

EDMUND HILLARY, whose conquest of Everest sets the seal on the new Elizabethan age, is a 34-year-old bee farmer from New Zealand.

He learned his mountaineering in the Alps of the little Dominion and was a pioneer in introducing winter ski-ing there.

Hillary's rugged independence made him one of this expedition's most valuable members long before the final assault.

He and George Lowe, the other New Zealander of the party, were making a free-lance climb in the Himalayas when Eric Shipton "look - see" expedition arrived in 1951 to choose a route up Everest.

Hillary and Lowe dropped their own project and trailed halfway across the vast range to join them. Shipton was so impressed by their performance that he gave them their places in the Coronation year attempt. Shipton said last night: "This is splendid. Once the South Col camp was established it seemed there was nothing to stop them, and I have been waiting for the good news."

Prophet Vicky

Malenkov going to the ball

Moscow, Monday. — Mr. Malenkov, Russian Prime Minister, will go to a Coronation Ball at the British Embassy in Moscow tomorrow night. With him will be Mr. Molotov, Foreign Minister, and 200 senior officials.

Yesterday's cartoon from Vicky on holiday.

Here the forecast is rain—hail—sun—storm, BUT the crowds are singing in the rain SO—

WHO CARES NOW IF IT SNOWS?

CORONATION DAY FORECAST: Northerly winds, sunny spells, showers with hail and thunder, cold. Mid-day temperature 55 deg.

NEWS CHRONICLE REPORTERS

REPEATED heavy showers lashed the packed campers lining the Royal Way last night—and the temperature dropped 13 degrees in a few hours.

Yet the drenched campers refused to quit for fear of losing their places—and moment by moment the throng grew as 18,000 cars an hour converged on London. And the trains had yet to come. . . .

Thousands of cheering people surrounded the Queen Mother and Princess Margaret as they drove from Buckingham Palace after spending two hours with the Queen in her private apartments—a last visit before the Coronation.

Reinforced police could not clear a way: the car was halted for 15 minutes beside the Victoria Memorial.

The Queen Mother, in a white feathered gown and off-the-face white hat, and Princess Margaret, in a low-cut smoke-blue gown, waved. Motor-cycle police came to the rescue. But a little later more crowds ran from their pitches and blocked the route to Clarence House.

DAMP DANCES IN THE MALL

The Mall looked like a gigantic refugee camp. Over 30,000 people were bedding down along the pavements. Twenty-thousand more were trying to find places.

Thousands sat in puddles of water hanging out their clothes.

Camping up to 12-deep on either side after squatting there all day they were thoroughly soaked by the intermittent storms. But not one gave up his pitch.

Of all ages, from toddlers to over-70s, they sheltered as best they could, some under improvised tents of tarpaulin slung between the trees.

Groups were singing, others dancing in impromptu fancy dress. Quieter parties listened to portable radios or played cards. A chain of mobile cafes issued tea, coffee and buns.

It was the same among the 6,000-7,000 camped out along Whitehall.

They seemed to have thought of everything. If the sun shines today—well, some had brought parasols. If it gets very cold: There were thick blankets and heavy coats.

TENT TOWN

But it was raining a slow, miserable, penetrating drizzle. And from Trafalgar Square to Parliament Square the kerbs were lined with people huddled under tarpaulins, blankets, newspapers, umbrellas—some of them hidden completely and looking rather like a pile of covered bricks: almost inanimate except for an odd rustle of nylon or corduroy from under the edge.

And the children . . . from five years upwards, they, too, had come with the family.

Even a newsboy outside the House of Commons caught the spirit of the hour, telling the crowd in case they did not want to read a paper, "every copy is waterproof."

As Big Ben boomed eight Whitehall's milkman, 32-year-old James Locke, handed out his 300th pint to the campers. Jimmy Locke, the man who

Turn Page Two, Col. 5

(mountains diagram: EVEREST 29,002 FT., LHOTSE 27,890 FT., NUPTSE 25,680 FT., NORTH COL, ICE FALL)

Stabbed girl dead in Thames

A MURDERED girl was found in the Thames yesterday; and last night the police feared her girl companion had been killed too.

The girl in the river was 16-year-old Barbara Songhurst, a chemist's assistant, of Princess Road, Teddington. She was stabbed three times in the back after being assaulted on Lovers' Towpath at Ham, Surrey.

On Sunday Barbara went cycling with her friend, 18-year-old Christina Reed, of Roy Crescent, Hampton Hill.

See Page Five

Flash kills 3 cricketers

Lightning struck three cricketers dead at a Coronation match yesterday. The flash shot through the dressing room at a soap factory's ground at Irlam, near Manchester.

The men killed were Ernest Taylor, 44, Herbert Vaudrey, 37, and George Perry, 31, all of Cadishead.

CENTRAL 5000

WEATHER. — Showers and short sunny intervals. Midday temp. 50-55. Sun rises 4.45 a.m., sets 9.10 p.m. Moon 00.35 a.m.-9.34 a.m. Lights 10.07 p.m.-3.49 a.m. tomorrow. High water at London Bridge 5.48 a.m.-5.54 p.m.

Weather map, Page Two

400 watch sea rescue

Watched by her 400 passengers, three brothers were taken aboard the Isle of Man steamer Snaefell from their crippled sailing boat, in a storm right miles off the island yesterday.

The brothers, Christopher, Frank and Ian Whipp, of Rochdale, had ridden the storm, which demasted their sloop, for 15 hours.

After the brothers had been taken aboard the steamer in heavy seas Douglas lifeboat took the sloop in tow.

No bread

All those Coronation sandwiches have started a bread famine in London and the suburbs. People yesterday toured from shop to shop in vain.

Said one group of bakeries: "We made half a week's normal supply to sell today. There is no time to make and distribute more."

Thousands went sight-seeing during the week-end; thousands decided to take up their positions on Coronation way yesterday instead of this morning; and thousands more arranged television parties at the last minute. And they all cut deeply into the loaf for sandwiches.

TO-DAY IN PICTURES

Evening Standard

40,142   TUESDAY, JUNE 2, 1953   Three-halfpence

THE CROWNED QUEEN
Pages of dramatic pictures

The Queen sits in King Edward's Chair, wearing the Crown, in Westminster Abbey to-day. The Crown has been placed on her head by the Archbishop of Canterbury, who now stands facing her. On her right is the Bishop of Durham, on her left the Bishop of Bath and Wells. The supreme moment of the ceremony has been reached.

From the Abbey the Queen drove in her golden coach home to Buckingham Palace. The streets were packed with millions of cheering people who had waited for hours in fleeting sunshine and in bitter rain to share the glory of the day. Beverley Baxter, MP, reports the Abbey ceremony on Page Two.

CORONATION SOUVENIR

HAPPY

This was the happiest picture of all

—AND GLORIOUS

SUNDAY PICTORIAL

December 27, 1953   No. 2,023   Twopence-halfpenny

She spoke words of comfort in a small suburban home

THE QUEEN SHARES IN A CHRISTMAS SORROW

From JOAN REEDER, Auckland, Saturday

THE QUEEN AND THE DUKE OF EDINBURGH, ON THE FOURTH DAY OF THEIR VISIT TO NEW ZEALAND, TODAY DROVE TO A LITTLE SUBURBAN HOUSE IN AUCKLAND TO TALK TO THREE SURVIVORS OF THE CHRISTMAS EVE RAIL CRASH IN WHICH 166 PEOPLE DIED.

Mr. and Mrs. John Falloon and their sixteen-year-old daughter Glenis were sitting in a friend's house wearing borrowed clothes.

Their own clothes—hosed down for two hours to get the mud off—were hanging in the garden to dry when the Queen walked in.

With the Duke, the Queen—wearing a mushroom brown and white silk suit—sat and listened with shocked sympathy as the Falloons told their story.

They heard how the coach in which they were travelling caught on the end of a broken bridge, and hung over the rushing river below. For a few moments the coach hung on the brink, and then finally plunged them down into the river.

'Stay at Home'

The Queen and the Duke smiled with pleasure as the Falloons told them: "As soon as we had borrowed some clothes we tried to go out and catch a glimpse of you, but the police warned us to stay at home.

"Little did we know then that you would be coming to see us."

The Queen told them warmly: "I am very glad to have been able to come and see you."

The Queen and the Duke drove to see the Falloons after attending the opening day of Auckland Racing Club's summer meeting.

Prime Minister Sidney Holland, the Minister in attendance on the Queen for the tour, had promised her the best Christmas New Zealand could make for her

Dash to Scene

But on Christmas Day the Premier had to dash 250 miles to the scene of the rail crash. He stayed there — a tired and unshaven figure, helping and comforting the survivors.

As soon as the Queen returned from church on Christmas morning and before she breakfasted, she sent a message of "heartfelt sympathy" to Mr. Holland—the man with whom she had been laughing and joking ever since her arrival here.

And then the Queen asked for her Christmas broadcast to be made a little longer so she could speak to the bereaved and anxious people herself.

So she was serious and subdued when, in her primrose yellow summer frock, she came out on to the front porch of Government House at ten o'clock to listen to rows of schoolchildren, all dressed in white, sing carols in the lovely flower-filled gardens.

The carols didn't help us much. Their melodies only reminded us of all those other children—their toys and presents strewn with wreckage and clothing along the mud, rocks and shattered railway carriages.

But then Father Christmas drove six little white ponies up to the porch, and jumped down from his present-packed sleigh.

The children said "Oo-oo-hh-hh-hh," and then the Queen suddenly smiled.

Father Christmas marched straight up to her and said in a loud voice, "Happy Christmas, Your Majesty, and now we have a present for you"

He gave her a walkie-talkie doll with a wardrobe full of clothes for Princess Anne, a huge set of trains for Prince Charles.

Then the Queen turned to Lady Pamela Mountbatten for her cine camera. Sighting quickly, she started filming the whole scene: Santa Claus, the little children in white standing on the lawn. . . .

So now Prince Charles and Princess Anne will see exactly how Father Christmas came and delivered their toys to their Mummy when she was in New Zealand

PRINCE CHARLES LISTENS IN

PRINCE CHARLES and Princess Anne heard their mother's broadcast on the drawing-room radiogram at Sandringham House. Earlier, they ate their own turkey—a small, plump bird sent to them by one of the Queen's tenant farmers.

The Queen's Christmas Broadcast—See Page 14.

The Queen, in a topless gown, broadcasting her Christmas message from Auckland.

3 DAYS' NEWS TODAY

RUSSIA: LET'S MEET LATER —Page 2	**Crossman's Suez cable** —Page 2
166 die in rail smash —Page 3	**LAST WAVELL DIES FIGHTING** —Page 20
YOUR 50,000 CHILDREN —Page 5	**Sport: All the results** —Pages 18 & 19

Largest Audited Circulation in Brisbane

Brisbane Telegraph

Telephone FB0101
Radio Newsroom—B0350

WEDNESDAY EVENING, FEBRUARY 3, 1954

36 PAGES—3d.
[Air Freight Extra]

Printed and published by Telegraph Newspaper Co. Ltd., of 93 Queen Street, Brisbane, at that address.

BUREAU FORECAST: Fine.

Registered at the G.P.O. Brisbane for transmission by Post as a newspaper.

CAPTURED ALL HEARTS
QUEEN TOOK SYDNEY IN HOLLOW OF HER HAND

From M. C. WARREN, "Brisbane Telegraph" Special Representative Travelling with the Royal Party.

● **SYDNEY: A gracious Royal Lady today held this city of 1,600,000 people in the hollow of her hand. Queen Elizabeth, at her landing in Sydney today with the Duke of Edinburgh captured all hearts with the charm and dignity that report had already woven round her.**

Looking younger than her 27 years she made history as the first reigning monarch to come to Australia.

The welcome to Her Majesty and to the Duke of Edinburgh was rousing and inspiring.

Australia could be proud of the gala demonstration by the first city to greet the Royal visitors.

The Queen must have been moved by the tumultuous reception expressed by the huge concourse of people on harbour craft, and lining the 10 miles of city streets.

The warm, sunny day typified the feelings of the Sovereign and people at this first direct acquaintance.

The Queen faced the cheering multitude with perfect poise.

It must have been an ordeal for her, as she was the centre of such concentrated attention for hour after hour.

But Her Majesty actually seemed to enjoy the occasion.

By a ready smile she showed she was far from indifferent to all this fuss, and as woman as well as monarch, she appreciated the admiration heaped upon her.

For the Duke it was not a case of first-view of Sydney — magnificent harbour and city — because he had had wartime service here.

But returning as husband of the Queen, he, too, must have been inspired by this warm demonstration of the nation's allegiance.

Sight not to be forgotten

The harbour was an unforgettable sight as the Gothic entered Sydney Heads.

As the Royal yacht in a coat of shimmering white made her appearance, the foreshores and bays were crammed with spectators.

From our Press launch we followed the Gothic to her moorings as hundreds of watercraft "dressed" from stem to stern edged round at respectful distance to bid welcome with sirens blaring.

There was colour and pageantry as a myriad craft from the smallest afloat to bright big pleasure boats, joined in the procession astern.

Flights of Vampires and Mustangs kept close formation and a solitary helicopter gave official cameraman and radioman a bird's-eye view.

Some 400 luxury yachts formed a colourful laneway for the Royal yacht as it moved to the landing pontoon at Farm Cove.

It was a memorable and moving spectacle as Her Majesty came ashore to greet her people.

Queen's speech

Her Majesty in her reply to the address of welcome by the Lord Mayor of Sydney (Ald. Hills) at Farm Cove, said:

"My Lord Mayor, I thank you and your aldermen most sincerely for the welcome you have given me and my husband on behalf of the citizens of Sydney.

"I would like to take this opportunity of telling you how delighted we both were by the spectacular greeting given to us this morning by the yachtsmen in the harbour and by the citizens on the shore.

"I have always looked forward to my first visit to this country but now there is the added satisfaction for me that I am able to meet my Australian people as their Queen.

"So this morning as the Gothic moved up the great expanse of this magnificent harbour and I saw before me the city of Sydney, I was filled with a sense of pride and expectation.

"Only 166 years ago the first settlement was made not far from where we stand, by Captain Phillip and his small band of Englishmen, and now there stands a fine city that has become famous throughout the world.

"In the same short space of time we have seen the rise of Australia as a great nation, taking her full share in the councils of the British Commonwealth and of the world.

"I am proud indeed to be at the head of a nation that has achieved so much.

"Standing at last on Australian soil, on this spot that is the birthplace of the nation, I want to tell you all how happy I am to be amongst you and how much I look forward to my journey throughout Australia."

Ignored V.I.Ps.

SYDNEY: The Royal carpet got a careful grooming on the landing pontoon at Farm Cove this morning.

Five workmen in overalls were oblivious to V.I.Ps. in morning suits, standing round in sartorial splendour.

The workers swept the carpet's surface and hand-scraped it to remove fluff.

It was another of those last-minute preparations for the Queen's arrival that give a human touch to the official ceremony.

HER MAJESTY ARRIVES: Ferries, yachts and rowing boats greeted the Queen's Royal yacht Gothic as the vessel made her way through Sydney Harbour this morning. A 21-gun salute roared as the Gothic passed through the Heads. Her Majesty and the Duke of Edinburgh landed at Farm Cove at 10.42 a.m. See Pages 2, 3. "Brisbane Telegraph" Daily Record of Royal Visit, Pages 17, 18, 19, 20.

Evening Standard

40,437   SATURDAY, MAY 15, 1954   Three-halfpence

THE HAPPY RETURN
Crowds line the Thames

FLAGS AND BANNERS ALL THE WAY

From GORDON HOLMAN

In the Evening Standard helicopter, Saturday.

At the moment of her homecoming the Queen paused today in the great sea gateway that leads to London.

As the sun rose the Britannia was lying at anchor little more than a mile from the North Foreland. We circled the ship.

Then, in 55 minutes, we flew over the sea and river course that the Queen will follow back into the heart of the Empire of which she has seen so much in the last six months.

The guards

The fields and orchards of Kent, shaded in the bright greens of spring, over which we flew to meet the Britannia again today, offered a soft English welcome after the sun-baked territories the Queen has trodden in recent weeks.

The Thames and the flat Essex foreshore wore an unexpected loveliness as the sun rose over them

With two destroyers guarding her, the Britannia looked small against the bold sweep of the Foreland and the wide expanse of sea.

As 7 a.m. approached ratings prepared to raise the anchors. In Britannia, with the Royal Standard flying from the mainmast, there was activity on the bridge and ratings were giving a final polish to deck brasses. One gangway was still partly down.

A barge, a collier

Small boats—some so small that they bobbed alarmingly on the quiet sea—clustered around. Among them was a red and blue painted lifeboat.

Beating up steadily from the Kent shore was a Thames sailing barge with sails fully

▲ Page Two, Col. Five

'Rain unlikely'

The weather forecast for the Queen's passage up the Thames was mainly fair, with moderate visibility becoming good, and moderate north to north-east winds.

For her drive through London this afternoon, the forecast was cloudy, with bright intervals, and with temperatures likely to be five degrees warmer than yesterday, reaching the mid-sixties.

The Air Ministry said: "Rain is unlikely."

The smiles that circled the Empire . . . This was a Malta moment . . . Today it is London's turn.

Dawn . . . the Britannia lies at anchor surrounded by craft large and small . . . Picture from the Evening Standard helicopter

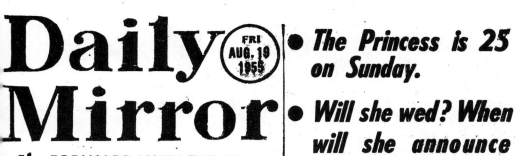

Daily Mirror

FRI AUG. 19 1955

1½d **FORWARD WITH THE PEOPLE**

No. 16,077

- **The Princess is 25 on Sunday.**
- **Will she wed? When will she announce her decision?**

COME ON MARGARET!

FOR two years the world has buzzed with this question:

Will Princess Margaret marry 40-year-old Group Captain Peter Townsend?—OR Won't she?

Five months ago, Group Captain Townsend told the Daily Mirror: '. . . the word cannot come from me. You will appreciate it must come from other people . . .'

On Sunday the Princess will be 25. She could then, if she wished, notify Parliament direct of her desire to marry without first seeking the consent of her sister the Queen.

♛

She could end the hubbub.

Will she please make up her mind?

Please make up your mind!

Daily Mirror

TUES NOV 1 1955

2ᴰ

FORWARD WITH THE PEOPLE

No. 16,140

MARGARET DECIDES:

DUTY BEFORE LOVE

PRINCESS MARGARET, in this dramatic announcement from Clarence House last night, told the world that she had renounced the love of Peter Townsend:

"I would like it to be known that I have decided not to marry Group Captain Peter Townsend. I have been aware that, subject to my renouncing my rights of succession, it might have been possible for me to contract a civil marriage. But, mindful of the Church's teaching that Christian marriage is indissoluble, and conscious of my duty to the Commonwealth, I have resolved to put these considerations before any others. I have reached this decision entirely alone, and in doing so I have been strengthened by the unfailing support and devotion of Group Captain Townsend. I am deeply grateful for the concern of all those who have constantly prayed for my happiness.

(Signed) Margaret."

Peter Townsend leaves—alone

SEE BACK PAGE

Daily Mirror

THURS DEC 22 1955

2ᴰ FORWARD WITH THE PEOPLE

No. 16,184

NIGHT OUT

THE Queen, the Duke of Edinburgh and Princess Margaret had their happiest family party of the year last night—at Bertram Mills Circus, Olympia.

At times, during the three-hour performance, all three rocked with laughter—especially at the clowns.

Margaret, wearing a mink coat over a black evening gown, seemed in high spirits. She sat at the Duke's side and often turned to whisper a private joke to him.

The Duke chuckled each time and passed on the joke to the Queen, who sat with Major E. W. S. Ford, an Assistant Private Secretary.

The Royal Party gasped during the show when crazy-wire performer Reco—Yorkshireman Herbert Wroe—fell 12 feet after struts on his apparatus collapsed. Reco was unhurt.

Daily Mirror

MON FEB 18 1957

2ᴰ FORWARD WITH THE PEOPLE

No. 16,542

Royal Visit Special

HEARTS ON HIS TIE

THE picture of happiness on the right was taken when the Queen and the Duke of Edinburgh were re-united in Portugal at the week-end—their first meeting since the Duke set out on his world tour more than four months ago.

The smiling Duke has his hand on his heart—and the Queen can see at a glance that he is wearing A TIE WITH A HEART-SHAPED MOTIF.

The Queen was dressed in a brand new fashion—navy blue dress and matching " Middy Line " jacket.

This is the newest line from the recent Paris shows.

The Duke greeted the Queen when she landed at Montijo.

Then they drove to the royal yacht Britannia, anchored at the fishing port of Setubal, to spend the weekend.

This morning the Queen and the Duke are sailing in Britannia to Lisbon to start their four-day State visit to Portugal.

FOR MORE PICTURES AND ANNE LLOYD'S STORY OF THE MEETING — SEE CENTRE & BACK PAGES.

Daily Mirror

TUES APR 9 1957

2ᴰ **FORWARD WITH THE PEOPLE**

No. 16,585

ROYAL SOUVENIR

TOAST of PARIS

AFTER a day of splendour, a day of cheering, a spectacular welcome-to-Paris day, the Queen and the Duke of Edinburgh went to a gala ballet performance at the Paris Opera last night.

The Queen was the toast of Paris in a magnificent, tight-bodiced, full-skirted robe of ivory satin embroidered in gold with the wild flowers of France.

Small golden bees, Napoleon's emblem, were dotted about the flowers. The design was set in a background of cream-coloured wheatsheaves.

In the vast square outside the Opera, 50,000 excited French people chanted "We want the Queen." And she appeared on the balcony to wave to them for three minutes.

More wonderful pictures inside and on the Back Page. The story of a glittering day—Page 7

The Queen, a glittering figure in a magnificent gown, at the Paris Opera last night. With her is the French President, M. Coty.

Daily Mirror

WED MAY 22 1957

2ᴰ FORWARD WITH THE PEOPLE

No. 16,621

ROYAL SOUVENIR
ALLOW ME!

Royal Visit to DENMARK

The Royal yacht Britannia passed this famous statue of Hans Andersen's character. The Little Mermaid, outside Copenhagen yesterday.

SO FRIENDLY—EVEN SENTRIES SMILED . . .

With a gesture that says " Allow me," King Frederik helps the Queen to drape her sable fur over her shoulders for the drive in an open carriage through Copenhagen yesterday. And the Danish people followed their King's example and gave the Queen and the Duke an oh-so-homely welcome. Why, even two Palace sentries, stiffly presenting arms, gave the Queen a friendly smile !

Yes, it was a wonderful, carefree day . . . a day of intimate moments.

● *More intimate pictures by Mirror cameramen Freddie Reed and Frank Woods inside and Page 24. Full story on Page 24.*

Daily Mirror

SAT AUG 3 1957

2ᴰ THE BIGGEST DAILY SALE ON EARTH
No. 16,684

THE QUEEN —BY A PEER

Island in the sun? Looks like US!

By the Daily Mirror Weathercock

A BRIGHT PHEWture for the holiday crowds—that is what the weather experts forecast.

Temperatures should be up in the eighties today and tomorrow, they say.

But they warn that there is an outside chance that the weather MIGHT be less settled on Monday.

Another warning comes from a doctor who says: "The fact that we had a poor July will mean that many skins that were well tanned during June will be tender again.

"So take the sun in small doses this week-end."

Yesterday's hot spots were Barmouth, Merionethshire, and Chivenor, North Devon . . . 80 degrees in the shade.

☆

WEATHER: Fine and warm. OUTLOOK: Similar on Sunday, possibly less settled on Monday.

SUNSET: London 8.46.

AN EASY START ON THE ROADS

A QUIET start to the Bank Holiday road rush in the South was reported by the Automobile Association last night.

They said that holiday car traffic on roads from London to the coast was "surprisingly light."

The rush is expected to start today.

The Royal Automobile Club reported heavy traffic on roads from the Midlands to the West Country.

DAILY MIRROR REPORTER

ASTONISHING criticism of the Royal Family and the Queen is made today by Tory peer Lord Altrincham in the National and English Review of which he is editor and chairman.

In an article in the August issue, he—

ATTACKS the "class" character of the Queen and Princess Margaret;

ATTACKS the Queen's "tweedy" entourage;

CRITICISES the Queen's style of speaking as "a pain in the neck";

DESCRIBES her broadcast personality as "that of a priggish schoolgirl";

CRITICISES the Court for "failing to move with the times.

Lord Altrincham writes first of King George V whose reign, he says, was a decisive one. He adds:

"George V was not a clever man and his constitutional sense was sometimes defective, yet his services to the Monarchy are beyond price, since he managed to adjust it, in essentials, to the new conditions."

Lord Altrincham goes on:

"When she has lost the bloom of youth the Queen's reputation will depend, far more than it does now, upon her personality.

"It will not then be enough for her to go through the motions; she will have to say things which people can remember, and do things on her own initiative.

"As yet there is little sign that such a personality is emerging. . . ."

'Upper-class'

After declaring that the Crown must not seem to be identified with any particular social group, Lord Altrincham writes of "The relatively 'classless' character of George V. . . .

"Unfortunately," he adds, "it is not to be seen in his granddaughters.

"The Queen and Princess Margaret still bear the debutante stamp.

"Why is this? The most likely reason is that they were given a conventional upper-class education. . . .

"'Crawfie,' Sir Henry Marten, the London season, the racecourse, the grousemoor, Canasta, and the occasional Royal tour—all this would not have been good enough for Queen Elizabeth I."

["Crawfie"—then Miss Marion Crawford—was the governess to the Queen and Princess Margaret. Sir Henry Marten, Provost of Eton, who died in 1948, was the Queen's senior tutor when she was Princess Elizabeth.]

Lord Altrincham continues: "It says much for

Lord Altrincham
He is thirty-three and was educated at Eton and Oxford. A bachelor, he succeeded his father, the first Baron Altrincham, in 1955.

the Queen that she has not been incapacitated for her job by this woefully inadequate training . . .

"But will she have the wisdom to give her children an education very different from her own?

"Will she, above all, see to it that Prince Charles is equipped with all the knowledge he can absorb without injury to his health, and that he mixes during his formative years with children who will one day be bus drivers, dockers, engineers, etc.—not merely with future landowners or stockbrokers?

"These are crucial questions."

'Tweedy'

The present composition of the Court, Lord Altrincham says, "emphasises the social lopsidedness to which the Monarchy is still prone.

"The Queen's entourage—those who serve her from day to day, who accompany her when she travels and sit with her when she eats—are almost without exception people of the 'tweedy' sort . . .

"In other words, the Court has lamentably failed to move with the times; while the Monarchy has become 'popular' and multi-racial, the Court has remained a tight little enclave of British 'ladies and gentlemen.' This cannot be right.

"The Queen should

'Priggish speeches'

surely now be surrounded by advisers and companions with as many different backgrounds as possible."

Lord Altrincham then comments on the Queen's speeches and the fact that this year her Christmas broadcast is to be televised for the first time. He adds:

"She will not, however, achieve good results with her present style of speaking, which is, frankly, 'a pain in the neck.'

'Hollow'

"Like her mother, she appears to be unable to string even a few sentences together without a written text—a defect which is particularly regrettable when she can be seen by her audience. . . .

"Phrases such as 'I am deeply moved' sound very hollow when they are read from a typescript. . . . But . . . with practice even a prepared speech can be given an air of spontaneity.

"George V, for instance, did not write his own speeches, yet they were always in character. . . .

"Not so the present Queen's.

"The personality conveyed by the utterances which are put into her mouth is that of a priggish schoolgirl, captain of the hockey team, a prefect, and a recent candidate for Confirmation."

'Idly by'

Admitting that his remarks may strike some readers as "intolerably disrespectful," Lord Altrincham says:

"Those of us who believe that the Monarchy can survive and play an even more beneficent part . . are not content to remain silent while needless errors go uncorrected.

"The Monarchy cannot afford to miss any chances now, nor can its devotees afford to stand idly by while they honestly think it is missing its chances."

● A Buckingham Palace spokesman said last night:

"Important speeches by the Queen are usually drafted by the Minister concerned. Other speeches are prepared by one of her private secretaries."

Talking to Women

● There are times when we all want to SCREAM!
There's a point where life itself becomes unbearable.
Some of us crack, and our misery is labelled "nervous breakdown."
A woman who travelled to the brink of madness tells you about her suffering and her joyous recovery.

● "I've never met a man who didn't make a pass at me," says the girl who will do anything for publicity.
She is the Blonde of the Age, the girl who plans to wed in a mink bikini.
What she is really like makes wonderful reading in
WOMAN'S SUNDAY MIRROR, on sale TODAY.

Printed and Published by THE DAILY MIRROR NEWSPAPERS, Ltd., at Geraldine House, Fetter-lane, London, E.C.4. Tel. Holborn 4321, and at Mark-lane, Manchester 4.—Saturday, August 3, 1957.

Daily Mirror

WED AUG 21 1957

2ᴰ FORWARD WITH THE PEOPLE
No. 16,699

THE ROYAL FAMILY

'LORD A' ATTACKS AGAIN

- He talks about our "Tourist Queen"
- He criticises the "old conception of monarchy"
- He condemns the "entire peerage" for grabbing the Coronation seats

LORD ALTRINCHAM, the peer whose criticism of the Queen and the Court set the world talking, has returned to the attack.

In an article published in several American and Canadian newspapers yesterday, he said that the time had come to make a living reality of the Queen's title "Head of the Commonwealth."

The Queen, he declared, is "still based upon the United Kingdom. When she goes elsewhere it is in the capacity of tourist."

"Canada is no more distant to her than the Scottish Highlands were to Queen Victoria. It can be reached by air in the same time that it takes to reach Balmoral by train."

He declared that the old conception of a monarchy, in which one country had controlling interest and the others were only minority shareholders, was "quite inappropriate now."

During her reign, Queen Elizabeth must come to feel hardly less at home in Canada and in other Commonwealth

- LONDON-BALMORAL by train and road: 14 hours.
- LONDON-OTTAWA by air: 12 hours 40 minutes.

countries than in Britain, said Lord Altrincham.

Her children also must be given the chance to feel completely at home in every part of the Commonwealth.

He suggested that the Commonwealth countries were not receiving their "full rights" to the Royal Family, although he attached some of the blame for this to the Commonwealth countries themselves.

For instance, Lord Altrincham said, Canada should have insisted that all her leading personalities should have been present at the Coronation. . . .

"Canada should have insisted that the Abbey should not be largely occupied, as in the past, by a host of near-mediocrities—not to mention the entire peerage —from the United Kingdom.

"Yet nothing of the kind was done."

Lord Altrincham said he was forced to conclude that Canadians did not seem to realise that the monarchy "was theirs as well as ours."

He hoped the Queen Mother would be appointed Canada's next Governor-General, but this, he said, would not happen unless the Canadian Government urged her most strongly to accept.

- THE QUEEN . . ." still based upon the United Kingdom."

THE QUEEN . . . and the 'Mirror'

THE Royal Controversy, started by Lord Altrincham, is still being sharply discussed by the public—and by politicians.

The battle has been reported, round by round and blow by blow, in this newspaper. That is its job.

But why has the Mirror maintained a monk-like silence about its own views? Is the Mirror "pro" or "anti" Altrincham?

The Mirror is not by nature a shrinking violet. It is rarely tongue-tied. It does not usually blush unseen. Its light has never hitherto been hidden under a bushel.

The answer is simple. The Mirror has ALREADY expressed without humbug—though more politely than Lord Altrincham—its constructive views on reforms now urgently required to strengthen the Royal Family's bond with the ordinary people of Britain and the Commonwealth.

In tomorrow's issue of this newspaper there will be published—

- What the Mirror has praised about recent Royal activities.
- What the Mirror has criticised.

TOGETHER WITH

- The Mirror's verdict on the Altrincham controversy.

Daily Mirror

TUES AUG 27 1957

2ᴰ FORWARD WITH THE PEOPLE

No. 16,704

The 19-year-old Lord Londonderry said last night:

"I HUMBLY APOLOGISE TO THE QUEEN'

THE Marquis of Londonderry, aged 19, who recently referred to the Royal Family "flashing their toothpaste smiles," yesterday apologised "for my bad manners."

In a statement written on notepaper headed with his Park-street, Mayfair, address, Lord Londonderry said:

❝ Public reaction to my letter has made it abundantly manifest that a personal attack on the Royal Family is much resented. Especially if the attack should come from someone both insignificant and unqualified.

Criticism of the monarchy must always be on a general level, and any attempt to make the Royal Family a target for personal criticism merely degrades the attacker in everyone's eyes and sets him up as an object of contempt.

I have been guilty of the latter crime and for that I am truly contrite. I fully comprehend and appreciate the resentment of those who accuse me of cowardice in pointlessly attacking someone who cannot retaliate.

For any personal attack on the Royal Family I am sincerely sorry and humbly apologise for my bad manners. ❞

Grandma Wanted to See Him . . .

In his criticism of the Queen and the Court—published in the magazine New Statesman—Lord Londonderry talked of the Royal Family. . . .

"Flashing their toothpaste smiles, displaying their latest hair-dos and exhibiting their deplorable taste in clothes."

The same day, Lord Londonderry was ordered to report to his grandmother, the Dowager Marchioness of Londonderry, aged seventy-seven, with whom he was staying.

A fellow-guest, Mr. H. Montgomery Hyde, Tory M.P. for North Belfast—he was private secretary to Lord Londonderry's grandfather—told him:

"I have been commanded by Granny to bring you in. She wants to see you."

The next day the Dowager Marchioness issued a statement describing her grandson's criticism as "vulgar, childish and silly."

The youthful Lord Londonderry's attack embarrassed not only the Dowager Marchioness.

It also greatly embarrassed the thirty-three-year-old Lord Altrincham, who was anxious to keep his own criticisms of the Royal Family on quite a different level.

Killed on way to dinner

DEATH ended the drive-to-dinner of former TV actress Pat Russell, 27, pictured left, and her husband's best friend, Geoffrey Neame, 30.

Both were killed when the car they were in hit a tree.

A second man in the car was injured.

Pat's husband, farmer Tom Hewer, 37, said yesterday that he and Pat entertained the Neames for cocktails at their farm near Winchester, Hants, and then they decided to dine at an hotel.

"Pat went in Mr. Neame's car," said Mr. Hewer. "So I took Mrs. Neame in my car."

STORY—PAGE 5.

★ **PARIS** Fashions   **FIRST PICTURES** —SEE CENTRE PAGES

4

Daily Mirror

THURS OCT 17 1957

2½ FORWARD WITH THE PEOPLE

No. 16,748

Ladies and gentlemen, today the Mirror gives you the loyal toast..

'THE QUEEN!'

Three reforms to make her reign happy and glorious

① MORE TRUE LOYALTY

to Her Majesty. The gulf between Palace and People is NOT the fault of the Queen or of Prince Philip.

② COMMONSENSE

about the right to criticise as well as to applaud.

③ SWIFTER CHANGES

In the age of man-made moons, the ghost of Queen Victoria should finally be laid to rest.

YESTERDAY—fresh from her personal triumph in Canada—the Queen began her visit to the United States.

The Mirror acclaims the Queen's achievements in Canada. She delighted everybody by her self-confidence and her warm, human speeches.

It is lamentable that the Queen's brilliant tour abroad should be accompanied by controversy about the Court at home.

The Mirror is angered when personal attacks are made on the Queen. The personality of the Queen should never become involved in argument about the Court.

Some recent criticism went too far. The Queen's voice and appearance should never be the target for ill-mannered comments.

But the Mirror declares that true loyalty to the Queen does NOT mean that all criticism of the Court must be stifled.

Indeed, full loyalty means that such criticisms should be voiced and examined.

If they are justified, then—in the interests of the Queen herself—reforms must follow.

Orders from Above?

The present controversy arises from criticisms of the Monarchy by Mr. Malcolm Muggeridge and Lord Altrincham. It has been fanned into flames by the folly of the B.B.C. in banning both these critics.

General Sir Ian Jacob, Director-General of the B.B.C. **(Better Be Careful)**, has turned himself into General Sir "Gag."

Is General Sir "Gag" acting on his own—or has he had orders from above?

Whatever the answer, this attempt to suppress debate is a blunder and a disservice to the Queen.

It has been alleged that Muggeridge and Altrincham attacked the Monarchy as an institution. That is claptrap.

Both applaud the Monarchy. Both urge reform to make the Monarchy more up to date.

Muggeridge wrote:

"The British Monarch does fulfil an authentic purpose providing a symbolic head of State transcending the politicians who go in and out of office and proving extremely popular with the majority of the people."

Altrincham wrote:

"Those of us who believe that the Monarchy can survive and play an ever more beneficent part in the affairs of the Commonwealth are not content to remain silent while needless errors go uncorrected."

Some people think that the answer to criticism like this is to ignore it.

Daily Mirror

TUES OCT 22 1957

2½ FORWARD WITH THE PEOPLE

No. 16,752

BELLE OF NEW YORK!

MORE than 600,000 wildly cheering Americans hailed the Queen as "Belle of New York" yesterday in a brilliant climax to her American tour.

FULL STORY—Back Page. MORE PICTURES—Centre Pages.

This was how Broadway, New York, looked yesterday as the Queen drove through in a storm of ticker-tape.

Daily Mirror

TUES JAN 14 1958

2½   FORWARD WITH THE PEOPLE
No. 16,822

MARGARET: THE SWAN NECK

A-bomber crash secrecy

THE United States Government last night confirmed a New York newspaper report that an American plane carrying an atom bomb had crashed on the United States.

The spokesman would not, however, reveal:—

● WHERE or WHEN the crash occurred; and

● HOW MANY CASUALTIES there were. All he would say was that—

● THE PLANE was destroyed by fire; and

● THE BOMB did not explode.

The spokesman said that since the bomb was "not armed no nuclear explosion was possible."

4

This is part of the famous portrait of Princess Margaret by Annigoni —a portrait that shows her as the Princess with the swan neck. The full portrait is on the Back Page.

Daily Mirror

TUES JULY 1 1958

FORWARD WITH THE PEOPLE
No. 16,965

2½

HATS OFF FOR THE PITHEAD QUEEN!

GOOD luck, ma'am! With a doff of the hat, three workers salute the Queen as she makes her first trip down a coal mine.

It happened at Rothes Colliery, Thornton, Fifeshire, yesterday. With the Queen is the colliery manager.

For her forty-minute tour 1,500ft. underground, the Queen wore a down-to-earth outfit of white helmet, white overalls and black gumboots.

But there was one touch of femininity—a white nylon scarf over her head, ears and neck which, besides keeping coal dust OUT kept her hair IN PLACE.

Four times while she crept, half-doubled, to the coal face, the Queen banged her helmeted head against overhead girders.

When she returned to the surface she was as fresh and immaculate as when she went down.

The Duke of Edinburgh went down another shaft. He had a go with a pick and when he mined some coal he asked a miner: "What would I get for that? Ten shillings?"

See John Rolls—Page 2.

ITV GIVES AWAY £100,000

SEE BACK PAGE

THE STAR

No 21,898   ★★   2½d

The Pictures Never Seen Before

IN the 500 years since the Sovereign opened Parliament no picture has been taken—until today. Here is the Queen in the House of Lords reading the Speech from the Throne. The whole place is a blaze of colour and light, of crimson, and gold and ermine.

She is wearing the Royal Robes and the Imperial Crown, Prince Philip the uniform of an Admiral of the Fleet.

On the right is Lord Montgomery, chosen this year to carry the Sword of State.

Picture on the left

shows the Queen in procession in the Royal Gallery, on her way from the Robing Room.

This was seen by millions of viewers in Britain and eight Continental countries.

More pictures and the Queen's speech Pages 8 and 9.

Govt to aid home loans

By ROBERT CARVEL

MR MACMILLAN told the Commons this evening that legislation will shortly be introduced to allow the Government to advance money to building societies and thus make it easier to lend to home buyers.

The Prime Minister continued : " Our aim is to bring about a general widening of house purchase in such a way that special aid will be given to purchasers of those houses —the older and smaller houses —which are most affected by the shortage of mortgage funds."

Ten ballots, but no Pope

THE Cardinals of the Roman Catholic Church, meeting in conclave in the Vatican City today, again signalled with black smoke that after ten ballots they still had not been able to choose a new Pope.

Lord Nuffield ill

Viscount Nuffield is suffering from gastric trouble at his home at Huntercombe, Oxon, it was learned today.

£1,000 hotel raid

Scotland Yard detectives today searched for thieves who stole property worth nearly £1,000 from Mrs L. Fletcher's room at the Stafford Hotel, St James's-place, Piccadilly.

'FOG TONIGHT'

DENSE fog will return to South-East England this evening and will stay until tomorrow, when it will be slow to clear, the Air Ministry warned.

Earlier today fog had disrupted London road traffic, stopped Thames shipping, delayed Southern Region suburban trains, and grounded planes at London Airport for 13 hours.

FORECAST

Forecast : Fog, but sunny later. Warm.
Outlook : Similar.
Lights up 5.11

TV and Radio—Page 13

Daily Mirror

TUES APR 28 1959

2½ᵈ FORWARD WITH THE PEOPLE ✦ No. 17,220

EVER SEEN THE 'ROYALS' LOOKING LIKE THIS?

THIS dramatic, strikingly unusual picture of the Queen and the Duke of Edinburgh was taken by Canadian photographer Donald McKague.

It was the Queen's own idea to have a Canadian as "Royal photographer" — to take some special pictures for the visit to Canada which she and the Duke are making this summer.

The Canadian Government chose McKague, thirty-seven-year-old Toronto man who took up photography only ten years ago.

He flew to London last December and spent four days setting up his camera and lights in Buckingham Palace. Then, in an hour-long session, he took more than fifty pictures of the Queen and the Duke.

Royal pictures with something DIFFERENT about them. . . .

Another new picture of the Queen

1

Daily Mirror

SAT AUG 8 1959

FORWARD WITH THE PEOPLE

2½

No. 17,308

The gay picture that was taken when (note the twinkle in his eye)

ONLY THEY KNEW!

OFFICIAL

It was announced from Buckingham Palace yesterday that the Queen has cancelled her public engagements. She is

OFFICIAL

expecting a baby early in the New Year. The Queen, who is 33, and the Duke are very happy about it.

OFFICIAL

Lord Evans, the Queen's doctor, said: "She is in the best health —this is very important."

See Page 3, Centre and Back Pages

Even today's Page One advertiser didn't know. He booked this "ad" on July 18, 1958. . . .

The Queen and the Duke pictured on their Canadian tour when ONLY THEY KNEW!

Daily Mirror

SAT AUG 8 1959

2½ THE BIGGEST DAILY SALE IN THE UNIVERSE

No. 17,308

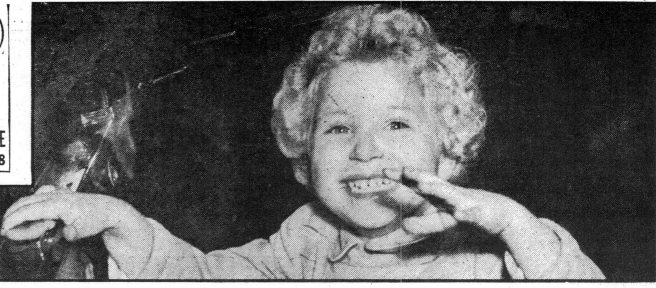

A GAY wave to the crowd from Princess Anne when she was four years old. Now the "baby" of the Royal Family is going to be "big sister." And the question is—

Will it be a brother? Or will it be a sister? for

DELIGHTFUL, MISCHIEVOUS ANNE

GAY, delightful, mischievous Princess Anne—what a lovely "big sister" for any baby to have! Here you see the Princess, who is nine on August 15, in a variety of moods matching the various meanings given to her name.

● FULL OF FUN . . . in Irish, Anne means "joyful."

● DETERMINED . . . in German, Anne means "courageous."

● FAIR LADY . . . in Welsh it means golden-haired.

EISENHOWER TELLS HIS CABINET

NEWS that the Queen is expecting another child was flashed round the world yesterday within minutes of the announcement in Britain.

In GHANA, West Africa —where the Queen was to have toured in November— the Prime Minister, Dr. Kwame Nkrumah, said: "I know that every man and woman will rejoice with me at this news, and wish me to convey their good wishes to the Queen and Duke of Edinburgh."

In WASHINGTON, President Eisenhower and his wife Mamie, who were told in advance, were said to be "delighted."

As soon as the public announcement arrived on the ticker-tape, the President read it to his Cabinet, which was meeting at the White House.

In OTTAWA, Canada, Prime Minister John Diefenbaker said: "This glad news will be greeted with happiness and acclaim by the Queen's subjects everywhere."

WEATHER: Dry, sunny intervals. **OUTLOOK:** Chance of thundery rain **SUNSET:** London 8.38

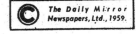

The Daily Mirror Newspapers, Ltd., 1959.

Printed and Published by THE DAILY MIRROR NEWSPAPERS, Ltd., at Geraldine House, Fetter-lane, London, E.C.4. Tel. Holborn 4321, and at Mark-lane. Manchester 4.—Saturday, August 8 1959.

Daily Mirror

SAT AUG 29 1959

FORWARD WITH THE PEOPLE

2½

No. 17,326

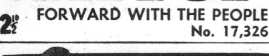

HOWDY!

Ike gives a "howdy" wave to the crowds at Balmoral yesterday as the Queen and Duke smilingly look on. Hidden behind the Duke is Princess Margaret. If you look closely you can see one of her shoes and a glimpse of her skirt.

The Queen drives Ike to a picnic

THE Queen drove President Eisenhower to a picnic tea with her children on the shores of Loch Muick, near Balmoral Castle, yesterday.

Ike, who was on a one-day visit to Balmoral, had lunch at the castle.

Soon afterwards he left with the Queen, Princess Margaret, and his son, Major John Eisenhower, on a brief tour of the estate.

The Queen was at the wheel.

Later the Duke of Edinburgh took Prince Charles and Princess Anne to meet them at the loch in another car.

Loch Muick is about three miles long and half a mile wide, set in hilly country.

The picnic was at a spot called Glas Allt, where there is a summer-house, now disused, which Queen Victoria used to visit regularly.

"How Nice of You to Meet Me"— SEE CENTRE PAGES.

Daily Mirror

TUES FEB. 9 1960

2½

No. 17,464

THE QUEEN: A CURIOUS DECISION

Some of her descendants will be called

MOUNTBATTEN-WINDSOR

By WILLIAM GREIG

THE Queen, who is awaiting the birth of her third child, announced last night that she had given her family the surname of MOUNTBATTEN-WINDSOR for use by those of her descendants who will not hold the title of H R H, Prince or Princess.

She has combined her own family name, Windsor, with the name Prince Philip took when he became a naturalised British citizen on February, 28, 1947.

There was little doubt last night that the decision had followed a conflict of views between the Queen and her Cabinet.

At one time there was undoubtedly pressure on the Queen to adopt for her family the name of Mountbatten **ALONE**. But this proposal had no appeal to Ministers

What the Cabinet said

The use of both names is a controversial compromise—said to have been arrived at only after very strong advice from the Cabinet.

This advice concerned the possible effect on public opinion of changing the name of the Royal House.

The Queen was reminded strongly of the history of the Mountbatten name, which was adopted by Earl Mountbatten's father, Prince Louis of Battenberg, during the First World War.

Because the new name will not apply until Prince Charles has grandsons, it is unlikely to be held by any member of the Royal Family for between thirty and forty years.

The first person to use it may well be THE SECOND GRANDSON OF PRINCE CHARLES.

Prince Charles's first grandson would not bear the new name, as he would still be a Prince of the House of Windsor.

Before the Queen made her decision the matter was discussed with Earl Mountbatten "as a matter of courtesy"—because he is head of the Mountbatten family

EARL MOUNTBATTEN
He was consulted

MY WILL AND PLEASURE
—Back Page

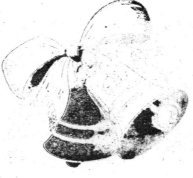

Daily Mirror

2½   **Saturday February 20, 1960**   **No. 17,474**

OH BOY!

Radiant and happy... the Queen pictured when she arrived in London from Sandringham to await the birth of her third child —the new Prince who is now second in line to the Throne.

TWENTY-ONE words thrilled the nation yesterday—the announcement that the Queen had given birth to a son.

It said: "The Queen was safely delivered of a son at 3.30 p.m. today. Her Majesty and the infant Prince are both doing well."

The notice, hung on the railings outside Buckingham Palace, was signed by Mr. John Peel, the gynaecologist, Dr. Vernon Hall, the anaesthetist, and Sir John Weir and Lord Evans, the Queen's physicians.

The baby Prince, whose weight has not yet been announced, is sharing a room with Sister Helen Rowe, adjoining the Queen's room.

A few hours after the birth, the Duke of Edinburgh took Anne to see her new brother.

Later, Prince Charles was given special leave from Cheam School and was driven home to the Palace. Immediately he arrived he, too, saw the baby.

Up and down the country bells rang and flags flew, and from all over the world messages of congratulation poured in to the Palace.

● More news and pictures on Pages 3, 9, 12, 13 and 24

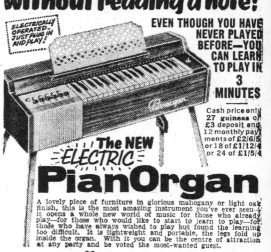

Daily Mirror

WED MAR. 23 1960

2ᵈ

No. 17,501

H.R.H.

INTRODUCING . . .

ANDREW ALBERT CHRISTIAN EDWARD

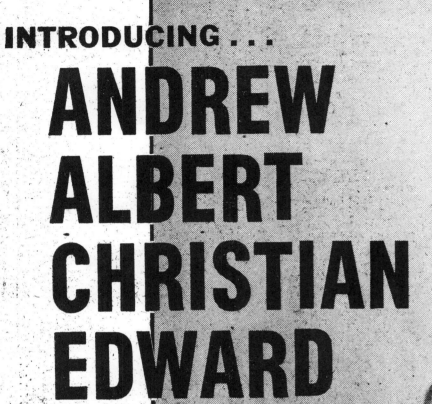

IT'S a Royal pat on the back for ANDREW ALBERT CHRISTIAN EDWARD!

And doing the patting is the Queen—in this first picture of the baby Prince, at Buckingham Palace.

The first two names are those of the little Prince's grandfathers—Prince Andrew of Greece and King George VI.

The third is that of his great-great-great-grandfather, King Christian IX of Denmark, and the fourth is of his great-great-grandfather King Edward VII.

The baby will be known as PRINCE ANDREW.

The Registrar at Caxton Hall, London, went to the Palace to register the birth yesterday.

His name—Mr. William PRINCE.

★ This picture was taken by CECIL BEATON. More Beaton pictures are on the Centre and Back Pages. THE FIRST PRINCE ANDREW FOR 500 YEARS—Page 9.

THE STAR

TUESDAY, APRIL 5, 1960

No 22,343   ★★   Twopence Halfpenny

CLOSING CITY PRICES

LATE NIGHT

LE JOUR DE GLOIRE

And the story of one little girl's father tells why we honour France today

Star Reporter

A ONE-ARMED ex-corporal of France, Nicola Caplan, of Westminster Road, Carshalton, will meet General de Gaulle in London tomorrow.

With his English wife he will watch as their five-year-old daughter, Nicole, presents a bouquet to the President.

The bouquet comes from the wartime Free French and Resistance Fighters.

Nicole has been chosen because of her father. And The Star proudly tells his story because he personifies the courage and the tenacity of his country.

Sent to Norway

In 1940 he was Senior Corporal Caplan, regular soldier and member of the French corps elite. He was sent to Norway following the German invasion there.

But the French were forced to make a Dunkirk-style escape. Senior Corporal Caplan was put in charge of a small detachment to cover the embarkation. One by one his comrades were killed. He was left alone firing his machine gun. Finally his right arm was practically severed and trapped in the wreckage of his gun.

With a pen-knife he completed the amputation. A German officer shot him in the head to finish him off.

Got French VC

Senior Corporal Caplan was officially posted as dead and posthumously awarded the French VC—and was made a Chevalier of the Legion d'Honneur with Military Cross. But the German officer's bullet had been deflected by his helmet.

Norwegian civilians rescued him. He was brought to England, and after a long convalescence he found himself at de Gaulle's Free French Headquarters in Carlton Gardens, Westminster, acting as messenger and as one of the General's security screen.

With the Liberation he accompanied de Gaulle back to France. But he did not stay. When the war was over he returned to marry Miss Helen Bacon, whom he had met in London. Now he works with British Railways at Victoria.

His return

But tomorrow he will take the day off to return to Carlton Gardens and meet the General again—one of the 500-600 Free French and Resistance Movement veterans invited to the occasion.

And ex-Senior Corporal Caplan will wear his medals—among them the Legion d'Honneur, the Norwegian Military Cross and the Croix de Guerre.

CLOUDY

Forecast until midday tomorrow : Mostly cloudy. Some bright intervals today. Drizzle or rain in places tomorrow. Winds fresh or strong. Warm. Barometer (9 am) : 29.99 in. rising

Outlook : Showers or outbreaks of rain, but bright periods also. Rather warm

Lights-up : 7.9.

Radio & TV—page 17

Madame de Gaulle, in navy blue, drove with the Duke of Edinburgh to Buckingham Palace after she and President de Gaulle had been welcomed by the Queen and other members of the Royal family at Victoria, when they arrived today. Story and more pictures on Pages 10 and 11.

Nicole

Who, me ?

Nicola

Left for dead.

Fur, gems haul

A fur coat and jewellery worth £2,000 were stolen from a house in Robin Hood Way, New Malden.

Blackmail girl, 13, 'saw it on TV'

A SCHOOLGIRL of 13 who had been blackmailing a warehouse manager told a detective who questioned her, "I have seen it done on television," North London juvenile court were told today.

The girl, dressed in a shortie coat, tight short skirt, nylons and stiletto-heeled shoes, admitted demanding money with menaces from the man. He was referred to as Alf.

She was committed to an approved school.

Detective - constable Arthur Page said the girl telephoned the man saying: "I want £5 and I want it in 20 minutes —or I tell your wife."

The girl told the magistrates: "He used to give me money. I took £10 from him, but he never touched me."

She broke down sobbing at the court's decision.

ONASSIS DIVORCE CASE OFF

Mrs Tina Onassis today discontinued her New York court suit for divorce from Aristotle Onassis, the shipping magnate.

It was disclosed that under a separation agreement the two children will reside with their mother, with Mr Onassis having joint custody.

Mrs Onassis neither asked for nor received alimony or legal fees, it was disclosed.

With the smiling Queen beside him, President de Gaulle waved happily to the crowds as they drove from Victoria to Buckingham Palace. The Queen was in sapphire blue with a high-crowned hat of stiffened tulle.

Protection men jailed—Page 2

Simone at the top — 3

African policeman hacked to death—5

£100 BOND WINNERS PAGE 16

Air fare cuts —Back Page

£300 cameras stolen

Cameras worth £300 were stolen today from a showcase at the shop of Boatmen & Co, Duke Street, Chelmsford.

Evening Standard

42,267 — FRIDAY, MAY 6. 1960 — ● 2½d.

ROYAL
WEDDING
EDITION

All England here, whose symbol is the Rose,
Prays that this Lady's Fortune may be fair

JOHN MASEFIELD TODAY

Together they make their vows

By Anne Sharpley

In splendour, sunshine and great sweetness, Princess Margaret married Mr. Antony Armstrong-Jones, the young man without title, without pretension, today in Westminster Abbey.

It was something that could have happened only in the 20th century—a Sovereign's daughter marrying a photographer

ON THE PALACE BALCONY

As seething crowds waited outside the Palace there were cries of "We want Margaret."

Suddenly, some of the crowd broke through the police cordon.

Twenty yards from the Palace railings they rushed forward in a wild stampede.

There were screams and shouts.

But the incident was over in less than a minute.

Then the bride and bridegroom appeared on the Palace balcony.

Princess Anne was standing behind them.

And then Prince Charles and the other members of the Royal Family joined them.

Every time they half-turned as if to leave the balcony the crowd stayed them with another tremendous burst of cheering.

with all the force of the centuries of this ancient land bringing dignity, grace and deep approval.

Princess Margaret — perhaps we have never known before how beautiful she is — kept a sweet gravity about her that we had never seen.

The simplicity and lightness of her gown, her quiet air. She was a woman surrounded by all the white mystery of womanhood.

Her young husband, Antony Armstrong-Jones, kept looking at her with what seemed to be tender astonishment, as though this was a Margaret he had never seen before.

Only a little earlier, before the Princess went up the aisle, he was a little pensive. But he whispered to Dr. Roger Gilliatt, his best man, who seemed to be encouraging him.

Together the couple made their vows, she in the light, sweet, steady voice that we know so well: he inexperiencedly in a low inaudible voice.

But they were brought so close by the moments they

▲ Page 14, Column Two

The ceremony is over. Hand-in-hand Princess Margaret and her husband walk down the aisle. For her a look of radiance. From him a reassuring grip. And outside the crowds wait to cheer them on their way.

Daily Mirror

2½d.   Friday, September 9, 1960   No. 17,646

HAPPY ANDREW

BALMORAL HOLIDAY No. 1

THIS gay new picture of the Queen with six-month-old Prince Andrew and smiling Princess Anne, was taken at Balmoral yesterday.

It is the Prince's first holiday in Scotland.

☆ Now turn to the Centre Pages for more pictures of HAPPY ANDREW.

Daily Mirror

2d. Thursday, October 20, 1960 ★ No. 17,681

AFTER YOU

GALLANTLY King Mahendra of Nepal waits while the Queen takes her seat in the Royal Box at the Royal Opera House, Covent Garden, last night.

Behind them the Duke of Kent, equally gallantly, holds the Queen's chair, ready to lend a hand. Also in the picture, the Duke's mother, the Duchess of Kent.

The Queen was a glittering figure in a diamond tiara, necklace and earrings and a white and gold satin gown embroidered with pearls and diamonds.

The opera they saw was Bellini's "La Sonnambula."

It was the last spectacular engagement of a three-day State Visit by King Mahendra and his wife Queen Ratna.

★

Story and more pictures—See CENTRE PAGES.

Daily Mirror

2½d.   Friday, March 3, 1961   No. 17,794

THE KILL!

DEATH OF A RHINO — the rare, "protected" animal whose shooting by the royal hunting party in Nepal last Monday brought protests from wild-life experts in Britain. The rhino lies dead in the jungle grass (left in the picture), killed by Foreign Secretary the Earl of Home—who had missed a tigress with four shots. In the background: part of the ring of elephants which had penned the rhino in a death-trap arena. The Queen is seen in her howdah—elephant-back passenger box—in the top right of the picture. The Duke of Edinburgh, spectator of the hunt because of his injured trigger finger, is aboard the elephant next but one on t Queen's right. Lord Home is in the front the howdah on the Duke's right.

More pictures of the jungle death tr are in the Centre Pages.

Daily Mirror

Thursday, March 16, 1961   No. 17,805

OUT GOES SOUTH AFRICA

JONES GETS 14 YEARS

—See Page Three

★

BIG TIP FOR THE BIG RACE

—See Page Twenty-seven

★

STORM OVER NEW £460-A-WEEK RAIL BOSS

—See Back Page

● Dr. Hendrik Verwoerd, South Africa's Premier, pictured yesterday. For three days he has been the key figure at the Commonwealth Conference —he will never attend another.

SOUTH Africa will cease to be a member of the British Commonwealth on becoming a republic at the end of May.

After three days of dramatic discussion, Dr. Verwoerd, South Africa's Premier, last night withdrew his application to remain a member.

It was a day of triumph for the Commonwealth.

Not 'Kicked Out'

The principle that all men are equal and that a White man is not better than a Black man has scored a tremendous victory over the policy of White supremacy followed by the South African Government under Dr. Verwoerd.

He and his country were not "kicked out." Mr. Macmillan and other Commonwealth leaders tried hard to get Dr. Verwoerd to modify his policy of White supremacy.

But he would not budge an inch.

By MICHAEL KING
Mirror Foreign Editor

The credit for the decision—by all the other members of the Commonwealth—to reject South African policy must be given to India's Mr. Nehru.

His influence on the outcome was paramount.

The Premiers were very near to agreeing on a formula which would enable South Africa to remain in the Commonwealth when Dr. Verwoerd announced his decision to withdraw his membership application.

He told the other Prime Ministers:

"The proceedings at today's meeting, which have obliged me to take this regrettable step, in my opinion, mark the beginning of the disintegration of the Commonwealth."

In fact, his decision will mean an enormous increase in the influence of the British Commonwealth in the African Continent—at a time when it is the chief target of Russia's foreign policy.

In his personal statement to the other Prime Ministers Dr. Verwoerd also said:

"The opposition to South Africa's continued membership is based on alleged discrimination and oppression of the non-White peoples of South Africa."

And he struck a defiant note in denying these charges when he declared:

"It is ironical that these allegations have come from Prime Ministers in whose own countries oppression and discrimination are openly practised and where the basic principles of democratic government are flouted."

But, Dr. Verwoerd also said that South Africa will "endeavour to co-operate in all possible ways with all those members of the Commonwealth who are willing to maintain their former good relations with us."

Statement Today?

Mr. Macmillan and his Government have been totally taken aback by yesterday's decision.

The Premier is expected to make a full statement on South Africa to the House of Commons today.

● The immediate reaction to the big news in South Africa last night was one of shock and resentment. The stock market is expected to be heavily shaken.

WHAT THE MIRROR SAYS—Page Two.

Daily Mirror

3d. Tuesday, June 6, 1961   No. 17,874

All smiles as Jackie meets the Queen

THE END OF A WONDERFUL DAY

By ALAN GORDON

IT was a great day for Londoners . . . and a great day America's President Jack Kennedy and his wife Jackie It was also a day of happiness.

And nothing could express that mood of happiness better than picture on the left of the Queen and Jackie at Buckingham Pal last night.

It is a picture to round off the great day perfectly . . . as the Que and Jackie, radiant in length gowns and spark jewellery, pause before go in to dinner.

Glittering

The dinner, at which the Qu and the Duke of Edinburgh w hosts to fifty distinguished gu besides the Kennedys, was a glit ing occasion.

President Kennedy and Jackie twelve minutes late in arriving . . . bec crowds, gay and exuberant, put the of schedule out of joint by swarming in path of their car.

Several thousand people were still ing when President Kennedy left Palace after dinner by car bound London Airport and the plane hom America.

The crowd cheered deafeningly. P dent Kennedy beamed at them.

Then the crowd began to s "Where's Jackie?" For in the car President Kennedy was Britain's Pre Mr. Macmillan.

In the middle of the shouts a car d out of the Palace following the Preside car . . . and in it was Jackie.

'Lovely'

Women shouted "There she is!" huge crowd surged round her car, kisses and said: "Isn't she lovely?"

Jackie grinned at them all. Clearly was enjoying every minute.

At the airport, after a triumphal through streets lined with cheer waving people, President Kennedy see in no hurry to leave Britain.

He shook hands with the police m cyclists who had escorted him. He s hands with airport officials.

Twice Mr. Macmillan began to walk wards the President's plane thinking President Kennedy had finished his g byes.

Goodbye

Each time an airport official pointed to Mr. Macmillan that the President still not ready to go.

Then just before midnight Presi Kennedy said goodbye to Mr. Macm and with a final wave entered his p . . . and was gone.

And Jackie? She is staying in Bri until tomorrow when she goes to Gr before returning to America.

● The guests at last night's Pa dinner sat at one large table. President Kennedy sat on the Que right and Jackie was next to the Du Edinburgh.

● Kennedys go to a christening— CENTRE PAGES; President Kenne meeting with Mr. Macmillan—BA PAGE.

● *Radiant smiles from two First Ladies.*

LONDONERS were cheering for the whole of Britain when they packed the streets to give the Kennedys a tremendous welcome on their brief visit.

THE MIRROR says: Thanks for calling in, Mr. President. It was fine having you with us.

We were eager to have a look at you and at your gay and lovely wife.

We were happy to see you because you are the leader of our greatest Ally. And because we think you are keen and on the ball (and we don't mean the golf ball, either).

But there is more to your visit than that.

We admire your initiative in tackling Mr. Krushchev in Vienna.

MIRROR PAGE ONE COMMENT

You're only forty-four years old. It is less than six months since you took over the biggest job in the Western World.

It is only just over a year since Mr. Krushchev publicly rebuffed your predecessor, Mr. Eisenhower, in Paris.

It needed courage, after that, for you to meet the world's toughest negotiator face to face.

It needed courage for you to override the doubts and the warnings on your side of the Atlantic.

You were right to do so.

The world is full of tired, cautious old men.

But world peace will not be achieved by just waiting for it to happen. It must be planned for, worked for, striven for—and travelled for.

Thank Heavens you've made a start.

Come back, soon, Jack. And stay longer with us next time.

Daily Mirror

3d. Thursday, April 12, 1962   No. 18,138

The Daily Mirror said it on Wed, Nov 13, 1957

NOW PHILIP IS SAYING IT, TOO!

Daily Mirror FORWARD WITH THE PEOPLE No. 16,711

Wake up, Britain!

WE'RE LIVING IN THE PAST WE'RE TOO SLOW, TOO SLEEPY, TOO DAMN SMUG!

URGENT... SEE TODAY'S CENTRE PAGES

HIS Royal Highness the Duke of Edinburgh, just back from his South American tour, told British industrial leaders in London yesterday:—

'There is no getting away from it, at the moment we have a reputation for being rather slow and rather old-fashioned.'

Prince Philip added that in South America people say of Britain—'You don't seem to have anything to offer now.'

WHEN WILL THE DAILY EXPRESS HAVE THE COURAGE TO COME OUT WITH THE SAME HOME TRUTHS?

Today's Editorial in the Mirror is written by Prince Philip.   See Page Two.

FORECAST: City: Cool. Few Showers, but Mainly Fine. Fresh Winds. Max. Temp. 68 Deg.

The Age

POSTAL ADDRESS: 233 COLLINS STREET, C.1. TELEPHONES: 63 0341; CLASSIFIED ADVERTISING: 63 0301.

No. 33,630 {Registered at G.P.O., Melbourne, for Transmission by Post as a Newspaper} MELBOURNE, TUESDAY, FEBRUARY 19, 1963 24 PAGES PRICE 4d.

Classified Index Page 18

"WE ARE DELIGHTED TO BE BACK"

Queen Begins Her Tour of All States

CANBERRA, Monday. — The Queen began her tour of Australia with a day which opened in sombre rain and ended in brilliant spectacle.

She was entertained by the Australian Parliament tonight and 3,000,000 Australians saw her, on television, as "the living and lovely centre of our allegiance"—in the words of the Prime Minister (Mr. Menzies).

The Queen spoke briefly in reply to national leaders and said: "We are both delighted to be back."

She wore white silk for her arrival at Fairbairn Airport. Tonight she wore white again—a State gown encrusted with pearls and diamente.

Despite the rain, 3000 people gathered at Fairbairn aerodrome to see her arrive from New Zealand. Twenty-five thousand lined Canberra streets to watch her drive from the aerodrome to Government House.

With the weather improving steadily, people began gathering outside Parliament House at 6 p.m. to await the Queen's arrival at 9.15 for the Parliamentary reception.

They brought rugs and meals, and children in pyjamas.

Floodlit

From 8.30 on they saw a procession of formally dressed Parliamentarians and their wives, uniformed service leaders and diplomats — many in national dress.

The crowd cheered as, on the floodlit portico, the Queen and the Duke of Edinburgh were met by the Prime Minister (Mr. Menzies) and Dame Pattie Menzies.

Under spotlights, the Queen mounted the main staircase to King's Hall, where the guests massed in welcome — the women curtsying and the men bowing.

With short speeches, Mr. Menzies, the Deputy Prime Minister (Mr. McEwen) and the Federal Opposition Leader (Mr. Calwell) welcomed the Queen to Australia.

A burst of applause interrupted her reply when she said — "I do not intend that this should be my last visit to Australia and next time I hope I shall see different places and many communities that could not be included this time.

"Tonight, on my arrival, I want to send greetings to all Australians and particularly to those we shall not be able to see on this occasion."

With the Duke, she spent several minutes inspecting the painting, now hanging in King's Hall, in which Ivor Hele depicted the opening of Parliament during the last Royal visit.

Then, obviously relaxed, the Queen spent more than half an hour talking with guests in the courtyards of Parliament House.

Guests Dine

Guests at the Parliament House reception dined on baron of beef, crowns of lamb, Russian, Waldorf, Japanese, French, Spanish, Californian and Harlequin salads, Scotch salmon, golden pheasant, and many other dishes.

About 800 guests attended the glittering reception, including Cabinet Ministers, senior service chiefs, members of the judiciary, heads of the Government departments, and members of the clergy.

King's Hall was a blaze of color with red carpets, trees and shrubs in pots lining the corridors and huge chandeliers shining overhead.

Guests dined buffet style in the cavernous Parliamentary dining-room.

Welcome by Leaders

Welcoming the Queen to the reception the Prime Minister (Mr. Menzies), speaking with emotion, said:

"We see you as our Queen, our Sovereign Lady, as the successor to monarchs who, in this very century, by their own standards and genius helped preserve our Monarchy in a world in which Crowns have tumbled and disasters have beset mankind.

"So far from abrogating any liberty because we are your subjects we add to our liberty because we are your subjects.

"Out of our allegiance to you comes an addition to our freedom and not a subtraction from it.

"You are the living and lovely centre of our enduring allegiance."

The Prime Minister added that the Queen was starting on a journey in which she would be seen by millions of Australians.

"This must be something that to you is almost a task," he said turning to the Queen.

With Joy

"I ask you to remember that in this country every man, woman and child who even sees you as a passing glimpse will remember it with joy in the words of the 17th century poet—'I did but see her passing by but yet I love her till I die.'"

The Deputy Prime Minister (Mr. McEwen) and the Federal Opposition Leader (Mr. Calwell), also welcomed the Queen.

Mr. McEwen told the Queen that in Australia loyalty was nowhere warmer than in the outback.

"For all our womenfolk it is an especial joy and pride that our monarch is a woman, a young mother with young children," said Mr. McEwen.

Great Future

Mr. Calwell said that Australians visualised a great future for their country.

"It is our prayer and our hope that events beyond our shores and beyond our control will not rob us and our children of our right to achieve it," said Mr. Calwell.

"It would be idle to pretend that in this rapidly changing world, changes in the relationship between Great Britain and Australia may not and will not occur.

"We all hope that these changes, if they occur, will not affect the relationship between Australia and the Crown, and that the Crown will become even more personal and intimate as it becomes increasingly the really significant link between Australia and Great Britain, between Australia and the rest of the Commonwealth of nations.

"We hope that this link, the only remaining tangible link, will never become cold and formal but that it will always be characterised by reciprocal warmth and mutual affection.

"That at any rate, it is guaranteed by the presence of the Queen in Australia tonight."

Nearly 15 minutes later than the scheduled time, the Queen emerged on the floodlit balcony to wave to several thousand people still waiting outside Parliament House at 10.40.

When she appeared a roar of cheering continued for several minutes while she and the Duke smiled and waved.

Then the Royal couple drove back to Government House.

Tomorrow morning the Queen will receive heads of diplomatic missions, preside at a meeting of the Privy Council and meet members of the press party covering her tour.

After lunch she and the Duke will fly to Adelaide on the first stage of the tour.

● **Summer Shower Fails to Mar Arrival, Page 3.**
● **Rain Could Alter Melbourne Plans, Page 3.**
● **Page of Royal Tour Pictures, Page 15.**

Inside Today

NEWS:

FEATURES:

SERVICES:

Classified Advertisements Index, Page 18.

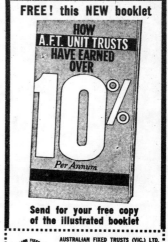

THE QUEEN, in a glittering formal evening gown, acknowledges the cheers which greeted her arrival at last night's State Reception at King's Hall, Parliament House.

Royal Promise of New Visit to See More of Australia

CANBERRA, Monday. — The Queen said tonight she would visit Australia again — and visit different places and different communities.

She spoke in King's Hall, Parliament House, in reply to speeches by the Prime Minister (Mr Menzies), the Leader of the Opposition (Mr. Calwell) and the Leader of the Country party (Mr. McEwen).

It was her first speech of the Australian tour. In it she said:

"I am delighted to forgive you and your two Parliamentary colleagues for your charming speeches this evening. I am also very happy to note that on this occasion you are all of one mind.

"My husband and I are deeply touched by the warmth and kindness of your welcome. Let me say at once that we are both delighted to be back in Australia for the jubilee celebrations at the capital city.

"As we flew over Canberra this afternoon I found it difficult to realise that all this has grown up in 50 short years. It is a wonderful achievement and an inspiring sight to see a great and gracious city taking shape almost before one's eyes.

Taken Root

"Even more remarkable and more important is that the plant of our ancient, free and democratic institutions has taken root here so firmly and is showing such vigorous independent growth.

"The first time I came to Australia everything was new, although not necessarily strange. This time I am looking forward to an even more interesting visit, as I shall be able to see many familiar places and old friends.

"I shall also be able to make comparisons with what I remember or our last visit, and I am quite sure that I shall be greatly impressed by the many developments and the progress of the past nine years.

"I many cases, I know what to expect, because I follow events in Australia with much interest and admiration.

World Stage

"Most impressive has been the rapid growth of a distinctive and independent Australian thought and culture, and I am very proud that this has led Australia to play an increasingly important part on the world stage.

"Perhaps even more significant for Australians has been the modern pioneering in the far north and northwest.

"The partnership of science and engineering with man and nature is harnessing precious water, coaxing the land into useful production and building new towns in remote areas.

"These are the foundations for what I hope will be thriving and prosperous communities in the future, and I am looking forward to visiting some of these areas with great interest.

Not Last Visit

"I do not intend that this should be my last visit to Australia, and next time I hope I shall see different places and many communities that could not be included this time.

"Tonight, on my arrival, I want to send greetings to all Australians, and particularly to those we shall not be able to see on this occasion.

"Thank you again, Mr. Prime Minister, Mr. McEwen and Mr. Calwell, for your kind words this evening. I pray that Australia will continue to prosper in a happy and peaceful future."

STOP PRESS

Scientists Appeal for Disarmament

GENEVA, Feb. 18.

More than 100 delegates to the current U.N. conference on science and technology today signed an appeal for general and complete nuclear disarmament.

Australia's Lord Casey was one of the signatories.—A.A.P.-Reuters.

Burge, 98, Rescues Australia

From Colin Macfarlan, "The Age" Sporting Editor

SYDNEY, Monday. — Peter Burge, dropped from the Australian team after the second Test for a fatal addiction to the sweep shot, swept himself back into the limelight with a fighting 98 not out, to almost guarantee Australia against defeat in the fifth Test match at the S.C.G. today.

At stumps, Australia were 6/285 in reply to England's first innings total of 321, and there are only two days left to complete the Test.

The weather forecast for Sydney for tomorrow is:—

Afternoon showers. Cold southerly winds developing. Expected maximum temperature, 77 deg.

Batted in Pain

There was more merit in Burge's effort than might have appeared to the spectators. He batted in pain, the result of a rib injury suffered when he made an attempt for a falling catch on Saturday morning.

The injury affected his breathing, but he is expected to be quite fit to continue tomorrow morning.

Percy Beames says that if Burge and Benaud can carry on tomorrow and form a productive partnership the foundation would be set for a handy Australian first-innings lead. If this was something like 100 runs then England could be in for trouble.

● See Page 24.

DAILY SKETCH

Thursday, June 20, 1963   Price Threepence   ★★★   WEATHER: Cool, but sunny

Just a wee deoch an' doris for Charles—then what a row

BEND OVER, YOUR ROYAL HIGHNESS!

Prince Charles . . . faces " disciplinary action " when he returns to Gordonstoun on Sunday.

By EDWARD CONNOLLY

PRINCE CHARLES may be in for a caning when he gets back to Gordonstoun School on Sunday—all because he drank a cherry brandy in an hotel cocktail bar.

Mr. Robert Chew, 55-year-old headmaster of Gordonstoun—Prince Philip is an old boy—said last night he was considering taking "disciplinary action" against the Prince, but could not say what form it would take until he had seen him to obtain the full story.

The 14 - year - old Prince's sip of liqueur in the Crown Hotel, Stornaway, Scotland, last Monday evening was admitted yesterday by Buckingham Palace after an earlier denial of the incident.

A Palace statement said Mr. Chew and the Queen's Press Secretary had been misled by a telephone call from the detective-bodyguard who was with the Prince when he toured the town.

STILL SAILING

Prince Charles left the bar—where he was sitting with Old Gordonstounian Mr. Harris Mackenzie, after Det.-Cons. D. Green walked in and said: "What are you doing in here?"

Outside in the hotel lobby, Det. Green asked the Prince: "What did you have?"

Said Charles: "A cherry brandy. That is all I knew what to ask for."

Last night Prince Charles was still on a training cruise off the Scottish coast.

At the time of the incident he and three other Gordonstoun boys were being shown round Stornoway by 32-year-old Mr. Mackenzie, and were hav-

⇨ *Back Page*

Yard men talk to Astor and Profumo

By REGINALD FOSTER

MR. JOHN PROFUMO was interviewed for two hours by police yesterday.

Chief Inspector Sam Herbert and Detective-Sergeant John Burrows saw him in the offices of his solicitors, Theodore Goddard and Co., in the Temple.

The two officers also spent three hours interviewing Lord Astor at Cliveden earlier in the week.

Other well-known people are to be interviewed during the next few days.

CONFERENCE

The Scotland Yard officers are in charge of an investigation which has involved Dr. Stephen Ward.

Their inquiries are not confined to the allegations against Ward, who is on remand accused of living wholly or partly on immoral earnings.

It was learned last night

that Chief Inspector Herbert has been in conference with security officers.

The Commons is due to pass judgment on Mr. Profumo today.

The Government last night published a motion, agreed with the Opposition, condemning Mr. Profumo for "grave contempt" of the Commons.

ON GUARD

Police are keeping a 24-hour guard on Christine Keeler after anonymous telephone calls threatening her life.

Last night uniformed constables were patrolling the pavement outside the flat where she is living, in Devonshire - terrace, Paddington, W.

The anonymous calls were made to three police stations and a newspaper office by a man who said he would kill Miss Keeler "within hours."

Daily Mirror

3d.   Wednesday, February 26, 1964   No. 18,719

ROYALTY:

A splendidly frank speech

BY THE DUKE

The Duke of Edinburgh pictured yesterday as he arrived at the Foreign Press Association lunch in London—ready for the tough questions.

THE Duke of Edinburgh spoke out frankly yesterday about the Monarchy, his own job, the Arts —and the Beatles.

Rarely has he been so outspoken and so direct in his comments.

He was speaking at a lunch of the Foreign Press Association in London, at which he was the principal guest. And he was the star of a sparkling question and answer session.

"Do you think that the monarchy has found its proper place in the Britain of the sixties?" he was asked.

The Duke replied: "Here we are in the sixties. What am I supposed to say? Perhaps you would enlarge on the question."

CRITICISM

Enlarging on what he meant, the questioner said: "One sometimes hears criticism in the Press that the monarchy has not found its place, although it is, of course, playing a useful role in this country, but has still not found the right approach to the problems of Britain today."

The Duke replied: "What you are implying is that we are rather old fashioned. Well, it may easily be true: I do not know.

"One of the things about the monarchy and its place—and one of its great weaknesses in a sense—is that it has to be all things to all people.

"Of course, it cannot do this when it comes to being all things to all people who are traditionalists and all things to all people who are iconoclasts."

CUNNING

"We therefore find ourselves in a position of compromise, and we might be kicked by both sides.

"The only thing is that if you are very cunning you get as far away from the extremists as you possibly can because they kick harder.

"I entirely agree that we are old-fashioned; the monarchy is an old-fashioned institution. The interesting thing is that it is not a monopoly of old people."

Asked whether he felt that fame was an asset or a liability in life, the Duke smilingly answered: "That is rather an awkward one. Without indulging in false modesty, I think the questioner is asking the wrong person.

"I do not consider myself to be famous. As you know, I may be notorious, but I would not describe myself as famous in the sense that I know of people who have achieved things and are famous.

"I am just here, so to speak, to be shot at.

"I should think that, on the whole, to those who are famous fame is probably an asset, because they can make something of it.

"As to whether it is an asset to be notorious and well known, that cuts both ways.

"In some cases it is helpful, and in other cases it is rather trying. That is as far as I can go."

When the Duke was asked what he considered the most important contribution he could make to the life and progress of the nation, he said "Perhaps what sometimes I consider to be a contribution other people merely consider to be time-wasting and interfering.

"The areas in which I can make the most useful contributions are fringe areas of voluntary and charitable activities.

"Frequently I hope I can inject a note of what I consider to be common sense, but I do not know what other people think."

Asked whether he thought the court did not show sufficient interest in the arts, the Duke replied, "That is a very interesting question, and I think the operative word in it is 'sufficient.' That is a matter of opinion.

SUFFICIENT

"It would be very easy for me to say 'Yes' in reply to the question, but what is sufficient interest, and how much more do we have to do?

"It seems to me that the answer is that we're doing very well.

"There is no art form in this country that has not got some member of the Royal Family at the head of it. Mark you, not every member of the Royal

Continued on Page Two

World Fight sensation: LISTON LICKED! — *Full story on Back Page*

DAILY SKETCH

Wednesday, March 11, 1964   Price Threepence   ★★★   WEATHER Rainy

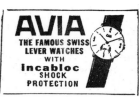

THE TIME—8.20 p.m. AND PRINCE PHILIP ORDERS CHAMPAGNE ALL ROUND FOR THE PALACE STAFF

A BOY—BOTH WELL

It's a boy . . . and the Palace crowd presses forward to read the announcement.

By JOAN MAINPRICE and KENNETH ROCHE

THE QUEEN gave birth to her third son at 8.20 last night—and at once Prince Philip ordered champagne for all the staff at Buckingham Palace.

A bulletin posted up on the Palace gates exactly an hour after the birth said:

‘ The Queen was safely delivered of a son at 8.20 this evening. Her Majesty and the infant Prince are both well. ’

The new Royal baby was born—with five doctors in attendance—in the Belgian suite on the ground floor of the Palace.

Prince Philip was waiting in a nearby room.

As soon as he heard he had become the father of a third son he telephoned the news to the Queen Mother, Princess Margaret—expecting her second child at the end of April—Prince Charles at Gordonstoun School, and Princess Anne at Benenden School in Kent.

OUTSIDE the Palace Mrs. Joan Balley, from Knightsbridge, said: "It's nice. It's a boy. I like boys."

After the birth the baby was placed in a cradle originally made for the birth of his mother—and which has been used for all her four children.

AN IRON CRADLE

The cradle is an iron one, cream-painted and trimmed with peach satin under a cream-spotted net.

It has an eiderdown of peach satin.

The Royal midwife, Sister Helen Rowe, who has attended the birth of all the Royal children was with the Queen until it was time to summon the five doctors.

They were: **Sir John Peel,** aged 59, surgeon-gynaecologist to the Queen since 1961.

The Queen's physician, **Dr. Ronald Bodley Scott.**

Sir John Weir, 84, a physician to the Queen since 1952.

Mr. John Brudenell, 38, a consultant at King's College Hospital.

Dr. Vernon Hall, 59, Dean of the Medical School at King's College since 1950.

OUTSIDE the Palace Mrs. Lindy Edward, from Roehampton, said:

"I'm glad of course. But I'm rather disappointed the Queen didn't have a daughter."

The weight of the new Royal baby—"full of grace" according to the old adage about Tuesday's child—was a secret.

That, said a Palace official, will be announced to-day.

[Prince Charles weighed 7lb. 6oz., Princess Anne 6lb., and Prince Andrew 7lb. 3oz.]

The Prime Minister, Sir Alec Douglas-Home, heard the news after addressing a

➡ *Back Page*

The smiling Queen.

Man in girl's clothes raids bank: Cashier shot

SKETCH REPORTER

BANK cashier Vernon Cran, shot in the chest when a man in woman's clothes held up the bank, was fighting for his life last night.

His parents sat by his hospital bedside at Darlington, Co. Durham. He was said to be "very ill."

And as the struggle to save him went on, tributes were paid to his courage.

Mr. Cran, 25-year-old son of a surgeon, was in Barclays bank branch in Albert-road, Darlington, yesterday afternoon when

the raider walked in with an automatic pistol.

The man wore a beige coat, nylon stockings, black court shoes, a black wig—and make-up.

He pointed the gun at Mr. Cran and demanded money. But he didn't see the bank's security guard, 67-year-old Mr. Jim Greenwood, who pressed the alarm.

Then Mr. Greenwood, a

former police sergeant, hurled himself at the raider and the two men fell to the floor fighting.

Mr. Cran went to Mr. Greenwood's help.

'Very brave'

There was a shot—and the cashier staggered back with a bullet in his chest.

There was a chase in which 33-year-old Mr. Fred Scott joined.

And later a man was arrested and taken to Darlington police station.

Last night at his home in Sedgefield, near Darlington, Mr. Greenwood said: "Vernon was very brave."

Mr. Scott, of Shelleyroad, Darlington, described Mr. Cran and Mr. Greenwood as real heroes.

And Det.-Supt. John Collinson said: "All three men did a magnificent job."

Late last night a senior police spokesman said a man had been charged and would probably appear in court today.

PRICES: BIGGEST TORY REVOLT—Back Page

4

Here Now
CONTINUING COOL
6 a.m. 36, 9 a.m. 38, 2 p.m. 46
Low tonight 34, high Wed. 57
(Complete weather page 8)

The Windsor Star

FINAL
★★★★

VOL. 93, NO. 30 | 36 Pages | WINDSOR ONTARIO TUESDAY OCTOBER 6 1964 | SEVEN CENTS

Two RCMP officers stand guard on the dock at Charlottetown today as the Royal yacht Britannia arrives with the Queen and Prince Philip. The dock area was literally swarming with Mounties and none of the crowd of hundreds was allowed in the general dock area.

Mounties Everywhere

Security Blanket

CHARLOTTETOWN (UPI) —Overcast skies, cold damp weather and strict security measures put a damper on the arrival today of Queen Elizabeth aboard the sleek 4,715-ton yacht Britannia.

With a band playing on board and flags flapping, the Royal blue and white yacht glided into this sheltered harbor followed by four destroyer escorts and flanked by four RCMP patrol boats.

On shore residents of this provincial capital were not allowed on the dock where the yacht tied up and a few hundred of them stood behind a wire fence framing the huge pier or along the shoreline.

The dock was covered with Royal Canadian Mounted Police officers in scarlet tunics and plainclothes.

When one reporter complained his identification pin put holes in his clothing, an RCMP officer said, "That's better than getting one in your head."

The Queen held a brief audience with members of the committee arranging the details of the eight-day Canadian tour, followed by luncheon on board with Prime Minister Lester B. Pearson, Governor-General George Vanier and the lieutenant-governor and premier of the province and their wives.

But the weather office said there was no danger of tropical storm Hilda bringing heavy rain and winds to the island as predicted earlier.

QUEEN HAILS CANADA'S HISTORY

Monarch Opens Memorial Site

By MAURICE JEFFERIES—Star Staff Reporter

CHARLOTTETOWN—Queen Elizabeth today praised Canada's 100 years of unbroken democratic government and called Confederation a "great act of political statesmanship." It was her first public speech of the Royal tour and was made at the dedication of the new Fathers of Confederation Memorial Buildings here, built to mark the Charlottetown conference of 1864, when union of the British North American colonies was first explored.

The Queen added a personal note to her speech. She recalled that Prince Edward Island was named after Queen Victoria's father and said:

"I feel an even closer connection now that I have a son called Edward."

Queen Elizabeth spoke after she and Prince Philip were driven three miles through this quiet, tree-shaded city, long known for its friendliness.

The drive was preceded by a luncheon aboard the Royal Yacht Britannia, docked here after sailing from Summerside, where the Royal couple arrived from London by jet Monday afternoon.

The warmth of the luncheon, attended by Governor-General George Vanier and Mrs. Vanier, Prime Minister Lester Pearson and Mrs. Pearson and Charlottetown and P.E.I. dignitaries, was in contrast to the cold weather which greeted the Royal motorcade as it made its way to the

(For other stories and photos on the opening of Queen Elizabeth's Canadian tour, see Pages 9, 20, 21 and 30.)

opening of the memorial buildings.

In her speech, she said it was a great joy for her and Prince Philip to be in Canada again, and that they both had happy memories of two previous visits to this island province.

"As Queen of Canada, I am proud and happy to share in the rejoicing of this centenary of the origins of the Canadian Confederation."

She spoke of the parts played by Lord Gray, governor-general of Canada in 1864, and Sir John A. Macdonald, leader of the delegates from Lower and Upper Canada (Quebec and Ontario), who came to Charlottetown 100 years ago.

Then, in French, she spoke of "the courageous initiative" of Georges-Etienne Cartier, leader of the Quebec delegation, who was premier of the old United Province of Canada in 1858 when the Confederation idea first was advanced in a Throne speech to Parliament.

"The dream has materialized thanks to the spirit of understanding and confidence which the delegates of the various provinces have shown," she added. "How right he was to believe in the possibility of an entente cordiale between men of good will."

Speaking in English, she called Confederation "the rock on which the Canadian nation has built its strength and authority, 100 years of unbroken democratic practices embracing the Crown, government and parliament."

Canada is one of the world's older and most stable nations, she said.

"We know the splendor of her achievements in peace and in the dark years of war, the esteem in which she is held in

See QUEEN—Page 6

VISIT ROYAL YACHT—Prime Minister Lester B. Pearson and Mrs. Pearson prepare to board royal yacht Britannia at Charlottetown dock for a luncheon with the royal couple. *(Canadian Press Wirephoto)*

HELLO TO CANADA!—Prince Philip waves to the welcoming throng at Summerside, P.E.I., as he follows Queen Elizabeth down the ramp of the jet which carried them from London, Monday. Queen Elizabeth stands with Prime Minister L. B. Pearson.

Drastic Change By RCs

Inter-Faith Rites Okay

VATICAN CITY (AP) — The Vatican ecumenical council voted approval today of an unprecedented new program of common prayer and public meetings between Roman Catholics and other Christians.

The council, a gathering of Catholic prelates from around the world, agreed that Catholics everywhere must undergo a "conversion of heart" toward others to further the goal on Christian unity.

Council fathers, meeting in St. Peter's Basilica, also approved a declaration that the church must be ready to reaffirm itself where errors may have occurred, and another declaration that Catholic teachings —both for priests and laymen —must conform to the principles of the Christian unity movement "to keep minds open to others."

Approval of these measures came in voting on the second chapter of the schema De Ecumenismo (On Unity), a fundamental goal of the council.

Passage of the provisions in the chapter, the second of three in the schema, was another major triumph for forces within the church working to overcome the barriers that have divided Christians for centuries.

The first chapter, which outlines principles of unity, was approved Monday 1,926 to 300 with 209 others in favor with reservations. That chapter states that the church must share in responsibility for the

See DRASTIC—Page 6

Cairo Cold

Moise Won't You Please ...Go Home!

CAIRO (UPI) — Congolese premier Moise Tshombe flew into Cairo today in defiance of official orders to keep out. But he soon was under virtual house arrest.

African heads of state met this morning to discuss Tshombe. Informed sources said later the view of the majority of African leaders that the Congolese premier should be barred from attending the unaligned summit conference remained unchanged.

The sources said a special meeting of the African heads of delegations voted to bar Tshombe and sent two delegates to tell him.

Inside Your Star . .

Let's Have Indian Summer

'Operation Longjohn' Coming Up

By Canadian Press

Signs of winter—Cold weather and snowflurries—are in evidence in many Ontario areas and the weatherman predicts more to come.

A blinding snowstorm that slowed highway traffic and dumped about 1.1 inches of snow was reported in the Cochrane - Kapuskasing area, 45 miles north of Timmins, early Monday.

The weather office reported about an inch of snow at Mount Forest, 40 miles south of Owen Sound, overnight Monday.

The snowfall was also accompanied by freezing temperatures in many parts of Ontario, and northwesterly winds pouring frigid Arctic air over the province were predicted to continue today.

Scattered snowflurries or rain was predicted for many districts as well.

White River in Northern Ontario was one of the coldest spots Monday night with a low of 12 degrees and a high of 34. The predicted low for tonight is 10 degrees.

The low at the Lakehead was 20 degrees, Sault Ste. Marie 24, North Bay 27, Trenton 28, Kingston 31 and Toronto 38.

A Smile

Mrs. Brown (to maid) — "Lizzie, do you and your husband quarrel as much as you used to?"

Lizzie—"No, indeed, ma'am."

Mrs. Brown — "What made you stop, Lizzie?"

Lizzie — "Well, ma'am, he died."

Automation Top Concern of OFL

By ANGUS MUNRO

NORTH BAY—Talk of automation has dominated the lobbies and off-the-floor discussions of the delegates to the Ontario Federation of Labor convention.

So concerned is the federation that a special booklet of some thirty pages has been printed and distributed to the delegates explaining what the eventual effects of improved technological improvements will mean.

One estimate is that in another 10 years, automation will have so far invaded production facilities that it will require 10 per cent of the present working force to meet requirements of the Canadian public.

David Archer, due for re-election today at the second day of the three-day annual conference, said "It is all very well for the politicians to assure us that before automated machinery is moved into a plant there must be consultation with the union. But what good is consultation if you have an agreement, and during the term of the agreement management calls you in to tell you hundreds of jobs have been eliminated because of new machinery or a new speed-up process?"

Mr. Archer warned that the automated age "hangs over us like a dark cloud."

Salary increases of $2,000 per annum for the federations two top officers also were approved Monday. This will give the OFL president a salary of $11,500 and the secretary treasurer $11,000.

Indian's 'Kill' Ruled Illegal

OTTAWA (CP)—The Supreme Court of Canada ruled today that treaty Indians in the Northwest Territories do not have the right under a 1921 treaty with the federal government to shoot migratory birds out of season.

Latin Crowd Erupts

Shots Mar De Gaulle Trip

CORDOBA, Argentina (UPI) —Shooting broke out in front of the justice palace here today as police sought to control crowds out to welcome French President Charles de Gaulle. Some persons were wounded.

The shooting was brief but intense. There was fire and answering fire between police and Peronist extremists.

The firing broke out after Peronists attacked police with stones.

Several ambulances converged on Sobremonte Square and several wounded were carried away on stretchers.

De Gaulle and President Arturo U. Illia were across town inspecting an automobile factory at the time of the shooting. They had planned to lunch at the justice palace in the square.

Police rushed heavy reinforcements into the riot area, which already was under heavy guard.

Earlier, police had brandished pistols and threatened to unleash police dogs to cow and dislodge Peronists who had threatened to block de Gaulle's passage past the General Workers Confederation headquarters.

Aftermath

East Berlin Threatens Pass Pact

BERLIN (UPI) — Communist East Germany today threatened to call off its border pass agreement with West Berlin because of the death of a Communist border guard Monday in the tunnel through which 57 refugees escaped.

The East German Communist Party newspaper Neues Deutschland charged West Berlin "bandits" killed Cpl. Egon Schultz as the tunnel was discovered early Monday.

But Western witnesses said neither the refugees nor the West Berliners who had helped them build the tunnel were armed. There was speculation Schultz was killed by mistake by another border guard, or had tried to flee himself.

Neues Deutschland warned West Berlin would have to choose between "continuation of the pass agreement or a continuation of the clashes and bloody provocations on the state border."

The agreement was concluded only last week. It pro-

See BERLIN—Page 6

East Berliner Leaving Tunnel

A Filip
SUNNY, WARMER
6 a.m. 32, 9 a.m. 36, 2 p.m. 41
Low tonight 30, high Sunday 60
(Complete weather, Page 6)

The Windsor Star

FINAL
★★★★

VOL. 93, NO. 34   52 Pages   WINDSOR ONTARIO SATURDAY OCTOBER 10 1964   SEVEN CENTS

POLICE GRAB AGITATORS

Separatists Demonstr... as Queen Tours

Police Struggle With Separatist Demonstrator
As Queen En Route to Quebec Legislature Rites

QUEBEC—Small knots of demonstrators who scuffled with police failed to slow the schedule for the Royal visit to Quebec today. The Queen heard some of the booing as her car drove away from the Legislature building but she didn't see a scuffle with thirty youthful demonstrators shouting "Quebec libre" (Free Quebec) as truncheon-carrying police grabbed 10 of them and whisked them off to a police station. The Queen also heard some scattered cheering and saw some flag-waving in the rather restrained reception. Police worked with well-ordered speed in their roundup of the young leaders of the demonstration and they were all speeding to police stations as the Queen, speaking in French, told a joint session of the Quebec Legislature in warm phrases of her appreciation for their invitation.

Her message was for moderation between the races. "Between compatriots, we must explain and present our points of view, without passion, respecting the opinion of others."

She went through generally cheerful crowds to the residence of the lieutenant-governor for lunch but at some points knots of young people chanted for Quebec independence and there was some booing.

But this was balanced by a good deal of hand-clapping and flag-waving along the Royal route through the beautiful residential area.

The arrests by police included former boxer Reggie Chartrand, well-known in Montreal separatist circles.

When the Queen left the legislature for the residence of Lieu-

(For other photos and stories on Queen's visit to Quebec City, see pages 2, 16, 29 and 44.)

tenant-Governor Comtois, the chant "Quebec pour des Quebecois"—Quebec for Quebecers—broke out in a group of about 50 young people among a fair-sized crowd. The chant disappeared in general applause as the Royal limousine under heavy police escort passed the spot.

About a quarter-mile from the Bois-de-Coulonge gates, 1½ miles or so from the legislature, another group of young people turned their backs as the Queen's automobile drove by.

Before it arrived on the scene they had sung "La Marseillaise"—hymn of the French Republic—and chanted "Vie la reine du carnaval"—long live the carnival queen.

It was a chanted association of Queen Elizabeth with the city's annual winter carnival which includes choice of a local girl as its publicity figure.

By the time that demonstration was broken up, a group of about 250—mostly young people and including a few girls and a few adults—started a procession around Quebec city hall, a half-mile away from the legislature buildings, where Reggie Chartrand was taken.

They paraded in pairs circling the city hall which contains police cells and set up a rhythmic chant calling for the liberation of the little dark-haired boxer who has figured in several separatist demonstrations in Montreal.

A few carried small Quebec fleur-de-lis flags and there was a boy who looked no more than 15. At times they raised their arms and spread their fingers in the V for Victory sign which some separatists have adopted as a salute.

Police were at the city hall in force and behind the building, crouched on a square across which Quebec Basilica stands, were an array of police cars, trucks and motorcycles.

Police did not interfere with the marchers for 20 minutes or

See QUEEN—Page 6

★ ★ ★

MAKES SPEECH—Queen Elizabeth addresses members of the Quebec Legislature today during her controversial tour of Quebec City.

Elizabeth Speaks In French

Thanks Lesage For Invitation

QUEBEC (CP)—Queen Elizabeth today thanked Premier Jean Lesage warmly for her invitation to this province and said, "It is most agreeable for me to think that there exists in our Commonwealth a country where I am able to express myself in French—one of the most important languages of our western civilization."

She was speaking to 340 Quebec government members and other officials in the red and gold Legislative Council chamber—Quebec's Upper House. The Queen devoted a large part

See SPEAKS—Page 6

Inside Your Star ..

Walter Reuther sees break in talks seeking end to General Motors strike.   Page 4

Provinces to seek a uniform code for private pension plans.   Page 2

Editorial and Comment, Centre Pages, First Section

Churches, Pages 48, 49

Financial, Pages 34, 35

Theatres, Amusements, Pages 21, 22, 23

Yanks Take 2-1 Edge In World Series Play

NEW YORK—The American League champion New York Yankees turned back the National League champion St. Louis Cardinals 2-1 today at Yankee Stadium to take a 2-1 edge in the best-of-seven World Series. Fourth game will be played Sunday at New York.

With two out in the Cardinals' second, Bouton walked Tim McCarver, who quickly moved to third base when Mike Shannon singled for the first St. Louis hit. But Bouton got Dal Maxvill to pop to first baseman Joe Pepitone to end the threat.

Simmons nailed Mickey Mantle on a grounder to open the Yankee half, but then Howard ripped a single. Tom Tresh fouled out, but Simmons walked Pepitone. Boyer then blasted the ball down the left field line. Howard scored, and Pepitone went to third as Clete legged it to second with a double. But Bouton flied out to prevent further scoring.

Tim McCarver, opening the Cardinals' fifth, singled to right

No Paper Monday

The Windsor Star will not publish on Thanksgiving Day, Monday, Oct. 12.

5,500 Athletes

Olympic Festivities Under Way in Tokyo

(See Also Sports Pages)

TOKYO (UPI)—The Olympic Games opened today to the sound of Oriental gongs and the spectacle of 5,500 athletes marching in rainbow-hued costume to the delight of a proud but rather reserved stadium packed with 72,000 Japanese and their overseas visitors.

As jet planes painted the five ring olympic insignia in the sunny sky and cannon boomed, a Hiroshima college boy ran around the track and up more than 100 green carpeted steps to light the Olympic flame.

Sunday the athletes get down to the business of competition.

Emperor Hirohito formally inaugurated the games in a one-sentence speech in Japanese: "I declare open the Olympic Games of Tokyo at the XVIII Olympiad of the modern era."

There are 94 nations in today's opening ceremony. North Korea, Indonesia, Ecuador and Barbados withdrew at the last moment but it was still the largest Olympic turnout in history—surpassing by 10 the number of nations at Rome in 1960.

So Near And Yet So Far

Red Firemen Watch U.K. Embassy Burn

MOSCOW (UPI)—Fire swept the left wing of the British Embassy Friday, destroying consular offices, food supplies and the embassy canteen, while Russian firemen stood around outside the building.

No one was hurt.

Britons and Russians clashed sharply today as to the reason for the firemen's delay in tackling the blaze. The Communist organ Pravda and the Tass agency said the British refused to admit firemen to the building, while the British said they didn't ask to enter until the fire had been burning for more than an hour and a half.

Tass, quoting Fire Lt. Fedor Malkin, said the British kept the firemen waiting until the blaze assumed proportions that "threatened the lives of people and neighboring buildings."

"In my 26 years of service, this is the first time I have ever seen firemen refused access to a Moscow fire," Malkin was quoted as saying.

Laser Tests

VANDENBERG AIR FORCE BASE, Calif. (UPI)—Scientists launched Explorer 22 into orbit Friday night and hoped to begin the first Laser tests in space today using the windmill-shaped satellite.

The pencil-thin and intense light beams will be bounced off hundreds of mirrors aboard the satellite.

A Smile

"Fine advice you gave me! You said if I was pally with the Judge he'd let me off easy."

"Well, didn't he?"

"No. I walked in and said, 'Good morning, Your Honor—how's the old kid today?' and he said 'Fine—twenty dollars.'"

Police Action 'Disgusting'

QUEBEC (CP)—Rene Letarte, well-known Quebec City lawyer, said today he was "disgusted" by the conduct of police in dealing with a demonstration at Quebec City Hall.

While no one appeared to have been seriously injured, Mr. Letarte told a reporter that when he was leaving his nearby office he saw police strike the young demonstrators with their sticks. He considered use of the sticks was not necessary.

Second Presumed Dead

Hunter Drowns

CHATHAM — One man drowned and another man presumed drowned after a boat carrying a hunting party of three, flipped over on Lake St. Clair this morning.

Dead is Clayton E. Spence of R R 2, Muirkirk, near Ridgetown.

Still missing is Stewart Ross, of Oriole Parkway, Chatham. Surviving the mishap is John Noel DeHoey of 8 Melrose, Chatham.

The trio were duck hunting on the lake about one mile from the mouth of the Thames River when their steel-hulled boat capsized at about 10 a.m.

The lone survivor swam to shore, while the others clung to the overturned boat. He was found staggering along a road by William Reaume, a worker at Bruce Bradley and Sons farm on River Road, Concession 1, Dover Township West. He was suffering from shock.

After he told Mr. Reaume about the accident, Bradley farm hands searched the area, finding the body of one of the hunters.

Chatham detachment of the provincial police have not yet located the third man.

Publicity Not Warranted, Quebec Minister Claims

QUEBEC (CP)—Alcide Courcy, Quebec agriculture minister, said Friday night the separatist demonstration in Quebec City was "absolutely nothing" but will get worldwide publicity anyway.

Some 200 members of Le Rassemblement pour l'Independance Nationale attempted a silent protest against the Queen's visit on the eve of her scheduled arrival today but they were forced to disperse.

"This demonstration came to absolutely nothing and tomorrow the newspapers will give it worldwide publicity," Mr. Courcy told a reporter.

The minister said he watched part of the abortive demonstration, which followed a meeting of Le Rassemblement attended by 500 persons.

	1	2	3	4	5	6	7	8	9	R	H	E
Cardinals	0	0	0	0	1	0	0	0	0	1	6	0
Yankees	0	1	0	0	0	0	0	0	1	2	5	2

All night they queue—at one time they reached Waterloo Bridge

FRIDAY · ·

SUN

JANUARY 29 1965   THREEPENCE   No. 116

THE INDEPENDENT DAILY NEWSPAPER

THE QUEEN'S HOMAGE

By ANTHONY CARTHEW and MAX MADDEN

QUIETLY and without fuss, the Queen made history in Westminster Hall last night. She became the first reigning monarch to pay public homage to a commoner.

Prince Philip, Princess Margaret and Lord Snowdon joined her opposite the catafalque bearing Sir Winston Churchill's coffin. All four stood in silence for about five minutes.

The royal party arrived at 7.50 pm. at the East door of the hall. All the time crowds continued to file past the coffin.

The Queen and Princess Margaret both wore small black hats—without veils—and full-length black coats. They stood with their hands clasped in front of them.

Once or twice they looked up and down the great hall at the slowly-moving crowd.

Slightly behind the Queen and the Princess stood Prince Philip and Lord Snowdon, wearing black suits.

As the four kept their vigil some of the crowd turned towards them. But most eyes looked only on the catafalque and Sir Winston's coffin, draped in a Union Jack.

It was a day of huge crowds, waiting in severe weather to pay homage.

RETURN

The peak hour was between six and seven o'clock last night, when the queue stretched for four and a half miles.

Between nine and ten o'clock 11,450 people passed through Westminster Hall. And at midnight a total of 165,530 people had paid tribute since the hall opened on Wednesday.

Some of the crowd had to wait four hours to reach Westminster Hall. Dozens of people collapsed with the cold.

It was also a day of personal memory for those closest to Sir Winston.

Lady Churchill paid another visit to the hall in the evening. With her were her daughter, Mary, and Mary's husband, Mr. Christopher Soames.

Just before midnight Mr. Soames returned for a personal vigil. He stayed 35 minutes.

EX-PREMIERS

Miss Sarah Churchill paid two visits.

The Duchess of Gloucester, the Duchess of Kent and Princess Marina joined the homage. The Duke of Kent and his brother, Prince Michael, both serving with their regiments in Germany, arrived in London last night to attend tomorrow's funeral.

Two former Prime Ministers, Earl Attlee and Mr. Harold Macmillan, both wartime colleagues of Sir Winston, stood together before the catafalque.

Sir Robert Menzies, Australia's Prime Minister, was there. He will broadcast from St. Paul's Cathedral after the funeral.

Detective - Sergeant Edmund Murray, for 15 years Sir Winston's Special Branch detective, filed through. With him were Sir Winston's chauffeur, Mr. J. Bullock, and 82-year-old Mrs. Georgina Landmare, his cook for 20 years.

About 200 disabled men and women—including blind people from St. Dunstan's—arrived together.

TRIBUTE

Tonight political leaders will pay their final tribute to Sir Winston.

Mr. Wilson has invited the leaders of the Conservative and Liberal parties, Sir Alec Douglas-Home and Mr. Jo Grimond, to join him and the Speaker of the Commons, Sir Harry Hylton-Foster, in mounting guard on the catafalque.

They will stand between the military guards.

Their vigil will begin at 10.30 pm. and is expected to last for five minutes as the public still file through.

The Duke and Duchess of Windsor will be represented at the funeral by Sir John Aird, who was equerry to the Duke when he was Prince of Wales.

Sir John is now an extra equerry to the Queen.

PICTURE BY GERRY WARNER

Joining in the people's homage—the Queen and Prince Philip arriving at Westminster Hall last night

Silent Eisenhower flies in for the funeral

EX-PRESIDENT EISENHOWER flew into London last night for the Churchill funeral.

With him in the Presidential Boeing airliner were the American Secretary of State, Mr. Dean Rusk, Chief Justice Earl Warren and Mr. Averell Harriman, Under - Secretary of State for Political Affairs.

Mr. Eisenhower, looking pale and drawn, was first down the aircraft steps. A Press conference which had been arranged for him was cancelled.

A U.S. Embassy spokesman said Mr. Eisenhower did not want to comment on "a very sad occasion."

Earlier the Soviet delegation flew in. First to leave the Ilyushin turbo-jet aircraft was Deputy Prime Minister Konstantin Rudnev. He was followed by 68-year-old Marshal Ivan Koniev, who led the Russian advance on Berlin in 1945.

Other arrivals yesterday included the Canadian Prime Minister, Mr. Lester Pearson, and Malta's Premier, Dr. Borg Olivier.

Queen Juliana of Holland will be at the funeral. Earlier it was believed that only her husband, Prince Bernhard, would attend the St. Paul's service.

Other world leaders will fly in today — including President de Gaulle, who will return home tomorrow night.

● The last mile home—Centre Pages
● The rival soldiers—Back Page

Princess Margaret and Lord Snowdon drive to Westminster Hall

Still the people came, despite the murderous cold. Last night 165,530 people had paid homage to Sir Winston Churchill.

FINAL

DAILY ☆ NEWS

NEW YORK'S PICTURE NEWSPAPER ®

10¢

Vol. 46. No. 226 Copr. 1965 News Syndicate Co. Inc. New York, N.Y. 10017, Tuesday, March 16, 1965★ WEATHER: Mostly sunny and cool.

QUEEN MEETS WALLY—AT LAST

'So Pleased' at Duke's Side

(UPI Cablefotos)

The Duchess Curtsies. Queen Elizabeth leaves the London Clinic (left) in rain-splattered limousine after dramatic meeting with the Duchess of Windsor (arriving, right) at bedside of the ailing duke. Meeting broke icy silence which existed for 29 years. "I'm so pleased to meet you," the queen told the duchess.
—Story on page 2

Daily Mirror

4d. Wednesday, April 21, 1965 ✱ No. 19,075

THE HAPPIEST ROYAL PICTURE

A fair deal for the kids

—CROSLAND'S PLAN

By TOM READ

EDUCATION Minister Anthony Crosland yesterday launched a dramatic crash programme to give "a fair deal for this generation of kids."

In a major speech, he announced the Government's eagerly-awaited 14-point emergency plan to fight the battle of Britain's bulging classrooms.

His aim—to almost double the present 290,000 teaching force in ten years and reduce the size of all classes to thirty children.

Help

Speaking to 2,000 delegates at the conference of the National Union of Teachers at Douglas, Isle of Man, he appealed for help from teachers, training colleges and local authorities to carry out his massive programme.

The proposals include:

MORE ROOM for trainee teachers in training colleges with outside annexes;

EXTRA HELP from colleges of further education.

FOUR OR FIVE more day colleges in big cities.

EDUCATION departments in some technical colleges next year.

PART-TIME training for teachers.

A NATIONAL effort to get more married women teachers back into the classrooms.

MORE nursery classes to help teachers who are mothers.

Thorny

A NATIONAL REGISTER to keep track of the teachers and try to cut down the "crippling wastage rate."

SIMILAR pension rights and a national pay scale to part-time teachers.

NON-TEACHER helpers to become a regular part of school life—in the playground, in libraries, and in laboratories.

EXTRA HELP for teachers INSIDE the classroom.

The last proposal is the most controversial.

"I know this is a thorny subject," Mr. Crosland told the teachers. "But the plain fact is that we have to tackle this subject now. If we don't,

Continued on Back Page

April in England. Daffodil time. A time for a family to walk in a garden, laughing as they go. Sister Anne plants a flower on Edward's head. Mother laughs. Father watches. Brother Andrew looks impish. The happiest royal picture I've taken, says Mirror Cameraman FREDDIE REED.

For other happy, informal pictures see Centre Pages.

DAILY SKETCH

Wednesday, May 19, 1965   Price Fourpence ★★★   WEATHER: Thunder showers

The Queen appeals to West Germany : Let's be partners in Europe

KAMERADSCHAFT!

(COMRADESHIP)

By GEORGE GORDON

NOW let's all pull together. That was the Queen's message to West Germany last night.

THE SETTING: The splendour of Augustusburg Castle in Bruehl, 10 miles north of Bonn. More than 2,500 guests thronged reception rooms ablaze with chandeliers and candles as, outside, German soldiers held flaming torches.

A gasp of admiration went up from hundreds of guests as the Queen descended the staircase on the arm of President Leubke, who had earlier entertained 98 guests to dinner in the apartments above.

The Queen's bell-skirted turquoise satin gown, worn with a white stole and a tiara, echoed the design and colours of the castle decorations.

THE QUEEN said: "We are anxious to play our full part within the European community.

"We must create an atmosphere of mutual confidence between the countries of Europe and a willingness to plan for the future in genuine co-operation.

"Without this, any thought of a genuine European unity will remain a dream."

She went on to say that her presence in Bonn was "testimony to the firm conviction of my Government and people that the important tasks ahead of us can only be solved in the closest co-operation, for which the earlier centuries of friendship provide an encouraging pattern and example today."

A MENTOR...

Earlier President Luebke talked of West Germany's determination to "make up for the past."

He said:

"At a time when Germany was engaged in a long and painful struggle for its political unity, Britain was already a leading nation of the world and a mentor for other nations."

He went on: "Britain and Germany are neighbours whose mutual relationship has over the centuries gone through all the degrees of human and political relations.

"Up to the outbreak of the first war there were hardly any serious conflicts between our two countries...."

Those ties remained unbroken until "the terrible event that took place between 1940 and 1945."

'SIGN OF TRUST'

He then quoted an extract from a speech by Sir Winston Churchill calling for a United States of Europe.

He said: "It is our hope and desire to see Your Majesty's country included in that European Union.

"We also regard your visit as a sign of the growing trust in our people.

"We believe that the

⇨ Back Page

To dinner in a Rhineland castle. The host last night: West German President Heinrich Luebke. Chief guest: The Queen, wearing a Hardy Amies bell-skirted turquoise gown.

Germans forbidden to 'heil'

—See
Centre Pages

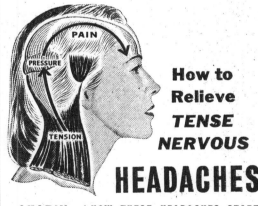

PAIN

PRESSURE

TENSION

How to Relieve *TENSE NERVOUS* HEADACHES

Daily Mirror

4d. Wednesday, May 19, 1965   No. 19,099

The Queen to 58,000,000 Germans:

'CLOSER.. AFTER 2 WARS'

We must make common cause, she tells them

THE Queen, welcomed to Germany with flowers strewn at her feet, had warm words tonight for the foes of two world wars.

She spoke them at a Presidential party which was seen on television by virtually all West Germany's 58,000,000 people.

Dressed in a turquoise evening gown, with her tiara and jewels glittering under the chandeliers, the Queen said:

"In the last twenty years the problems facing our two peoples in Europe have brought us closer together after two world wars in which your country and mine stood on opposite sides."

'Tensions'

The speech was the highlight of a crowded day which began on the stroke of noon when the Queen—the first British monarch to make a State visit to Germany for fifty-six years—stepped from her aircraft on to German soil.

Guests at President Heinrich Luebke's magnificent reception in the Schloss Augustusburg, just outside Bonn, listened in silence as the Queen spoke.

"This tragic period in our relations is happily over," she said.

"In the tensions and uncertainties of the modern world the peoples of Europe can no longer afford the clashes and divisions of earlier ages."

It was the gentle but firm voice of reconciliation —the hand of friendship— after the two great wars.

The Queen turned to the bright promises of the future, not only of Britain and Germany, but of Europe.

"If we wish to preserve the best of our great heritage," she said, "we must make common cause."

'Trust'

White - haired President Luebke, in his speech of welcome to the Queen, said that after the "appalling catastrophe" of the last war, Britain and Germany were moving closer 'together.

The Germans, said the

From DENIS MARTIN and HOWARD JOHNSON
Bonn, Tuesday.

President, regarded the Queen's visit as a sign of growing trust in the German people.

"We believe," he said, "that the German people have clearly demonstrated their determination to make up for the past."

The Queen was twenty-five minutes late arriving at the reception—because the big crowds repeatedly stopped the car in which she was travelling with the Duke of Edinburgh.

During the reception, the Queen and the Duke moved separately among the guests.

Posies

Earlier, the Queen driving into Bonn from her hilltop residence, 1,000ft. up on the other side of the Rhine, saw massed German crowds throwing posies of spring flowers in the path of her car.

The Queen did not forget one man who could not be there to greet her. Konrad Adenauer, 89-year-old ex-Chancellor, who is ill. She sent him a bouquet of red roses

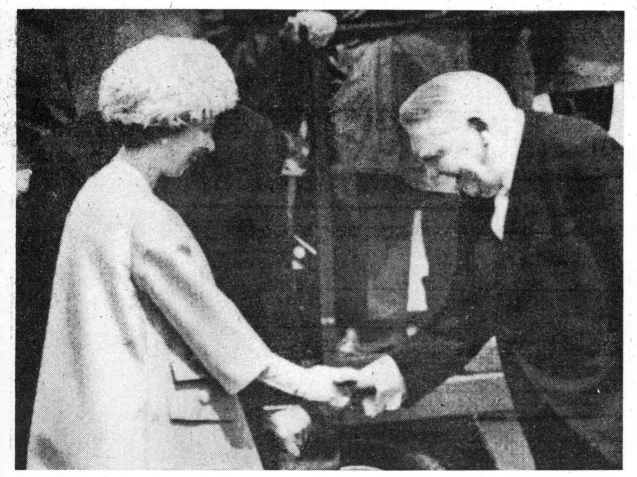

Hand of friendship   The Queen in West Germany yesterday . . . and a handshake greeting from Chancellor Erhard.

NEW ITV PROGRAMME BOSS SACKED

By JACK BELL

STUART HOOD, 49, the ex-B B C-T V chief hired by the Rediffusion company last summer as £10,000 a year programme controller, was sacked yesterday.

The sacking—Rediffusion called it the "termination of his contract"— came a week after the company announced the dropping of a planned Diana Dors detective series at an estimated loss of more than £70,000.

Rediffusion is the London weekday ITV company which produces such network top ten programmes as "No Hiding Place" and "Our Man at St. Mark's," and the quiz shows "Double Your Money" and "Take Your Pick."

Mr. Hood left at noon yesterday, after a meeting with the board of management.

Last night Mr. John MacMillan, Rediffusion's general manager, whose former job as programme controller was taken over by Mr. Hood last September, announced: "Mr. Hood's contract has been terminated.

"We will not explain the reasons for the termination because it concerns his personal future."

Mr. Hood quit his job as B B C-T V programme controller last June, after policy disagreements.

He arrived at Rediffusion with a high reputation— after initiating such BBC successes as "Z Cars," "Compact" and "Dr. Finlay's Casebook."

But an ITV executive commented last night: "To be a programme controller in I T V is a vastly different proposition.

"I T V works to stringent budgetary control."

Mr. MacMillan is resuming his chairmanship of the programme board, the job he did before Mr. Hood joined Rediffusion.

Stuart Hood—his contract is "terminated."

Daily Mirror

4d. Friday, May 28, 1965   No. 19,107

Red border guards look in by telescope

THE QUEEN AT WALL OF DEATH

Beside the tragic Berlin Wall with its barbed wire barricade yesterday . . . the Queen and the Duke of Edinburgh.

HERE was a moment of history . . . a moment that silenced the tumultuous cheering of hundreds of thousands of West Berliners.

It was when the Queen's car stopped near the hated Wall between East and West.

For a moment the Queen looked at the Wall—the "Wall of Shame" as West Berliners call it, the "Wall of Death" as the world knows it.

Her glance was grave, and did not linger. Soon she turned her eyes away.

The Duke of Edinburgh took a longer look. He took photographs, too.

And he smilingly waved at East German soldiers who were watching through binoculars and telescopes

The soldiers smiled . . but did not wave back.

But there were East Berliners who had turned out in the hope of seeing the Queen.

About 500 of them — mainly elderly people and teenagers—stood silently at a police barrier 300 yards back from the Brandenburg Gate.

It was the most tense and dramatic moment in the Queen's six-hour visit to Berlin.

Away from the fateful atmosphere of the Wall of Death—away, too, from the

Huge Berlin welcome

From DENIS MARTIN and HOWARD JOHNSON

Berlin, Thursday.

East Berlin guards who watched the Royal cavalcade through telescopes — the Queen had a fantastic welcome from the West Berliners.

It was a day of a million cheers. At least that number of people, it is estimated, packed the West Berlin streets.

For miles there were forests of Union Jacks, balloons and bunting.

It was the same all the way down Berlin's famous street of nightlights, the Kurfurstendamm. And it was the same outside West Berlin's Town Hall this afternoon when the Queen spoke from the step.

She told the crowd: "Nowhere is the tragedy of a divided world made more evident than in this city.

"The courage and persistence of the people, and your tremendous achievements in spite of every

difficulty, are a glowing inspiration to the whole free world."

Later the Queen flew to Hanover . . . and another tumultuous reception.

And if there was ever a tailpiece to this "hand of friendship" State tour, three banners held up by university students told the 1965 story of Germany and Britain . .

The Queen and the Duke laughed aloud as they passed the banners which read: "We want you to invade us," "We love your Queen," "We want her for us."

Tomorrow it is Hamburg's turn — and then home.

DIMBLEBY MAKES A ROYAL GAFFE

Dimbleby

RICHARD DIMBLEBY, the man nothing seems to ruffle, made his first gaffe on a great royal occasion last night.

It was during the special BBC-1 programme on "The Queen In Berlin."

The programme should have started at 8.50 p.m., but there was a technical hitch and music was put on. Then the programme started —but went off again.

Loud and clear came Mr. Dimbleby's exasperated comment: "Jesus wept!" And when the programme really started a few minutes later, he looked just a shade flustered.

As viewers flooded the BBC— and the Daily Mirror—with phone calls, a BBC spokesman said: "We are sorry Mr. Dimbleby's remark was overheard. It was understandable in the circumstances."

Evening Standard

43,979   THURSDAY, NOVEMBER 11, 1965   4d.   3

UDI—SMITH BREAKS WITH BRITAIN—official

IAN SMITH . . . his voice trembled with emotion.

'End of the road' he tells the nation

SALISBURY, Thursday.—Rhodesia today seized independence in defiance of Britain. It is the first rebellion of the kind since America broke away as a colony in 1776.

Action to bring Rhodesia to her knees?

ROBERT CARVEL

The Rhodesian Government is now in open rebellion against Britain and it will have to take the consequences.

There is no doubt, it was stated in Whitehall, that Mr. Ian Smith and his men have acted illegally and are to be treated as rebels.

At 10 Downing Street the Cabinet held a session as Mr. Smith made his fateful broadcast and the unilateral declaration of independence.

Emergency action

Mr. Wilson asked his Ministers immediately to approve the signal he gave for emergency British counter-action which is aimed at bringing the rebellious Rhodesian regime to its knees.

The moment had come for dealing with what Mr. Smith had been repeatedly warned would be regarded as "treasonable action."

The Prime Minister was making a special statement to Parliament later today as a prelude to emergency legislation authorising financial and other sanctions against Rhodesia.

There remains no question of

◆ **Back Page, Col. Two**

The unilateral declaration of independence was broadcast to the nation of 217,000 whites and 4,000,000 Africans by 46-year-old Prime Minister Ian Smith, in a voice, at times trembling with emotion.

Mr. Smith said today's action did not mean that the principles enshrined in the present constitution would be torn up. The Union Jack would continue to fly in Rhodesia and the National Anthem would continue to be played.

He proclaimed unswerving loyalty to the Crown and said : "God save the Queen."

After the speech . . .

It was only when Mr. Smith had finished speaking that the announcer said that Rhodesians had just heard a proclamation of independence.

Then shortly after the broadcast the Government announced the imposition of censorship. The announcement said no one shall print or publish any publication without prior authority of the Director of Information.

The declaration was made despite an early morning telephone appeal to Mr. Smith by Mr. Wilson.

Rhodesians, black and white crowded tensely and silently round radio sets to hear the Prime Minister read the proclamation, which was couched in formal, stylised language.

Mr. Smith said provision had been made for MPs, judges and civil servants and members of the armed forces to carry on their work.

Mr. Smith said he had promised Rhodesians that he would negotiate with the British Government to the bitter end. "It now falls on me to tell you that negotiations have come to an end."

The British Government had been playing the Rhodesian government along and "the end of the road has been reached," he said.

No revenge, he says

His Government, he said, would never take revenge on neighbouring African states for sanctions imposed against Rhodesia. But he warned that, if the Rhodesian economy contracted as a result of sanctions, Rhodesian Africans would be given priority in jobs and that Africans from other countries would suffer first.

"I do not believe that any of the extreme consequences suggested both here and abroad will come to pass but I have that utmost confidence in our people

Ⓒ **Back Page Col. Three**

The proclamation
'Justice ...beyond question'

SALISBURY, Thursday.—The Proclamation of Independence read by Mr. Smith said:

"**Whereas** in the course of human affairs history has shown that it may become necessary for a people to sever the political affiliations which have connected them with another people and to assume amongst other nations the separate and equal status to which they are entitled :

"**Whereas** in such event respect for the opinion of mankind requires them to declare to other nations the causes which impel them to assume full responsibility for their own affairs :

"**Now, therefore,** we, the Government of Rhodesia do hereby proclaim that it is an indisputable and accepted historic fact that since 1923 the Government of Rhodesia have exercised the power of self-government and have been responsible for the progress, welfare and development of their people.

"**That** the people of Rhodesia, having demonstrated their loyalty to the Crown and to their kith and kin in the United Kingdom and elsewhere through two world wars, and having been prepared to shed their blood and give their substance in what they believed to be the mutual interests of freedom - loving people, now see all that they have cherished about to be shattered on the rocks of expediency.

'**Steadfast . . .**'

"**That** the people of Rhodesia have witnessed a process which is destructive to those very precepts upon which civilisation in a primitive country has been built: They have seen the principles of western democracy, responsible government and moral standards crumble elsewhere: nevertheless they have remained steadfast.

"**That** the Government of Rhodesia have for a long period patiently and in good faith negotiated with the Government of the United Kingdom for the removal of the remaining limitations placed upon them and for the grant of sovereign independence.

"**That** in the belief that procrastination and delay strike at

▲ **Back Page, Col. Four**

QUEEN SUSPENDS SMITH AND HIS MINISTERS

SALISBURY, Thursday.—Mr. Smith and all his ministers are now suspended from office —on the Queen's instructions.

The Rhodesian Governor, Sir Humphrey Gibbs, announced this immediately after Mr. Smith declared independence.

But what was not immediately clear was how the Governor could implement the Royal instructions : and how the country's government is to be carried on in the critical interim period.

Sir Humphrey, in his prepared statement, said:

"The government have made an unconstitutional declaration of independence.

"I have received the following message from Her Majesty's Secretary of State for Commonwealth Relations.

"'I have it in command from Her Majesty to inform you that it is Her Majesty's pleasure than in the event of an unconstitutional declaration of independence, Mr. Ian Smith and other persons holding office as Ministers of the Government of Southern Rhodesia or as Deputy Ministers cease to hold office.

"'I am commanded by Her Majesty to instruct you in that event to convey Her Majesty's pleasure in this matter to Mr. Smith and otherwise to publish it in such a manner as you may deem fit.'"

The City takes it calmly

The news from Rhodesia was taken calmly in the City today. On the Stock Exchange the immediate reaction was to mark all shares down. But the falls in most cases only amounted to a few pence.

Whitehall flashed good news to the City. Against most expectations our trade gap—the difference between what we buy and sell overseas—narrowed very slightly in October.

Most encouragingly, exports showed a further small increase. —See Page TWO.

Daily Mirror

4d.   Saturday, July 8, 1967   ◆   No. 19,762

The picture that needs no headline

It was taken by Freddie Reed. More pictures and full story inside.

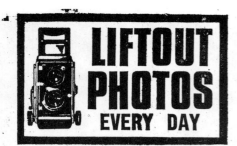

LIFTOUT PHOTOS EVERY DAY

BIGGEST WEEK-DAY SALES IN NSW

THE INDEPENDENT PAPER

Daily Mirror

LATE FINAL EXTRA

Registered at the G.P.O., Sydney, for transmission by post as a newspaper.

Sydney, Thursday, October 3, 1968

No. 8493 — 5c

Phone 2-0924

● Lotteries: Special 1665 and Ordinary 6088 P 42 ● Finance P 56 ● TV P 54 ● Weather: Sunny, W winds | Weather Bureau details, P66

A DELIGHTFUL FAMILY PORTRAIT BY PRINCE PHILIP

The Queen, in bed at Buckingham Palace

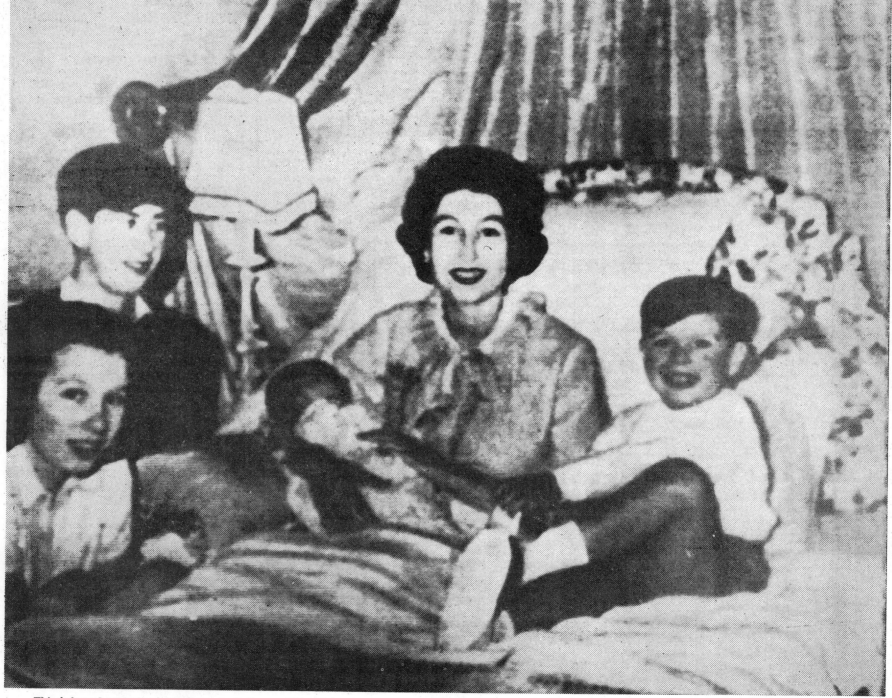

This informal portrait of the Queen in bed at Buckingham Palace, surrounded by her family, was taken by Prince Philip.

It is one of the most delightful series of photographs ever taken of the royal family.

The Queen is nursing her youngest son, Prince Edward. Also on the bed with her is Prince Andrew. And kneeling alongside are Princess Anne and Prince Charles.

This picture and one taken by Princess Anne were first published in Paris Match this week. The publication brought a reaction from the Palace.

But the London Daily Express published one of them yesterday, telling its four million readers that the pictures, "by their very informality, cannot but add to the public affection for the Queen."

Prince Edward was born on March 10, 1964, and the pictures were taken only a few days later by a very happy father and sister.

The Queen is wearing an embroidered bedjacket as she sits up against a satin pillow.

—Radiopicture

Anne's photo, Page 3

Sunday Mirror

7d. March 2, 1969 No. 307

YIPPEE!

That's the new Royal word .. on the big day for Charles and Anne

SUDDENLY Princess Anne and Prince Charles emerged yesterday as Britain's liveliest youngsters. Charles, 20, set the pace. Giving his first radio interview he talked candidly of what it is really like to grow up as the future king. He quipped: "I didn't suddenly wake up in my pram one day and say 'Yippee!'" Turn to centre pages for his highly personalised account of the royal life—including his debut as a comic in Cambridge, recorded in the picture above. Anne, 18, also made a debut yesterday. In her first official engagement she took the salute and presented St. David's Day leeks to the Welsh Guards at Pirbright, Surrey. A proud day. Or to use a royal word—YIPPEE!

Daily Mirror

YOUR PRINCE

5d.   Wednesday, July 2, 1969   •   No. 20,377

MY MOST DEAR SON

THIS was the moving climax to a crowded day of breathtaking pageantry. The moment when the Queen presented the Prince of Wales to his people after his Investiture in Caernarvon Castle. She presented him as "my most dear son." That was the official description laid down in the Letters Patent, the historic form of words to be followed in creating any Prince of Wales. But no choice of words could have been more appropriate. For this was so clearly a mother proud of her son, raising his hand so gently.

With the world looking on, he had come through the pomp and the ceremony, the long ordeal, with compelling poise and dignity. And now, at last, he was ready to meet his people. As his mother raised his hand in the traditional manner of presentation, they smiled. At their people . . . and at each other.

MIRROR INVESTITURE SPECIAL on Pages 2, 3, 4, 5, 11, 15, 16, 17, 18, 19 and Back Page. Donald Zec's report starts on Page 15

Daily Mirror

5d. **Tuesday, November 11, 1969** → No. 20,490

Prime Minister will make Commons statement

WILSON TO STEP IN TODAY ON ROYAL CASH

Premier slams the City's rumour mongers

By JOHN DESBOROUGH

CITY rumour-mongers cost Britain more in one day than all the motor industry strikes during the last six months.

This was claimed by Premier Harold Wilson last night.

The day was Friday, December 6 last year, when "inexplicable panic" swept the markets and for a time "threatened incalculable harm to sterling," he said.

The rumours had hinted at the resignation of the Prime Minister, Chancellor Roy Jenkins, and the Governor of the Bank of England.

Attack

And Mr. Wilson, who made his attack on the rumour-mongers at the Lord Mayor's banquet in Guildhall, revealed:

"According to every expert observer in the City, the rumours started on the basis of nothing more startling than that I had a sore throat.

"In the centre of a square mile which contains more professional expertise than almost anywhere else in the world feverish rumours were believed, acted upon, telephoned abroad."

Yet the rumours "could have been dismissed by a phone call to any junior reporter in any newspaper office," said Mr. Wilson.

As a result of the rumours people abroad, who were free to sell sterling short, were panicked into doing so

Earn

The losses were recovered within a few days, but it could have been serious for sterling and for Britain

Mr. Wilson said that managements and men, who sweated to earn exports the hard way, could get disillusioned when their hard work was thrown away "even temporarily, by occasional manic-depressive action."

Mr. Wilson also returned to the theme of "shop floor power."

This was not a British monopoly, but was growing throughout Europe.

No country had yet found the answer to it "whatever its pattern of legislation about industrial relations."

By VICTOR KNIGHT
Chief Political Correspondent

PREMIER Harold Wilson decided last night to step into the row over whether the Queen should have a pay rise.

He will make a Commons statement today in reply to questions raised by MPs following Prince Philip's comments on American TV that the royal finances would soon be "in the red."

Tory leader Edward Heath and his shadow cabinet have also joined the controversy.

They urged the appointment of an all-Party select committee of MPs to review the Queen's official allowance of £475,000 a year.

Liberal chief whip Eric Lubbock also agreed to the idea.

Mr. Wilson is not expected to commit the Government to proposing a select committee at the moment, but he could leave the door open for action later.

He is expected to give details of the Queen's allowance which was fixed after she began her reign in 1952.

Mr. Wilson decided to make his statement after it became clear that a flood of questions from MPs was building up.

Mr. William Hamilton, Labour MP for West Fife, a persistent critic of the Royal Family, is seeking facts about the Queen's revenues from her Duchy of Lancaster estates.

Burden

Mr. Hamilton said: "I think Prince Philip has a colossal nerve to plead poverty in general for the Royal Family and in particular for himself on American TV."

He said that taxpayers should not shoulder any further burden on behalf of the Royal Family.

A motion sponsored by Tory MP Sir Gerald Nabarro gives strong support to the demand for a select committee.

He said that the Queen's yearly allowance of £475,000 should be increased to £800,000 to allow for declining money values since it was fixed nearly eighteen years ago.

In a second pre-recorded TV interview shown in New York yesterday, Prince Philip dismissed as rumour recent speculation that the Queen might abdicate in favour of Prince Charles.

Excerpts of the interview were shown on BBC-2 last night.

Prince Philip said: "Abdication has its attractions, obviously, but no, I don't think it's been thought of very seriously.

"In fact, I am not sure the advantages necessarily outweigh the disadvantages.

"The idea that he

The Tories press for a 'pay review'

[Prince Charles] would only be capable of making a contribution if he were sovereign is really not true."

Asked about his role as the Queen's husband, Prince Philip replied: "Inevitably it's an awkward position to be in.

"There's only one other person like me—and that's Prince Bernhard of the Netherlands. We occasionally discuss the matter. He's the only other member of the union, so to speak."

Surprised

Many Labour MPs strongly oppose increasing the Queen's pay while there are compulsory curbs on wage increases.

If a select committee is set up, some of them will demand that it should have full power to inquire into the whole of the Queen's assets.

Prince Philip's abdication comments on American TV surprised the Buckingham Palace Press office.

A Palace spokesman said: "The question of the Queen's abdication has never been considered.

"It has not arisen so there is nothing we can add."

THE REAL STAR OF THE SHOW

THE QUEEN, the real "star" of the Royal Variety Performance, is about to spend an evening watching the stars of show business. She is pictured last night as she was escorted into the world-famous London Palladium by impresario Bernard Delfont. Behind them is Prince Philip. He — with the Royal Family's money worries—was the subject of the show's opening gag. Compere Des O'Connor told the story about "a certain gentleman" who appeared on TV "He said he might have to give up polo and leave his house because of the expense," said Des. "I understand about the house, but Polo's only 3d. a packet."

Picture by Alisdair Macdonald.

Daily Mirror

5d.   Monday, November 17, 1969   No. 20,495

QUEEN AND COUNTRY: THE PEOPLE'S VERDICT

PRINCE Philip blows his top. Parliament hears about the Queen's cash problems. The Royals are in the limelight.

In the middle of the great controversy the Mirror goes to the country.

What do the British people think about the Monarchy? Has it got a future? Should it change its role and image?

In a restless and changing age, what do the British people **REALLY** think about the "Royals"?

The Mirror asked Social and Community Planning Research, which has no connection with this newspaper, to conduct an authoritative survey of public attitudes towards the Monarchy and its members.

The detailed results will be published in this newspaper this week.

Today the Mirror outlines the main majority findings of this important survey:—

● **MOST PEOPLE**—9 out of every 10—would choose a Monarchy for Britain rather than a Republic.

● **MOST PEOPLE**—almost 9 out of 10—think that Royalty will survive in its present form during the whole of their lifetime.

● **MOST PEOPLE**—practically 9 out of 10—say that the Queen and Prince Philip are of real value to Britain.

● **MOST PEOPLE**—8 out of 10—disagree with the idea of changing the role of the Royal Family.

These are the major issues where there is overwhelming mass agreement about Queen and Country.

The independent survey has also revealed Royal issues which split the nation down the middle. You have given your answers.

SHOULD the Queen abdicate so that Prince Charles can become King at an earlier age?

SHOULD the Royal Family live in less luxury?

SHOULD the Queen's children go to State schools?

THE NATION'S VERDICT WILL BE GIVEN THIS WEEK IN THE DAILY MIRROR.

The man who 'pulled his finger out'

SEE CENTRE PAGES

Sunday Mirror

8d. February 22, 1970 No. 358

THE QUEEN

As you have never seen her before

A STARTLING new painting of the Queen by the Italian artist Pietro Annigoni will be unveiled at the National Portrait Gallery on Wednesday. It will take the art world by storm. The SUNDAY MIRROR has secured exclusive rights to publish this important new work in advance of the official ceremony. A detail appears on the right and there is a fuller version on the Centre Pages. Lionel Crane writes about Annigoni and the mysteries behind the painting on Page 20.

Great souvenir portrait CENTRE PAGES

47 DIE IN AIR BLAST

Arab bomb blows jetliner out of sky

—SEE BACK PAGE

The Queen through the eyes of Pietro Annigoni .. detail from the controversial portrait

Canberra SUNDAY POST
ROYAL VISIT
SPECIAL FOUR - PAGE LIFT-OUT

The Queen and the Duke of Edinburgh after laying a wreath at the Australian War Memorial yesterday

Los Angeles Times

LARGEST CIRCULATION IN THE WEST, 982,075 DAILY, 1,317,220 SUNDAY.

| VOL. XC | SEVEN PARTS—PART ONE ★★★ | THURSDAY MORNING, MAY 20, 1971 | 128 PAGES | Copyright © 1971 Los Angeles Times | DAILY 10c |

QUEEN CAN'T LIVE ON MILLION A YEAR

NEWS SUMMARY

THE WORLD

CAIRO PLOT—As the full extent of the plot against Egyptian President Anwar Sadat unfolded, it seemed clear that the president came within an ace of being ousted from his job. (Part 1, Page 2.)

HEATH-POMPIDOU — British Prime Minister Edward Heath and French President Georges Pompidou meet today in Paris prepared to achieve at last the unity of Europe. (Part 1, Page 6.)

A SHAU CLASH—South Vietnamese troops battled Communist units for six hours in the first major clash of the A Shau Valley campaign. (Part 1, Page 8.)

THE NATION

GEN. KOSTER DEMOTED — The Army demoted Maj. Gen. Samuel Koster, the commanding general at My Lai. (Part 1, Page 2.)

TRAINS ROLL — Stalled freight started moving again and commuters found their regular trains running, as the nation's railroads struggled back to normal after the two-day signalmen's strike. (Part 1, Page 2.)

SST DEFEAT—The White House conceded, before a showdown vote in the Senate, that the move to revive the SST was obviously doomed to defeat. (Part 1, Page 2.)

CITY AND STATE

FREEWAY OVERPASSES—A bill require screening of state freeway overpasses to prevent rocks or objects from being dropped on motorists was given final approval and sent to Reagan for his expected signature. (Part 1, Page 3.)

CONSOLIDATION — Reorganization of more than 50 Los Angeles departments into 10 to 14 consolidated departments or agencies recommended by the City economy and Efficiency Committee which said an annual saving of $30 to $40 million is possible. (Part 2, Page 1.)

BUSINESS-FINANCE

STOCKS EDGE UP—The market closed slightly higher, ending a two-day selloff. The Dow industrials closed up 1.48 at 920.04.

SPORTS

NEW HERO—Canonero II, the winner of the Kentucky Derby and the Preakness, has one leg to go in racing's Triple Crown but he clearly is a hero—back home in Venezuela. The Venezuelans have gone wild over the new turf favorite. Plaques and statues to Canonero are planned. Students have even stopped rioting in the wake of his success.

AT SEA FOR TALKS—East Coast lobster fishermen and U.S. officials approach the Russian fishing fleet's command ship off Cape Cod to begin talks on differences over fishing on the continental shelf. This view of the Soviet craft was made from U.S. cutter Duane.
Story in Part 1, Page 16

UPI Wirephoto

SHERIFF RULED INNOCENT—Lucius Amerson, sheriff of Alabama's Macon County, greets friends on leaving courthouse in Opelika where an all-white jury found him innocent of beating a black prisoner. Amerson is Alabama's first Negro sheriff since reconstruction days.
Story in Part 1, Page 5

UPI Wirephoto

She Asks Parliament for Raise

LONDON (AP)—Queen Elizabeth II, just back from putting in overtime on a royal tour of Canada, put in for a pay raise Wednesday. It is the first time Elizabeth has asked for an increase since she became queen in 1952.

Her bid comes at a time when Britain is experiencing trouble in business and the government is having little success trying to keep pay settlements down to 9%.

In restrained and regal words, the queen told the House of Commons in a message read by the speaker, Selwyn Lloyd, that she couldn't make the palace budget balance on the 475,000 pounds ($1.02 million) annual allowance she now gets from the government.

The word around Westminster was that Parliament would appoint a 17-member committee to consider the queen's message, with every likelihood that the royal budget would be bolstered.

Elizabeth's request for a raise came as no particular surprise. In recent years she has had to dip into her private purse to pay bills.

The queen pays about $2.4 million a year for the upkeep of Buckingham Palace and other royal residences.

The government receives all the income from Crown estates, running about $8.4 million a year.

Queen Elizabeth's personal fortune is estimated at $144 million.

Senate Rejects 2 Troop Cut Moves

WASHINGTON (AP) — President Nixon's forces scored a decisive victory Wednesday in rejecting the first and second in a series of Senate proposals to cut U.S. forces in Europe.

By an unexpectedly large margin of 63 to 26, the Senate defeated a proposal by Sen. Gaylord Nelson (D-Wis.) for a phased 50% cutback of the 300,000 U.S. troops over a three-year period unless East-West talks start promptly on the possibility of mutual withdrawals.

The heavy vote underscored the view of White House backers that they would be able to block all moves for a unilateral U.S. troop reduction.

A second proposal, by Sen. Birch Bayh (D-Ind.), was defeated by a vote of 81 to 13. It urged talks by the U.S. with its allies to share a greater share of the defense burden and providing, if they fail to, for a reduction of American forces to 150,000 by the end of 1972.

Principal target for Administration forces is an amendment to draft-extension legislation offered by Senate Majority Leader Mike Mansfield (D-Mont.). This would cut U.S. forces in half by the end of this year.

Chief threat to the Administration's no-compromise position and its desire to defeat the Mansfield amendment directly was a bipartisan proposal urging U.S. talks on possible troop cuts, both with its European allies and the Communist

Please Turn to Page 15, Col. 1

DAILY Mirror

BRITAIN'S BIGGEST DAILY SALE

2½p   Friday, June 4, 1971   No. 20,967

A magistrate (HOBBY: LANGUAGES) makes that ★★★★★★★★ word legal

THAT seven-letter word beginning with F is no longer obscene, a magistrate ruled yesterday. He dismissed a charge of obscene language brought against a man who used the word F＊＊＊＊＊g twice in the street.

The magistrate is 43-year-old Mr. Ian McLean, of London's Old Street Court.

Mr. McLean lists "languages" among his hobbies in Who's Who.

By ALAN GORDON

The case before Mr. McLean concerned motor fitter James Lawson, 43, whose van was stopped by a policeman.

Lawson was said to have shouted to workers on a nearby building site: "Look at this f＊＊＊＊＊g idiot making a fool of himself."

Search

"I am a working man. I am twice the man he is. What f＊＊＊＊＊g right has he got to search me?"

After hearing evidence from the policeman, Constable Andrew Richardson, Mr. McLean said: "Is this really obscene in 1971? It is used as an adjective by some people who know no other."

Lawson, of Queen's-road, Walthamstow, had denied using obscene language to the annoyance of passers-by.

The charge was brought under the Metropolitan Police Act, 1839. —when Victoria was Queen.

Constable Richardson said that when Lawson used the seven-letter word there were several women and children around, and they looked upset.

Mr. R. A. Prior, defending, submitted that there was no case to answer. He said: "This was not quite within the meaning of the Act."

Magistrate McLean agreed and dismissed the charge. A further charge against Lawson, alleging he used insulting words, was not proceeded with.

Afterwards, Mr. McLean, who has two daughters, laughed when told his ruling would probably cause a sensation. "I did not appreciate it would cause such a fuss," he said.

"It is true that some people seem to know of no other word. They don't mean it obscenely. We just have to decide each case on its merits."

Mr. Lawson, father of five, said after the case: "I used the words in the heat of the moment. No women or children were in earshot, or I would not have said it.

Church

"You hear the word on T V and in films. Obviously, this beak is a man of the world."

A Scotland Yard spokesman, asked if they would appeal or drop further prosecutions under the Act, said: "We can make no comment."

The Law Society said: "A different magistrate might take a different view. It might be different if a chap said this word coming out of a church.

"Things prohibited under these old Acts are quite odd. People must not fly kites or slide on the snow in certain places. But changes in the law take place very slowly."

A spokesman for the Magistrates' Association said that all cases were judged on their merits.

He added: "Words used to a group of building workers might be viewed differently from the same words used at a parish meeting."

James Lawson . . . He spoke "in the heat of the moment."

THE QUEEN: HER PAY AND THE PEOPLE

The Mirror (with plebeian cheek) comes to the rescue

FOUR out of five Daily Mirror readers who replied to our recent question think that the Queen is being paid enough.

Mr. Wallace of Enfield, a postman, expressed a human reaction pungently when he wrote:

A plan to end her embarrassment. . . .

"If the Government treats the Queen's claim as they did the postman's, God save the Queen."

Thank you, Mr. Wallace.

Of course, this simple issue has been brilliantly complicated by one of Her Majesty's Privy Councillors.

Mr. Richard Crossman, former Labour Cabinet Minister, now Editor of the New Statesman, knows how to be offensive.

PAGE ONE COMMENT

To talk about "truly regal cheek" was a trifle excessive even by the Right Honourable Crossman standards.

Yet the problem remains. More dough or no?

Certainly the argument about "how much— and when?" will not be answered by subtle asides from Prince Philip in response to explosive broadsides from R. H. S. Crossman.

A Select Committee of MPs has already been appointed to sort out this business of Pay and the Palace.

The cost of Royalty is a palatial bill that has

Continued on Page Two

On the day the Queen told Hirohito: We cannot pretend the past did not exist...

HOMAGE
at the Abbey

Hirohito: 'We have been feeling the warmth . . .'

Wilson offers Roy let-out on Six

By WILFRID SENDALL

IN a cynically brilliant manoeuvre, Mr. Harold Wilson yesterday offered a deal to pro-Market Mr. Roy Jenkins and his friends which will put Mr. Edward Heath and the Government in a fix.

In simple terms the scheme is this :—

NO REPRISALS against deputy leader Mr. Jenkins and other 'pro-Marketeers' if they vote with the Tories for entry into Europe in the Commons on October 28.

BUT IN RETURN, Mr. Jenkins and his followers will be required to obey party discipline and vote against the legislation which the Government must pass during 1972 to get Britain into the Market.

There is little doubt that most of the Jenkins faction will pick up Mr. Wilson's offer.

Tactics

It conforms with Mr. Jenkins' own tactics, which are to resign the deputy leadership before the October 28 Commons vote then immediately seek re-election in the new parliamentary session.

PART of the implied understanding between Mr. Wilson and Mr. Jenkins is that Mr. Wilson will do what he can to influence Mr. Jenkins' re-election as Deputy Leader.

Without doubt Mr. Wilson would rather have Mr. Jenkins at his back than either Mr. Jim Callaghan, Mr. Denis Healey or Mr. Anthony Wedgwood Benn.

A successful Wilson-Jenkins deal will prove dangerous for the Government.

It means that even if only 20 of the Tory anti-Marketeers stick to their guns, it will be virtually impossible for the Government to get through Parliament the mass of complex technical legislation necessary to give effect to a decision to enter Europe.

Mr. Wilson yesterday spelt out the Government's problem. He said : " October 28 is not an end but a beginning. The whole Parliamentary Party will fight against the mass of consequential legislation, main legislation, subordinate legislation, statutory instruments, orders-in-council which the Government will endeavour to force through.

Pressure

" I cannot imagine a single Labour member who, faced with this legislation, will not be in the lobbies against the Government."

Mr. Wilson's plans will obviously lead to the most severe pressure being brought on the anti-Marketeers in the Tory Party.

They will be urged to abandon their convictions to save the Government. They will be told that Government defeat would bring about a General Election on the Common Market in its present form, the Tories would be catastrophically defeated.

But Tory anti-Marketeers insist that defeat on the Common Market legislation need not bring about the Government's resignation and an election.

All Mr. Heath need do if he is defeated, they say, is to drop the Common Market project and stay in office.

Conference report : Page 4
Opinion : Page 8

Mass burial

BRUSSELS, Tuesday.—Thirty-eight of the victims of Saturday's B.E.A. plane disaster whose bodies cannot be identified, will be buried in a mass grave near the crash site.

Wall Street down

NEW YORK, Tuesday.—The Dow Jones Index on Wall Street closed 4·45 points down today at 891·21 after trading in 12·3 million shares.

Dog bites 22 children at school

Express Staff Reporter

THE owner of a dog that bit 22 children at a school was being hunted by police last night.

The dog ran amok in the playground as several hundred children, all under 11, waited to start lessons.

Many ran screaming into the cloakrooms at High Greave Junior and Infants' School in Rotherham, Yorkshire, with the dog in pursuit.

Ten children were taken to hospital and several were given anti-rabies injections.

'Ties Britain must keep'

Close ties with the Commonwealth and the United States must be maintained if Britain is to survive as a world Power, said yesterday.

Australia's High Commissioner to London, Sir Alexander Downer, said yesterday.

He called on the English-Speaking Union to help re-create Britain's " former outward look " through publicity and Government pressure.

Still missing

Ann Bellenger, the 20-year-old student who vanished on July 25 during a walking holiday on Dartmoor, did not turn up at Durham University yesterday.

Driver dies

Motorist Mr. Arthur Peaver, of Sevenoaks Road, Orpington, Kent, was killed when his car was in collision with a fire engine at Sidcup last night.

Metro strike

PARIS, Tuesday.—Army lorries were pressed into service today when 2,000 Metro Underground train drivers went on strike.

OLEG'S 'FRIEND DEFECTS'

BRUSSELS, Tuesday.

A RUSSIAN trade official, said to be a close friend of super-spy Oleg Lyalin, was last night reported to have defected in Brussels.

He is said to be 38-year-old Anatole Thoibov.

Lyalin's defection in London led to the expulsion of 105 Russian diplomats and trade officials accused of spying.

Today, sources close to the Belgian government are not commenting on what information Thoibov might have.

However, as Brussels is the capital of both NATO and the Common Market, this latest defection could prove important for Western Intelligence.

According to the unconfirmed reports, Thoibov defected 10 days ago.

IN LONDON Lyalin will know soon if he has to appear in court on a drink-driving charge.

The papers have been passed to the Director of Public Prosecutions.

Murder charge

Graham Wood, a 23-year-old Scunthorpe, Lincs, police constable, was sent for trial to Leicester Assizes yesterday charged with the murder of his 23-year-old wife, Glenis, on June 29.

FANCY THAT

COUNCILLORS at Ryde, Isle of Wight, burst into laughter last night on hearing from Whitehall that Seaview Pier was officially listed as a building of historic or architectural interest. The pier was demolished in 1952.

Express Staff Reporters

ONCE he was a godlike king whose armies savaged half the world : now the picture is of a little grey man in a baggy suit at the journey's end of all war—the Tomb of the Unknown Warrior.

With all the reverence of his race, Emperor Hirohito lays a wreath in Westminster Abbey of red roses for England and white chrysanthemums for Japan. Flowers of peace.

Of course, as the Queen told him later at Buckingham Palace, " We cannot pretend that the past did not exist."

Indeed it seemed that the British people—whether embittered old soldiers who remember Japanese brutality or happy-go-lucky youngsters who admire Japanese technology—really did not know what to make of Hirohito and his empress arriving on a state visit.

The big silence

Crowds were lining the streets of London. *But so quiet.* Hirohito, riding in a carriage with the Queen, soon stopped waving. Even Prince Philip, with the empress, was looking uneasy by the end.

There was one stir of excitement when a man threw his coat in front of the cavalcade : it turned out this was a case of private grief not connected with the Japanese.

Later Hirohito paid his tribute at the Abbey. Then came a banquet at the Palace.

The magnificent setting was the white and gold ballroom. The Queen, wearing white satin and the Supreme Order of the Chrysanthemum, sat at the head table with the emperor and empress. The emperor wore the Order of the Garter which was taken away from him during the war but recently restored.

Absent

Most of the Royal Family were there, though Lord Mountbatten, wartime Supreme Commander in South-East Asia, was absent : he had, it was said, a previous engagement and intended no disrespect. The Prime Minister, Mr. Heath, was present.

The food was entirely occidental : chicken soup, sole, saddle of lamb, and pineapple and ice cream.

The Queen, recalling that " we are both island people " highly industrialised, said that Japanese life " has been studied sometimes with admiration and sometimes with apprehension, but always with interest."

Then : " We cannot pretend that the past did not exist. We cannot pretend that the relations between our two peoples have always been peaceful and friendly. However, it is precisely this experience which should make us all the more determined never to let it happen again.

" Your Majesty's own actions and example since the dark days of 1945 make it only too obvious that you are dedicated to peace and friendship. The tremendous success of Japanese industry and commerce over the last 25 years should also be an object lesson to all nations that success and prosperity can be achieved by peaceful means "

Warmth

Hirohito, whatever he may have made of the silence of the crowds, replied : " We are very happy that from the very moment we landed we have been feeling the warmth of the heart of Your Majesty's people."

He expressed hopes for " preservation of tranquility in the world and promotion of the welfare of mankind." About those " dark days " he said nothing at all.

This painful charade:
PAGE 8

At the state banquet:

PHOTO NEWS

PAGE 7

Bomber crash

An R.A.F. Canberra jet bomber crashed and burst into flames in a field at Lobthorpe, Lincolnshire, last night, after its crew of three bailed out.

Faulkner date

Ulster Premier Brian Faulkner flies to London tomorrow for Downing Street talks with Mr. Edward Heath.

LATEST

TV-Radio programmes Page 12

'PEACE' CALL

Soviet Premier Kosygin called for guarantees of lasting peace and security and a halt to the armaments race, in speech during State visit to Algiers.

Daily Mirror

BRITAIN'S BIGGEST DAILY SALE

3p   Thursday, December 16, 1971   No. 21,130

The Mirror writes an open letter to:

Her Majesty, Queen Elizabeth II, Buckingham Palace, London, SW1

'DEAR QUEEN..'

Dear Queen,

DON'T be too upset. Of course, Willie Hamilton, that well-known maverick and Scottish MP, was very rude to your sister, Princess Margaret.

To call her 'this expensive kept woman' was going too far. All that can be said in his favour is that he had the right to say it.

After all, as Mr. Hamilton had to admit, Princess Margaret had three or four public engagements a week last year—and she is, of course, married to that brilliant photographer, Antony Armstrong-Jones.

Indeed, the highest mountain in Wales is named after him.

Guilty

And Wild, Wild Willie was also guilty of a little *lese majeste* towards Queen Elizabeth, The Queen Mother.

For Willie to call her Princess Margaret's "old mum" was being a bit familiar.

She certainly does her share of the Royal chores.

She had 211 official engagements last year—and carried out every one of them with impeccable graciousness

As a constitutional monarch, Your Majesty, you are in the unfortunate (or fortunate) position of being unable to lay down the law — unlike your predecessor, the First Elizabeth. She would have clapped Wee Willie into the Bloody Tower.

You must have seen her on the telly.

Facts

But you have a fair point when you say: "If I am Sovereign, why shouldn't I be Sovereign of my own household?"

All right. Loyalty is loyalty. Affection is affection. But facts are facts.

For every ONE reader of the Daily Mirror who wrote to this newspaper approving the new financial arrangements EIGHT were AGAINST.

And a high proportion of those eight were pensioners.

This doesn't mean that

PLEASE TURN TO PAGE 2

'BLACK HAND' STRIKES IN LONDON

See Back Page and Centre Pages

Haunting prospect for School Board
Page 10

Candid comments by Liza Minnelli

Showcase

A kilowatt crisis here this summer?
Viewpoint

WARM
Mostly sunny Sunday. High in the middle 80s. See Page 84.

Chicago Sunday Sun-Times

★★★★★
FINAL
City, Suburbs: 30c
Price Elsewhere 40c

Vol. 25, No. 35, 296 Pages (Mail 9 sections)
©1972 by Field Enterprises Inc.

Sunday, May 28, 1972

Duke of Windsor is dead at age 77

THE DUKE OF WINDSOR

By Philip Magnus
Special from the London Observer

LONDON — The Duke of Windsor, the former King Edward VIII of England who gave up his throne for "the woman I love," died in his Paris home early Sunday, Buckingham Palace announced. He was 77.

A Buckingham Palace statement said, "It is announced with deep regret that His Royal Highness, the Duke of Windsor, has died at his home in Paris at 2:25 today, Sunday, May 28, 1972." This was 8:25 p.m. Saturday Chicago time.

His decision in 1936 to become the first of 60 British rulers to abdicate rocked the 1,000-year-old British monarchy. But his determination to marry American divorcee Mrs. Wallis Warfield Simpson became one of the great love stories of all time.

Prince Edward Albert Christian George Andrew Patrick David — known to his family as David and to the world successively as Prince of Wales, King Edward VIII and Duke of Windsor — was born on June 23, 1894, at White Lodge, Richmond Park. His childhood was spent mostly at Sandringham, in isolation from his contemporaries, under the educational regime of a bored and inefficient private tutor, H.P. Hansell; and his upbringing was handled badly, despite the best intentions, by his parents.

The duke's father, George V, had been educated in the royal navy. He himself had enjoyed an ideally happy relationship with both his parents. But its pattern, unique in the annals of the royal family during the previous 200 years, was not repeated in his relationship with his own children.

The Duke of Windsor was nervous and sensitive and his childhood lacked warmth. Queen Mary, who intervened frequently to shield him, had no instinctive understanding of young people's minds, and the duke's tutors thought that he ought to be sent to a good preparatory school. His early education was conditioned wholly by the requirements of the entrance examination into the Royal Naval College; but Hansell urged that he should be allowed to acquire first, like other boys at private schools, the protective armor of a communal habit of thought and code of conduct.

King George pooh-poohed that appeal. "My brother and I," he said, "never went to a preparatory school. The navy will teach David all that he needs to know." At Osborne and subsequently at Dartmouth the Prince took some hard knocks before learning to hold his own. Attractive and popular, he displayed a morbid anxiety "to be treated exactly like any other boy."

In 1911, for example, he provoked a family row when required to dress up, at Lloyd George's behest, to be invested as Prince of Wales. "What would my navy friends say," he protested, "if they saw me in this preposterous rig?" However, he became happy in the navy and was distressed when his father told him abruptly in 1912 that he must quit. King George explained that his mind needed to be broadened by undergraduate residence at Oxford and by educational trips to France and Germany during vacations.

Between August, 1919, and October, 1925, when he was 31,

Turn to Page 18

Soviets view Nixon today
Story on Page 2

Donohue wins Indy at 163 m.p.h.

Driver Gary Bettenhausen pilots his Penske McLaren-Offenhauser (right) past the careening car of Mike Mosley at the Indianapolis 500-mile auto race Saturday. Mosley was burned in the crash, which happened while he was in the lead. Mark Donohue won the race at a record speed of 163.465 m.p.h. Story, more pictures on Back Page. (AP)

WEATHER:
Mostly dry.
Lighting-up time:
9.42 p.m.
Details—Back Page.

46,006

Evening Standard

London: Monday June 5 1972

A King's funeral—only a crown was missing

THE SHARED MOMENT OF GRIEF

THE COFFIN, borne by Welsh Guardsmen, is carried in St. George's Chapel.

NPA Rota

By ANNE SHARPLEY

WINDSOR, Monday.

THE FUNERAL service is over ... And the Queen and the Duchess of Windsor, heavily veiled, leave St. George's Chapel, Windsor, today.

When the coffin of the Duke of Windsor was brought into the chapel the small frail figure of the Duchess, head slightly bowed, stood between the Queen and Prince Philip.

It had taken his death for them to be here surrounded by the family, the pageantry, the Establishment and all the expanding wave of contact that in the end include the whole Kingdom on such a day.

Of English oak

There was grandeur in plenty for this abdicated King now. In fact, but for the absence of a crown on the coffin and the burial later at the Royal private cemetery rather than in a vault, it was almost a King's burial.

A great procession had made its way round the Chapel carrying the coffin of English oak which was gently rested on the catafalque of purple. A strangely empty chapel, however. Only half filled, for this was a private funeral service.

Yet they were all there. The Constable and Governor of

Continued Back Page, Col. 3

A prayer for a King: News on Camera—Page THREE

THE FUNERAL service over, the Queen and the Duchess of Windsor leave St George's Chapel.

Press Association

THE NEWS

Phone (Editorial and other business) 51 0351
Classified 51 0191

Adelaide: Friday, October 13, 1972   7c*

BROKEN HILL, 8c

LAST

WEATHER   Fine. MAX. TEMP. (to 3 p.m.): 15.6 C. Sunset 6.29.

STUDENTS SCREAM ABUSE AT QUEEN

A MIXTURE of cheering and jeering students, with some just looking, surround the Queen's car as it drives from Stirling University. Today's AAP-AP radio picture.

SHOCKING ORDEAL

STIRLING, Scotland, Thursday: Students screamed abuse and obscenities at the Queen when she visited Stirling University today.

In violent, unprecedented scenes, several hundred students mobbed her and many yelled "Queen out" and "Sieg Heil" along with other insults that included four-letter words.

They shook their fists at her and sang filthy songs as she walked within feet of them.

Many of them were drinking from beer cans and bottles of cheap wine.

Police, pressmen, and Palace officials formed a cordon round Her Majesty

as the students surged towards her.

Throughout the ordeal, the Queen remained calm and showed remarkable presence of mind.

The scenes were the worst in the Queen's 20-year reign.

They were described by

From Frank O'Neill

Press Association staff reporter Alan Smith as the most frightening he had witnessed in more than a decade of covering Royal tours.

The trouble started as the Queen entered the university library.

A huge crowd gathered outside, students began jostling police, and a stink bomb was let off.

As she left for the university theatre, obscene shouting broke out and there were cries of "Queen out."

Then the crowd surged forward and a cordon was quickly thrown around the Queen.

In the cordon were her lady-in-waiting, Mrs. John Dugdale, the Lord Polwarth, Minister of State for Scotland, Squadron Leader Peter Beer, the Queen's Equerry, the

Queen's private detective, Mr. Edward Frizell, and Mr. James Milne, deputy constable of Stirlingshire police.

Still seemingly unruffled, she made her way slowly to a small foyer leading to a theatre inside the Mac-Robert building.

There, as she met university staff, a shouting student tried to push his way in.

Police were restraining him when Mrs. Marie Cottrell, wife of the principal, ran from behind the Queen, up some stairs to the door, and pushed the student outside.

● CONT. P. 57

No. 15,321—Registered for posting as a newspaper—Category B.

DAILY Mirror

HAPPY ANNIVERSARY

BRITAIN'S BIGGEST DAILY SALE

3p   Tuesday, October 31, 1972   No. 21,398

The smiles that say everything about the silver years together

THE Queen and her husband the Duke of Edinburgh are pictured together in the grounds of Balmoral Castle.

This is what is described in the bare language of the Court Circular as "an official portrait."

But this picture by the Queen's second cousin, Patrick Lichfield, loses the starchy emptiness of most "official" portraits. No severe looks, no regalia, no stiff uniform.

Just two people relaxed and informal, the Duke in an open-necked shirt, the Queen in a light summery dress.

Two people who celebrate their twenty-fifth wedding anniversary on November 20 . . . their silver anniversary, for which this picture was taken.

PLEASE TURN TO PAGE 7

INFLATION CRISIS: HEATH'S ULTIMATUM

PREMIER Edward Heath gave the unions an ultimatum last night in the pay-and-prices crisis. He warned T U C chiefs that unless there was voluntary wage restraint, laws would be introduced to curb prices and incomes. The T U C will give their reply tomorrow.

Full story—See Page 2.

The toast is...
THE QUEEN!

Pictured foreground: The Lady Mayoress, Prince Philip, Mr. Heath, The Queen, Lady Templer, the Lord Mayor, Sir Gerald Templer, Mrs. Ramsey, the Archbishop

By CYRIL AYNSLEY

THE QUEEN ... that was the toast, and the flashing goblets were raised amid the splendour of a great occasion. But the Queen herself gave it an air of informality, wit, and personal happiness that revealed the woman behind the symbol.

A service of thanksgiving at Westminster Abbey, a luncheon at Guildhall, a walkabout in the Barbican, and a family party at Buckingham Palace marked 25 years of marriage.

On such a day, she said with Prince Philip by her side at Guildhall, the speech really should start with *"My husband and I."* Everyone roared at the way she recognised that royalty can be the target of satire, and can answer back too.

Terrorist 'flown to Britain for cure'

By JOHN HAMSHIRE

THE Home Office was last night investigating a report that an Arab letter bomb expert was flown to Britain for treatment after the bomb he was making accidentally exploded.

The man, believed to be Lebanese, was taken to London's Westminster Hospital, where he paid for private treatment in the wing where Lady Churchill is now a patient.

After several days treatment he was declared fit by the hospital and allowed to leave.

A hospital spokesman said last night : " This man did not get free medical attention. He paid for it.

" We cannot say whether the police were informed. When he left the hospital we do not know where he went to."

A Foreign Office spokesman said : " If the hospital suspects that a patient may have been involved in a criminal act, then they should contact the police."

Freeze Bill rebels

The Government had a majority of 29—292 votes to 263—in the Commons last night for the Third Reading of the pay-prices freeze Bill, which now goes to the Lords.

Mr. Enoch Powell (Tory, Wolverhampton S.W.) voted against the measure and two other Tories abstained : Mr. Jock Bruce-Gardyne (Angus South) and Mr. John Biffen (Oswestry).

Grandma's at the Palace

COMPLETE with her battered black hat and ancient fox fur, Giles's Grandma was right in there at the Buckingham Palace silver wedding dinner last night.

The dinner was given by Prince Charles and Princess Anne in their parents' honour.

And by royal request Grandma's creator, Express cartoonist Carl Giles, produced the cover for the dinner programme — that's part of it on the left.

The caption, as the loyal but unpredictable Grandma's anniversary gift is examined at the Palace gate :—

" *Six silver spoons for Her Majesty and His Royal Highness from a lady with the initials B.R.*"

Says Giles : " It was a great honour and I had tremendous fun producing the cartoon. I hope the Royal Family like it."

This great day—in great pictures
PAGES 3, 6, 7, 8 AND 9

Also at the royal table were the Archbishop of Canterbury and Mrs. Ramsey. So for a definition of married life the Queen said:—

❛When the bishop was asked what he thought about sin he replied with simple conviction that he was against it. If I am asked today what I think about family life after 25 years of marriage I can answer with equal simplicity and conviction : I am for it.❜

Blank

As it happened, the only unmarried person at the table was Prime Minister Mr. Edward Heath. There was a blank on the guest list, seat No. 6, which might have marked the fact.

Other guests on Table One were Field Marshal Sir Gerald Templer, Lieutenant for Greater London, and his wife, and, of course, Lord Mais, the Lord Mayor, and Lady Mais. That made nine. Other top tables had 10.

Lord Mais said : " As we enter Europe as a nation for the first time not under arms, we go under your Majesty's banner, and that assures us a special welcome.

" It will also, I hope, ensure that differences and doubts will be cast aside and all will do their utmost to see that our entry and the outcome are a lasting success."

Party

The rest of the celebrations were private—a party at the Palace for 200, arranged by Prince Charles and Princess Anne.

Outside, it was miserable with rain, but there was a crowd to watch guests arriving—including members of European Royal families—and to give a special cheer for the Queen Mother.

Inside a classical concert opened the evening. But after dinner pop took over for a dance, and it looked like developing into a swinging night.

Family

Then, on the family theme again, he added : " But while we are making new friends and finding new markets, may we remember that your Majesty is not only Queen of Great Britain but Queen of Canada, of Australia, of New Zealand, and other countries who are still members of the Commonwealth."

The Queen said that she and Prince Philip had attended the service at the Abbey—the scene of their wedding—" with the spirit of real thanksgiving for our good fortune," and now she thanked London for its good wishes.

Afterwards she expressed those thanks person-to-person in a walk with her family to the Barbican, talking to children, office girls and City gents in the informal crowds while confetti poured down from the new concrete skyscrapers.

POCKET CARTOON
By OSBERT LANCASTER

" *Personally dear, I'm only too delighted to think that she's happily chasing foxes when she might be chasing us!*"

DID YOU FANCY THAT?

PUNTERS with an eye for a royal gamble scored yesterday when Silver Delight won the first race at Folkestone at 7—2. It was tipped by the Scout, naturally.

Big Tory revolt goes ahead

By DANIEL McGEACHIE

TORY M.P.s last night had a confrontation with Home Secretary Mr. Robert Carr, over the new immigration rules.

Mr. Carr was said to have received " an almost totally hostile " hearing at the Commons meeting, attended by about 120 backbenchers.

The M.P.s failed to get any assurance that members of the old Commonwealth should have at least the same rights of entry to Britain as Common Market Europeans after January 1.

Mr. Carr *did* promise that he would alter the entry system at London Airport to avoid embarrassing Commonwealth citizens.

It was a pledge that failed to satisfy the M.P.s and one later called it " more of a joke than a concession."

FOUR

Mr. Carr said he hoped to have four entry channels at all times—a move exclusively disclosed in the Daily Express last week.

The channels would be United Kingdom, Commonwealth, Common Market, and Aliens. This would avoid Commonwealth citizens having to go through the Alien barrier if their own entry point was unmanned.

If it was not possible to man all the gates, said Mr. Carr, then he would introduce a system of one gate for everyone.

Mr. Carr spoke to the M.P.s about what he described as " a grossly distorted Daily Express campaign." And he called on M.P.s to emphasise the advantages that Commonwealth immigrants would enjoy, rather than the disadvantages.

They would be able to vote, to join the Army, or the Civil Service — " privileges " that would not be available to Market citizens.

But he was only repeating

➥ PAGE TWO COL. SIX

... 20 PAGES

Hickey :	Page 3
Big Crossword :	Page 7
Weather :	Page 11
Contest :	Page 13
Target :	Page 13
Appointments :	Page 14
Money :	Page 15
Mary Peters :	Page 17
Racing :	Page 18
Fight preview :	Page 19
Soccer :	Page 20

Going East...

BONN, Monday.—Mr. Edward Heath is to visit West Germany for personal talks with Chancellor Brandt early in the new year following Brandt's election victory.

...going West

NEW YORK, Monday.—The United Nations Secretary-General is prepared to accept an application by East Germany for observer status, a UNO spokesman said today.

Wall Street boom

NEW YORK, Monday.—The Wall Street boom continued today with the Dow Jones Index 0·53 of a point down at 1,005·04.

Savings boost

Customers with ordinary accounts in the National Savings Bank are to have the interest rate raised from 3½ to 4 per cent from January 1.

MacStiofain waits it out

A massive demonstration by Provisional I.R.A. supporters was staged in Dublin last night in a bid to free their arrested leader, Sean MacStiofain, who was held on Sunday.

Time was running out for Prime Minister Jack Lynch if he wants to hang on to his prisoner. MacStiofain has to be charged within 48 hours—or go free.

Soldiers killed

Mystery surrounded the death yesterday of two soldiers in a booby-trap bomb blast at a derelict farmhouse in Co. Armagh.

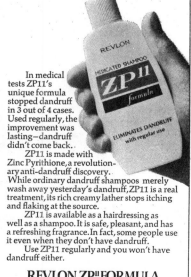
PHONE STD CODE 01

353 8000

TELEX 21841

THE Sun

FORWARD WITH THE PEOPLE 3p

Thursday, November 15, 1973

THE CAPTAIN'S LADY

BE THERE WITH THE SUN ++ BE THERE WITH THE SUN ++

JUST MARRIED! The handsome Captain and his Princess. Their witnesses: 500 million viewers all over the world. Picture by ARTHUR STEEL

PAGES AND PAGES OF PICTURES INSIDE

The New Zealand Herald

Telephones | Classified Advertising - 78-999
| Other Departments - 78-988

AUCKLAND, THURSDAY, JANUARY 31, 1971   2   Price 6c

'This Is Certainly a Family Gathering...'

Reunion at Christchurch International Airport: Pictures taken on the arrival of the Air New Zealand DC-8, which brought Queen Elizabeth, Princess Anne and Captain Mark Phillips from Rarotonga. The Duke of Edinburgh and Prince Charles met the Royal party.

Christchurch Welcomes The Queen

Staff Reporter   **Christchurch**

Warmth was the keynote at Christchurch yesterday when thousands turned out in 30-degree (86 Fahrenheit) temperatures to welcome the Queen.

The welcome at the airport by the Governor-General, Sir Denis Blundell, the Prime Minister, Mr Kirk, and other dignitaries was formal, but the Queen herself generated and responded to the warmth of popular feeling when she replied to the address of welcome.

"Above all, I am looking forward to being once again in this beautiful, kindly and hospitable land, of which I am proud to be Queen," she said.

"I am delighted to be back in New Zealand and I am extremely grateful to you for your loyal and generous welcome to me and to the other members of my family.

"This is certainly a family gathering! We have converged on Christchurch by different routes and by different means. But one thing is the same . . . we

Naval Uniform

The Prince of Wales, in naval uniform, arrived soon after 4 p.m., followed by the Duke of Edinburgh, also in naval uniform.

The Royal flight, a specially-fitted Air New Zealand DC8, under the command of Flight Captain R. Johnson, landed at 4.19 p.m., four minutes late, and the Duke and Prince Charles climbed the gangway.

A few minutes later the Queen appeared at the head of the gangway, smiling and waving. She was dressed in an emerald and white silk jacket and skirt, with a hat of swirled organza and was quickly joined by Prince Philip, Princess Anne — in

are all glad to be here . . . and glad to be together."

Crowds began gathering at the airport at 1.30 p.m., more than two and a half hours before the Queen was due to arrive.

a sapphire jacket, skirt and hat — Captain Phillips and Prince Charles.

Captain Phillips wore the uniform of the Queen's Dragoon Guards.

"The Government and people of New Zealand extend to you, our most Gracious Sovereign, and to Her Royal Highness Princess Anne and Captain Mark Phillips, a most sincere and warm welcome," said the Prime Minister, Mr Kirk.

The Hub

"For the past week New Zealand, and in particular this city of Christchurch, has been the hub of Commonwealth activity. The Commonwealth spirit of friendship and co-operation is very strong at these the tenth Commonwealth Games."

Referring, in her reply, to "the great family of the Commonwealth" gathered here for the Games," Her Majesty said:

"In this country, which has always given firm support for the Commonwealth association, I know they will find the happiness and satisfaction which come from friendship and co-operation.

"Today, Christchurch is the centre of the Commonwealth and, as its Head, I am especially pleased to be here.

"Mr Prime Minister, New Zealand's achievements have often outstripped those of larger countries and you can imagine how much I am looking forward to seeing something of these — and of the changes that have taken place since I was last here."

From the airport the Royal party made a ceremonial progress through the city.

The cathedral bells rang out as the cars passed through Cathedral Square, where crowds stood five and six deep.

Her Majesty will officiate at the closing ceremony of the Games on Saturday.

Greatest Range War Of Gordon's Life

Staff Reporter   **Christchurch**

A 17-year-old marksman, Maurice Gordon, yesterday won the full-bore rifle gold medal at the Commonwealth Games in a thrilling finish at Christchurch.

Few New Zealand successes at the Games were more popular than that of the Hastings apiarist, who, for many years, has not only shone as a competitor but even more as a coach of national teams.

But Gordon knew he had been in one of the greatest

range wars of his life before he could claim the gold.

In hot pursuit over the final rounds were the Scot Colin McEachran, and the Englishman James Spaight.

At 900 yards Gordon scored 73 out of a possible 75 with 14 bulls. But even then the

Britons were still not beaten.

Then came the final 1000-yard. Could the New Zealander, now feeling pretty weary, keep that precious one point lead from McEachran, with Spaight only a few points behind?

The wind was switching with a frontal fishtail swinging far right.

Some might call the conditions atrocious. Perhaps they were, and yet they were made for Gordon.

Marksmen up and down the country say that when it comes to switching breezes no one can handle them better than the Hastings man.

He shot magnificently and yet in the middle of the 1000 he feared he was going to "blow it."

His shots were going too high and this was costing him points.

No Panic

But Gordon is not one to panic.

The elevation was corrected and higher scores followed.

He and McEachran dropped nine points each for 66 and New Zealand had won its first Games gold medal for shooting.

Gordon's score was 387 out of a possible 405. McEachran was a point behind with Spaight scoring 383.

All that was now required was to place the modest Gordon in the rifle victor's chair —a charming custom of the sport—and to present medals.

Gordon looked a bit embarrassed about it for he is no publicity seeker.

Act as Boost

He did say, however: "The victory was naturally of a great personal satisfaction and I am delighted that it will act as a boost for the sport."

Gordon's gold was matched yesterday by the 23-year-old Pukekohe Golf Club greenkeeper, David Aspin, who came first in the middleweight wrestling.

It was New Zealand's best day at the Games in terms of medals won. Two golds (wrestling and shooting), one silver (weightlifting) and five bronze, two in wrestling and three in boxing.

● Details in Section 2.

Maurice Gordon being chaired by fellow competitors after winning his gold medal.

ART BOOM HIT BY FORGERIES

Art lovers were warned yesterday that the signatures of famous New Zealand painters might be forged by people trying to cash in on the current art boom.

The warning was given for £2000, he said, he had been informed of the forgeries.

The dealer said he had sold a landscape by an unrecognised 19th century artist." It later turned up in an Auckland shop bearing the signature "J. C. Hoyte."

who said there were a "lot of very wide people . . . in the job at the moment."

He claimed that unscrupulous people were buying some virtually worthless old New Zealand oil and water colour landscapes and adding the signatures of such better-known painters such as Hoyte, Blomfield and Chevalier.

The dealer, who declined to be named, alleged that several such paintings had been sold at vastly inflated prices in Melbourne.

An art gallery had bought one such painting

The forging of signatures had become apparent only in the last five or six years since the price of paintings began to soar.

A spokesman for the Auckland Criminal Investigation Branch said yesterday that the police had received no complaints about the forgeries.

Tears as Games Wrestler is Disqualified

Many of the Indian Commonwealth Games wrestling team were in tears yesterday morning following the debarring of their flyweight, Radhey Shyam, from further competition because he was too heavy by about the weight of a needle.

The deadline for making the correct weight was 8.30 a.m.

Shortly before this, Shyam was running about the weighing-in room trying everything—towelling, running, spitting and even vomiting—in an attempt to get rid of those extra drops.

His target was to weigh in under 106 pounds. The manager of the Indian team, Mr D. P. Chand, appealed to the weighing controller, Mr Jack Prestney, for some relaxation.

"This can't be done," said Mr Prestney. "I have got to be fair. Other teams have weighed in correctly."

"Two minutes to go," announced a steward.

But there was sympathy for the desperate young wrestler. Even the scale platform was rubbed continually in an effort to remove any perspiration.

Just before 8.30, a pair of scissors was produced. Large chunks of Shyam's thick black hair fell to the floor in an effort to reduce his weight.

Shyam once more stepped on the scale, but Mr Prestney shook his head.

Once more Shyam mounted the scale to weigh in correctly, but the clock had moved to 8.34.

"Shyam cannot wrestle," declared Mr Prestney. "He has not weighed in at the correct weight by 8.30."

The scissors hacked away again as the clock hand moved to the half-hour mark. The wrestler was told now that he should not step off the scales.

However, in the confusion he failed to follow the directions. And still the scissors sheared away.

Chand, who sought a meeting with Mr Prestney, Mr Jacob and other officials. They soon returned with the verdict unchanged.

Mr Chand then urged Mr Prestney to put details of his decision in writing and he would do the same.

Mr Prestney shook his head saying: "There is no point in taking such an action. All the rules have been adhered to. Nothing more can be done."

It only remained for a few to offer their sympathies to the Indian team. The tears, however, still flowed.

There was one final desperate bid by Mr Chand turned to Mr H. Jacob, of England, representing the International Wrestling Federation.

There was no reprieve. Mr Jacob indicated quite clearly with a wave of his arm that Shyam was out.

TWO MAJOR RALLIES CANCELLED

Two major car rallies have been cancelled this year because of the fuel crisis—the Heatway International and the Marlboro Rally Championship.

Both sponsors—Heatway Industries Ltd and Philip Morris (N.Z.) Ltd—will continue to plan for future rallies in the hope the fuel situation will improve.

ON OTHER PAGES

As Heath loses his big gamble…

QUEEN BACK TO A CRISIS
Who rules Britain?

By ROBERT CARVEL

THE PRIME MINISTER is expected to report to the Queen tonight on the grave political crisis in which the nation is plunged by the apparently indecisive outcome of the General Election. Nothing like it has been experienced in British politics for half a century.

Mr Heath has suffered a moral defeat. A period of minority government seems to be signalled. And today it was not quite clear which party will rule although Labour looks like being the biggest one. Another General Election soon cannot be ruled out—daunting and damaging as the prospect for the country must be.

The initial shock of the new political uncertainty was immediately evident in the City. This was bound to be followed by unfavourable reaction abroad.

The Treasury was braced for new strains on sterling. This was a most powerful incentive for the party leaders to get the machinery of government under proper control quickly.

During the campaign they had said it would be imperative to act without delay after polling day to steady the pound and consider extra support in the form of new international loans.

With an unstable government Britain is not going to be an attractive proposition for the lenders.

It was almost certain that neither Mr Wilson nor Mr Heath would be in a position to form a one-party Government able to command a parliamentary majority on its own.

Immediate and desperate secret bargaining is likely as party leaders manoeuvre this weekend.

The situation was complicated with the election of a handful of Nationalists declared during the night and with that of a number of dissident Ulstermen coming this afternoon.

It was not clear that Mr Thorpe and his Liberals would

Cont. Back Page Col. 1

Evening Standard: Tim Graham

THE QUEEN at Heathrow this morning returning from Australia to political crisis.

Shares dive, the £ is hit

By DAVID MALBERT

THE CITY was devastated today by the Election result and share prices were crashing in what looked like becoming the most catastrophic one day fall ever recorded.

Hundreds of millions of pounds were slashed from the values of leading shares which had been climbing over the past weeks on hopes on a clear-cut Tory victory.

Industrial gians such as ICI, Unilever, British Leyland, Turner and Newall and a host of others slumped heavily as soon as the Stock Exchange opened.

Government stocks tumbled with War Loan down 61½p to an all-time low of £26¼.

Stores and property shares were also hit badly and indeed, the only sectors to avoid the carnage were gold shares which were rising as the metal price raced ahead by nine dollars to 172 dollars an ounce.

The pound took a beating too, losing two cents against the U.S. dollar to 2·2840 in a confused and worried foreign exchange market.

Also reflecting the depression was the dollar premium — the extra that has to be paid by U.K. investors for overseas securities.

This jumped to a quoted rate of more than 50 per cent, based on the old exchange rate of 2·60 dollars. Effectively with the pound at around 2·28 dollars, this is a premium of a highest ever 33 per cent.

Underlying these gnawing City fears was the prospect of gathering inflation, difficulties in raising overseas loans, out-of-control labour relations and a general lowering of the credit-worthiness of Britain.

After the first shock waves had passed through the Stock Market, however, the feeling was growing that the dramatic collapse may have over-emphasised the gravity of the situation.

The Financial Times index was down 25·5 at 312·3.

Full story: Page 42

State of the parties

Labour	-	-	-	-	-	-	255
Conservative	-	-	-	-	-	-	177
Liberals	-	-	-	-	-	-	5
Others	-	-	-	-	-	-	5

Seats declared: 442	Still to be declared: 193

Computer forecasts

WITH 442 results declared, the computer-based predictions of the final outcome of the election were:

PRESS ASSOCIATION

Tory	298
Lab	310
Lib	13
Others	14

ITN

Tory	297
Lab	303
Lib	18
Others	17

BBC

Labour majority of nine over Tories.

These forecasts indicate that the Liberals and Others will hold the balance of power in the new Parliament.

Results in detail

Pages 23-26

● Other election news : Pages 3, 6, 7.

Sandringham rebuilding plan halted

THE QUEEN CUTS HER HOUSEKEEPING

Sandringham House : Only 270 rooms left

Wood Farm : Six bedrooms.

THE Queen has decided to set an example to the nation by not having the builders in at Sandringham, her home in Norfolk.

Cancellation of the work will save £250,000 of her own money.

And she is having an economy drive at Buckingham Palace.

By BARRY O'BRIEN

The central heating has been turned down and staff have been told to re-use envelopes for internal memos.

'Everyone has been asked to tighten their belts a little. That is what the Queen is doing,' the Palace said yesterday.

Sandringham House with its hundreds of rooms may be abandoned altogether as a royal residence.

In that case the Queen and her family would probably use Wood Farm, a six-bedroomed house on the Sandringham Estate where they stayed last month.

Demolished

The work that was to have been done was itself planned to cut the cost of running the 361-room, Jacobean-style mansion built in the mid-19th century by the Queen's great-grandfather, Edward VII.

As a first stage, 91 staff- and guest-rooms and old-fashioned kitchen, service and dining room areas on separate floors were demolished.

These were to have been replaced by quarters for a much smaller staff of 18 modern, labour-saving kitchens and a new dining room.

But although public funds were not involved—Sandringham is the Queen's private property, inherited just 23 years ago yesterday from her father George VI — she decided to call a halt as inflation pushed up the cost of the work.

'The Queen feels it would be inappropriate to go ahead at a time when many people are facing economic difficulties,' the Palace said.

Some work will have to be done to make Sandringham waterproof. The Queen will decide whether or not it would now be practical to stay there.

'One of the problems,' the Palace spokesman said, 'is that the house now has no kitchens.'

Part of Sandringham House will be opened to the public from next year. The 75-acre gardens and grounds have been open between April and September for 20 years.

The Palace said that a charge would be made for admission to the house but stressed that this would not be used to finance building work—'if there is any profit after operating costs have been met it will go to charity.'

With 'rising costs and general inflation' the Queen had asked for all royal expenditure to be closely studied.

Reduced

There was the central heating reduction — 'by several degrees' — and the cutting down on stationery. And the Master of the Household, Vice-Admiral Sir Peter Ashmore, 'has been asked by the Queen to keep a particular eye on items like food bills.'

Also, the Queen was asking public bodies giving her meals not to go to the expense of formal banquets — t h r e e courses would be enough.

● Prince Charles was forced to land his Navy helicopter on a disused airfield at Weston Zoyland, Somerset, 'as a precaution' after engine trouble on January 27, it was revealed yesterday.

'Dear old Sandringham'—Page Six

Onassis in jet dash

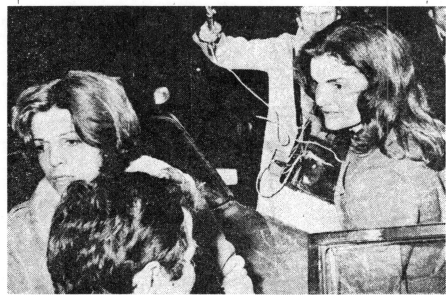

Jackie Onassis, right, and the tycoon's daughter Christina last night.

GREEK shipping tycoon Aristotle Onassis flew to Paris last night for hospital treatment after an attack of flu affected his heart.

Mr Onassis, 69, had been in an oxygen tent for 24 hours after developing breathing difficulties.

But he managed to walk up the steps of his plane at Athens airport after travelling from his villa near the city in a seven-car convoy.

And on arrival in Paris he was driven to his home near the Arc de Triomphe and was able to walk unaided from the car.

His wife Jackie — widow of President Kennedy — went with him. So did his only child, Christina, and French heart specialist Jacques Caroli.

Sources close to the family said that after the onset of influenza Mr Onassis suffered a relapse of myasthenia gravis—a muscular complaint—which impaired his breathing a n d affected his heart. Myasthenia can induce paralysis.

But members of his family said simply that the flu affected his heart.

A doctor said Mr Onassis would be admitted to the American Hospital this morning.

Mr Onassis fell ill last week during negotiations with the Greek Government for the transfer of Olympic Airways from his ownership to the State.

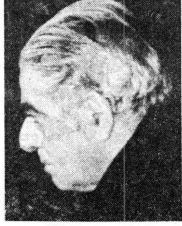

Onassis in Paris last night

Pickets moved to closed prisons

Daily Mail Reporter

THE two Shrewsbury strike pickets have been secretly moved from an open prison to closed jails at Leicester and Lincoln.

Their transfer was exclusively forecast in the Daily Mail last week. The move from the open prison at Sudbury in Derbyshire, took place on Tuesday.

But it was a closely guarded secret and Home Secretary Mr Roy Jenkins, although questioned in the Commons about the two men yesterday, carefully avoided any mention of the transfer.

Protests

The men, Dennis Warren and Eric Tomlinson, are serving three-year and two-year sentences for conspiring to intimidate others during the 1972 building workers' strike.

The decision to split them up and move them from Sudbury was taken by prison authorities because they refused to work or wear uniform.

But protests about the men's treatment were again firmly rejected by Mr Jenkins in the Commons yesterday.

Left-Winger Mr Norman Atkinson claimed that their trial had been politically motivated.

He alleged that notes which passed between the then Attorney-General, Sir Peter Rawlinson, and the Director of Public Prosecutions at the time of their trial, had been destroyed.

DAILY EXPRESS

No. 23,214 Thursday February 13 1975 Weather: Cloudy; some rain Price 5p

Royal row as miners get £15 offer

THE QUEEN and KING COAL

OPINION

'A demonstration of something that is increasing: the politics of envy'

SEE PAGE 8

POCKET CARTOON
By OSBERT LANCASTER

"I'm told that the trouble with Willie Hamilton is that he was once badly frightened by a corgi in his pram."

THE QUEEN was attacked by the Left last night for wanting more money, but her Household was looking like a poor relation compared with the miners.

Union leaders were ready to break the social contract with rises of 33 per cent (£15 a week) for face workers. The Queen, while keeping her staff rises within the contract, was still digging into her purse to help meet costs increasing at over 18 per cent.

Chancellor Healey, faced with a crumbling wage policy, warned T.U.C. chiefs that unemployment will grow unless militant unions toe the line. The T.U.C. demanded Government action to save jobs.

As the miners make a final decision today Labour rebels, despite a hammering from Mr. Wilson, will be calling for a debate on royal finances.

Every little helps

Jesse Hill hands the Queen a 10p gift yesterday

By Tony Craig

FOUR-YEAR-OLD Jesse Hill yesterday gave his Queen the 10p piece he saved . . . just for her. For the Queen, it was one of those special moments that must give meaning to her busy working day.

Later, with regal thoughtfulness, she handed the coin back to one of Jesse's teachers.

Her visit to the Thomas Coram Foundation for deprived children in London's Bloomsbury was just one of her duties yesterday.

Tuesday evening was busy too. Prime Minister Wilson's audience at six. A quick change, then dinner for 35 at 8.15.

Followed by a reception for 500 guests, including showbiz personalities Morecambe and Wise.

It ended at 2 a.m.—but the Queen was up as usual by 8.30 for eggs and toast with Prince Philip.

Meeting

Then a chat with her private secretary about the thousand and one items that are always cropping up.

At noon, an investiture. At 12.20, she saw the Privy Council.

Then a meeting with the new Archbishop of York, the Most Reverend Stuart Blanch.

Lunch followed . . . but the Queen found time to check the day's Government business piling up in official scarlet boxes.

At 3.15, the Thomas Coram Foundation.

At five, back to the Palace . . . and two hours with the scarlet boxes. Then dinner — with another busy day ahead and a crowded West Indies tour looming on Sunday. She will miss Prince Andrew's 15th birthday — just one sacrifice the Queen must make.

Wilson: It's in contract

JAMES WELLBELOVED, Labour, Erith and Crayford, demanded a full debate on royal finances but would not attack the miners. He said: "There is no parallel between miners, who pay income tax, and the Queen, who doesn't."

MICHAEL ENGLISH (Lab, Nottingham West) said: "There is no comparison with the miners. Anyone with a private fortune pays tax on it." Willie Hamilton is to propose a Bill to make the Royal Family "bejewelled civil servants."

By Walter Partington

A SUPREMELY unruffled **Mr. Wilson** yesterday brushed aside furious Labour protests in the Commons after he announced a £420,000 rise in the Queen's expense account.

The Premier said the Queen had offered to provide £150,000 of her own money this year—thus reducing to £270,000 the cost to the Treasury.

That was not sufficient to still the scoffing cries from his own backbenches and a violent protest from arch royal critic **Mr. William Hamilton** (Lab., Fife Central).

But Mr. Wilson dealt with the near-mutiny in brilliant fashion. It was a telling lesson for **Mrs. Margaret Thatcher,** making her first Front Bench appearance as Tory leader.

Staff pay

Mr. Wilson said the rise in the Queen's allowances—from £980,000 to £1,400,000—was needed largely to meet Royal household staff pay increases.

He told M.P.s: "The pay increases are within the T.U.C. guidelines" [*on the social contract*].

The Civil List expenditure did not represent any increase in real expenditure, said the Prime Minister. He insisted: "This cannot be regarded as an increase in pay . . It is, in fact, a reduction, not an increase in the real value of the finance made available."

He was jeered by Labour M.P.s for saying that the Queen had contributed £60.000 from her own purse to cover 1974 costs. There were groans and shouts of: "What a shame!"

As for the Queen's £150,000

Page 2, Column 7

£3,000 pitmen go on talking

By Barrie Devney

A DEAL for miners which looks certain to bust the social contract was hammered out in London yesterday.

Final negotiations will take place today between the Coal Board and the full executive of the miners' union.

It is by no means certain that there will be a recommendation to pitmen to accept this deal put forward by management.

The offer is to step up the basic rate of face workers to £3,000 a year—from £45 to £60 a week. That is an increase of 33 per cent but would include a current £4·40-a-week threshold bonus.

Price

Other underground workers would get an extra £10 lifting their basic rate from £36 plus £4·40 threshold to £46. Men on the surface would have a 25 per cent increase, from £32 to £40.

As revealed in the Daily Express yesterday the effect of the offer—costing over £100 million a year—will be at least £2 a ton increase on the price of coal next month.

The package would also give valuable fringe benefits.

There would be a bonus of £3 a week for all workers whenever output topped a figure based on an annual production of 115 million tons.

Management made clear yesterday that it is also prepared to improve on sick pay and pension schemes. And it will consider union demands over "anti-social hours," which would give 90 per cent of workers an extra £1 a week at least.

Last night neither union leaders nor Coal Board officials would give an opinion about whether the deal would be accepted.

Both sides made a determined attempt to insist that all the improvements were in line with the social contract. But there is no doubt that if the deal goes through it will lead to many embarrassing questions for the T.U.C.

And there will be a stream of demands for similar rises from other key workers.

Yesterday leaders of 38.000 Merchant Navy seamen submitted a claim for a five-day 40-hour week with a basic rate of £40—which could step up actual earnings by 80 to 100 per cent.

Whitelaw, the deputy

IT was consolation day for Mr. William Whitelaw yesterday.

The man defeated in the Tory leadership fight was named deputy leader by the woman who beat him, Mrs. Margaret Thatcher.

Grandpa Willie: Page 2

Fiona's present

MOSCOW, Wednesday. — British girl Fiona Cummings celebrated her seventh birthday today with news that she may have been saved from blindness by Russian doctors treating her for a rare disease.

Pope's plea

VATICAN CITY, Wednesday.—Pope Paul today marked the beginning of Lent by calling on Christians to reject the materialistic attitude to life. He was speaking to pilgrims in St. Peter's.

Into port

LISBON, Wednesday. — The Portuguese Government tonight said it had set up a "strict inquiry" into the alleged use of synthetic alcohol to fortify port wine.

Warning on jobs—and prices

By David Buchan

AS BRITAIN'S bosses warned of "intolerable" wage claims, Chancellor Denis Healey told T.U.C. leaders last night: The social contract must be tightened up."

Mr. Healey called in members of the T.U.C.'s Economic Committee for urgent talks.

He told them that dole queues would stretch unless the 25 per cent of unions who were ignoring the guidelines on pay fell into line.

Earlier Mr. Healey snubbed Mr. Tony Benn's State takeover dreams by warning that industries under Government control must be made to pay.

He told a private meeting of Labour M.P.s that the money saved by ending subsidies to industry could pay for two and a quarter power stations, or 66,000 council houses. or 30.000 new hospital beds. But prices on gas and electricity would have to go up again.

BOSSES told Mr. Wilson there would be "terrible unemployment" if steps were not taken soon to control inflation. C.B.I. president Ralph Bateman said: "We have no confidence in this Government. We told Mr. Wilson that the Industry Bill [on State takeovers] was a deliberate attack on private industry.

"We felt that we were failing to get through to Government over high taxation, price controls and profit freeze."

Big hunt for killer of Alison

By John McCormick, Owen Summers and Frank Howitt

PIECE BY PIECE detectives were building up a dossier last night in the hunt for the killer of 10-year-old Alison Chadwick, the girl who set off for a friend's home—and never arrived.

And back at her house the family who waited for eight agonising months were left with just memories.

MEMORIES of her room with pictures of the Osmonds and Wombles on the wall.

They kept her room as she had left it.

MEMORIES of the Brownie girl who was always smiling and friendly.

Alison's mother, Mrs. Peggy Chadwick, always hoped her only daughter would be found alive, even though big police hunts failed to find her.

She said at the time: "I fear the worst, but I will never give up hope until I have proof that my daughter is dead."

Yesterday there was tragic proof.

Alison's body was found in a sack—buried in a flooded gravel quarry. Her head was discovered a few yards away.

Police believe it was dragged there by an animal—and they think she could have died on the day she disappeared last June.

Alison Chadwick . . . in shallow grave

Discovery

A pathologist's report on how she was killed is expected today.

The discovery was made on Tuesday by a construction worker on the site of a new yachting marina at Sunbury, Middlesex, just eight miles from Alison's home.

He stumbled across her skull and raised the alarm.

Police sealed off the spot near Felix Lane—the haunt of young courting couples.

Senior detectives called for dental evidence before confirming yesterday that the teeth matched those of Alison.

Last night Mrs. Margaret Richardson, whose Isleworth home Alison was visiting on

Where Alison was found

the day she vanished, told of the anguish her family had felt.

Her daughter Fiona was Alison's best friend. She has not cried since Alison disappeared.

Mrs. Richardson said: "I took her round to the Chadwick home and Mrs. Chadwick let her have the pick of all Alison's things to try and break her.

"We were hoping that she would burst into tears and get rid of it."

The main clue to Alison's killer is the sack she was found in. Forensic experts will now put it under a microscope to try to discover where it was made. Then the hunt for the killer will move on again.

Fancy that

LOCAL government officer Derek Craske is to get a £5 a week pay rise—because his bosses forgot to sack him when his job as Registrar in Martley, Worcestershire disappeared under the reorganisation.

Wall Street up

NEW YORK, Wednesday.—The Dow Jones index on Wall Street closed 7·43 points up today at 715·3 after trading in over 19·7 million shares.

Master stroke

ROME, Wednesday.—Sicilian Antonio Arcidiacono was today charged with the theft of three priceless Old Masters.

London rail strike chaos today

By Terry Pattinson

MORE chaos faces rail travellers today when signalmen stage another 24-hour stoppage.

Worst hit will be London commuters, with the probability of no trains at all into Waterloo.

And last night Western Region signalmen at Swindon voted to join the 24-hour stoppage. Trains from London to Bristol and South Wales will be affected.

Some trains would run on alternative routes but cancellations could be as high as 50 per cent, said a British Railways spokesman last night. Commuter services would not be disrupted.

But British Railways advise all tralvellers: "Check your trains are running before starting out for the station."

Southern, Eastern, and Western Regions are all affected by the signalmen's unofficial action over a pay dispute.

Lines from Kent will be particularly chaotic. From many places any trains at all are unlikely.

There will also be disruption on London Midland Region. All Manchester-Euston trains have been cancelled.

Talks

The signalmen's stoppage—stemming from the last rail pay rise—comes on the eve of new overall wage talks with demands for "substantial" increases.

N.U.R. secretary Sidney Weighell said last night he hoped the negotiations would be entered into "without a shot being fired."

But he warned of a likely revolt by railmen if the miners are allowed to crash through the social contract guideline.

And he called on the T.U.C. to take the same tough line with rebellious unions as it did against the Industrial Relations Act.

Abortion traffic

ROME, Wednesday. — About 1,000 Italian women have had abortion operations in Britain in the last 16 months. Women's Lib groups claim.

ENGLAND WIN BY INNINGS

England won sixth and final Test against Australia in Melbourne by innings and four runs.

(See Back Page)

PHONE STD CODE 01
353 8000
TELEX 21841

Daily Mirror

EUROPE'S BIGGEST DAILY SALE

5p Monday, August 4, 1975 ◆ No. 22,243

ON THE OCCASION OF HER SEVENTY-FIFTH BIRTHDAY

(Photographed by PETER SELLERS) **BRITAIN'S GREATEST GRANDMOTHER**

THE proud grandmother. The Queen Mother and the Prince of Wales pose on the eve of her seventy-fifth birthday for the camera of actor Peter Sellers. In her time Elizabeth Bowes-Lyon has lived through many momentous events. Two world wars, the Blitz, the atom bomb, the Space programmes.

She has seen great kingdoms fall and famous statesmen depart. Now she holds the arm of Prince Charles, the young man who is heir to a thousand years of British history.

Holds it proudly—and with affection.

PLEASE TURN TO PAGE 5

DAILY Mirror

EUROPE'S BIGGEST DAILY SALE

6p   Wednesday, April 21, 1976   No. 22,465

50 TODAY!

Why Jim couldn't go to the party

By JOHN DESBOROUGH

PREMIER James Callaghan turned down a personal invitation from the Queen to attend her fiftieth birthday party at Windsor Castle last night.

Instead, Mr. Callaghan stayed at his Sussex farm and kept working on his official papers.

A Buckingham Palace spokesman said: "The Prime Minister was invited but was unable to come."

The official reason for his absence was pressure of work. Mr. Callaghan had spent the Easter weekend deep in his official papers and was still "reading himself in" last night at his farm.

Accepted

Now the Queen has invited Mr. Callaghan and his wife Audrey to dinner at Windsor next week. This will give him an opportunity for a long informal chat with her.

There was a swift reaction to any suggestion that Mr. Callaghan might appear to be snubbing the Queen by not going to her birthday party.

"Not true," it was said. The Queen quite understood why he could not attend.

And if there had been the slightest hint of a snub, there would have been no invitation to dinner at Windsor next week.

Among those who accepted invitations were former Prime Minister Harold Wilson and his wife Mary, who had been holidaying in the Scillies over Easter.

And ex-Tory leader Edward Heath flew back from Spain specially for the celebration.

Also there were the present Tory leader Mrs. Margaret Thatcher and her husband, and Liberal leader Jeremy Thorpe and Mrs. Thorpe.

Wonderful

Before the Windsor Castle party there was a private dinner for the royal family and close friends.

A Buckingham Palace spokesman said last night: "Obviously we can only tell it from our point of view. The Callaghans were invited and were not able to go.

Today the 180 holders of the Victoria Cross and the George Cross will go to a special birthday tea with the Queen.

The president of the heroes' association said: "It was entirely her own doing. We thought it was a wonderful thing she should give up half her birthday for us."

From the Mirror's 12,500,000 readers..

At 21 1947, year of her engagement. She told her people: "I'm devoted to your service."

At 50 The Queen today. Her promise is fulfilled. But perhaps too, the strain is showing.

The BEST of British birthdays, Ma'am!

A HAPPY and glorious birthday, Ma'am.

The Mirror toasts your half-century with affection, warmth and pride.

We haven't always seen eye to eye. Particularly over some of the Royal pay rises. But our criticism has never been personal.

Today we would like to be very personal indeed. We think you are the tops. And damned good at your job.

Like Queen Elizabeth I and Queen Victoria, you've shown that being a monarch is something a woman can do every bit as well as any man. And in some cases better.

The monarchy in Britain today is immensely popular. No small thanks to you.

We've had our troubles since your Coronation in 1953. But the status of the monarchy has gone from strength to strength.

Today the Mirror wishes you the best of British birthdays. And many more of them.

ELIZABETH, THIS IS YOUR LIFE—PAGE 9

Daily Mirror

BRITAIN'S BIGGEST DAILY SALE

6p   Thursday, September 16, 1976   →   No. 22,592

What Her Majesty said about that Jesus sex venture

THE FILM-MAKER: Danish producer Jens Jorgen Thorsen, who plans to come to Britain later this month.

THE QUEEN: She finds the proposed film on the sex life of Christ "quite as obnoxious as do most of her subjects."

OBNOXIOUS!

THE QUEEN has joined the protest over plans to make a film about Jesus Christ's sex life.

In an unprecedented move, she has attacked the idea as "obnoxious."

Her action, described by Buckingham Palace as "quite unusual," came after she received more than 150 protest letters.

The letters, many in the form of petitions, called on the Queen to use her powers to stop Danish film producer Jens Jorgen Thorsen entering Britain.

Mr. Thorsen revealed his plan to make the

By JOHN PENROSE and KEN ROGERS

controversial film in Britain after being refused permission in Denmark, Sweden, France and Italy.

The Queen's views about the planned film were revealed in letters she sent to each protester.

But she told them there was nothing she could do.

Each letter said: "While Her Majesty finds this proposal quite as obnoxious as do most of her subjects, the prevention of the making of such a film in the UK or the exclusion from this country of Mr. Thorsen could only be accomplished within the laws of the UK."

The Queen has ordered each protest letter to be sent to the Home Office who will decide whether Mr. Thorsen should be allowed into the country.

Mr. Thorsen said yesterday he was flattered that the Queen had joined the protest.

But he added: "No matter what her general idea is about the sex life of Jesus Christ, she doesn't know anything about my film."

Mr. Thorsen, who was speaking on BBC Radio One's Newsbeat programme, said he intended to try to enter Britain at the end of the month.

He said: "It would be completely illegal to refuse me entry. I have done nothing illegal."

Mr. Thorsen has three actors—one English—in mind for the part of Jesus.

Last night he refused to reveal the identity of the English actor.

All he would say was: "It's not Laurence Olivier."

Leyland rebels snub peace plan

A LEYLAND plant was crippled by a walkout yesterday—hours after a dramatic plea for peace from top union leaders.

Copies of the "work or sink" message from Hugh Scanlon and Jack Jones lay unread at the factory as ninety labourers staged their unofficial stoppage.

Last night 1,600 workers at the Coventry engines plant had been laid off. The strikers left before copies of the company newspaper—which carried the union chiefs'' appeal—arrived for distribution.

But a management spokesman said: "They must have known about it."

The strikers meet today to discuss their next move. No talks with management had been arranged last night.

The walkout started when a man who disobeyed an order was told he would not be paid.

£90 MILLION RIDDLE OF SLATER WALKER

By ROBERT HEAD, RICHARD STOTT and SIDNEY WILLIAMS

A MULTI-MILLION pound question mark hung over Slater Walker last night as pressure grew for an inquiry into the company.

A highly-critical report has revealed that the financial empire lent £90 million. More than

half went to just four customers. This is against the normal business practice of spreading your risks.

Now the City wants to know: Who got the money?

But the names are expected to stay secret unless Parliament or the

courts step in to order that they be made public.

The disclosure of these loans—and the fact that Slater Walker lent large sums to its own directors —adds fuel to demands for an inquiry.

Last night Labour MP

Gwilym Roberts was pressing for a Parliamentary Select Committee to probe the workings of the City.

Earlier yesterday, Stock Exchange chairman Nicholas Goodison said that the law dealing with loans to directors

was "inadequate." The report on Slater Walker — called for by new chairman Sir James Goldsmith — sent the value of the company's shares crashing.

● Downfall of a whizz-kid—Centre Pages.

BURTON ON LOVE LIZ AND SUZY

SEE PAGES 22 and 23

The Sun

Wednesday, March 9, 1977   6p   TODAY'S TV: Pages 14 and 15

SPECIAL IN THE SUN TODAY

YOUR PAY

Healey v Joseph
SEE CENTRE PAGES

'Killer tax' plan in new war on smoking

By LESLIE TOULSON

SMOKERS should be made to pay higher taxes on cigarettes which are most dangerous to health, said Social Services Secretary David Ennals last night.

A plan on these lines' to curb the top-risk smokes has been proposed to the Common Market. And manufacturers have agreed to try to eliminate all high-tar brands in the next two years, he said.

Crack-down

British sport could also be a victim of the crackdown. For the tobacco companies may withdraw their millions of pounds of sponsorship . . . by Government order.

Mr Ennals, also announced that:

● Cigarette packets will carry a stronger health warning that smoking can "seriously" damage health.

● Advertising of high-tar cigarettes will be stopped immediately and of middle to high-tar brands by the end of next year.

● There will be a crack-down on smoking in public places.

● An extra £1million will go to the Health Education Council to put over the anti-smoking message.

Smell

Mr Ennals appealed to all smokers: "Stop. It is worth the effort.

"You feel better, you smell better, you taste better and you have cash for other things."

Cigarette smoking was

Continued on Page Two

'QUEEN OF SHEBA' JIBE

Sophia . . . "Hopping mad" with police

Sacked Australian Premier in shock a a Royal party

From SALLY MacMILLAN in CANBERRA

THE QUEEN was publicly insulted yesterday by Australia's sacked Prime Minister Gough Whitlam.

She sat only a few yards away as he mocked her role as a Sovereign.

And she was visibly upset as he asked sarcastically: "What will she be next — Queen of of Sheba?"

Mr Whitlam made his amazing outburst in Canberra at a reception following the opening of Parliament by the Queen.

More than 1,200 people witnessed the most embarrassing moment she has suffered on a Royal tour.

Mr Whitlam said directly to the Queen: "Some of your British subjects want you to be Queen of Scotland, but somehow I find Queen Elizabeth of the Scots sounding somewhat strange."

Prime Minister Malcolm Fraser glowered from his seat as Mr Whitlam went on:

"But perhaps Queen of the Scots is not as strange as Queen of Queensland."

SACKED

This was a reference to a constitutional move two years ago when it was hoped the Queen would become Sovereign of the State.

Mr Whitlam added: "A week ago, it was proposed that you be Queen of the Solomons.

"What next? . . . Queen of Sheba?"

Mr Whitlam is now leader of the Opposition Labour Party.

Whitlam . . . Amazing outburst at party

He was sacked as Pri Minister in Novem 1975 by the Queen's r resentative, Govern General Sir John K in a bid to avert a c stitutional crisis

Mr Whitlam also po fun at the Queen's jub celebrations.

He said: "Twenty-years is but an even gone. A twinkling eye."

Earlier, about demonstrators booed the Queen arrived Parliament building a massive security.

But the protesters heavily outnumbered 6,000 people who chee the Queen.

● PRINCE CHARLES unlikely to become Aus lia's next Govern General. The Queen believed to have vetoed idea for "personal political reasons."

SOPHIA LOREN HELD IN CASH QUIZ

FILM STAR Sophia Loren was arrested last night as she tried to board a plane out of Italy.

Finance police seized her at Rome Airport and took her baggage off a flight to Paris.

She was quizzed for more than four hours. Airport officials said she was "hopping mad" with her interrogators.

Police sources said Sophia and her film producer husband, Carlo Ponti, have been under investigation for tax evasion and the illegal export of foreign currency.

The couple's phones have reportedly been tapped for some weeks.

Sophia, who lives in Paris, refused to answer questions until her lawyers arrived.

She was allowed to telephone her husband in Paris.

Sophia, aged 43, has been in Rome shooting the final scenes of a film with Marcello Mastroianni.

A month ago 10 police agents spent seven hours searching the couple's villa near Rome but refused to say what they were looking for.

At the time, Mr Ponti's assistant denied the illegal currency transactions. He said: "A producer of Mr Ponti's character obviously needs money for the films he has to make abroad."

Sophia and her husband have been living in Paris for the past three years.

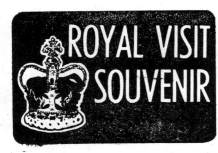

IT'S THAT ROYAL SMILE

A ROYAL WAVE and smile from Queen Elizabeth as she stands on the balcony of the Elizabeth Council chambers today.

INSIDE

52 pages

THE Evening Standard is 52 again today! For the second time in 1977 support from readers and advertisers has pushed our size up to 52 pages, enabling us to give more coverage to news, sport, regular features and entertainments in and around London this weekend.

The Standard is now regularly bigger than any other tabloid-size national or evening paper. So keep up your Standards, and read on . . .

Simenon's 10,000 women

After Georges Simenon's boast that he has made love to 10,000 women, Sam White asks how he found the time. **Page 17**

The dangerous Miss Brodie

Geraldine McEwan is to play the formidable school-teacher in a new series for Scottish TV. Miss McEwan, says Michael Owen, admires la Brodie for her dedication —"but she was dangerous of course . . . a liberated woman." **Page 27**

Missing out on skateboards

London looks like missing out on a great opportunity to establish skateboard arenas because of the authorities' reluctance to recognise it as a growing sport. **News on Camera: Page 3**

Diana Dors in court move

Diana Dors is to take action in the High Court in a bid to prevent the publication of her life story. **Page 7**

Jack Charlton quits Middlesbrough

Jack Charlton today resigned as manager of Middlesbrough. He will stay with the club until the end of the season. **Page 50**

● Friday Forum—2. Sam White—17. Londoner's Diary—18. TV and Radio—20, 21. Shopping, Angling—23. Cookery, Gardening—25. Critics, Weekend Out—32. Katina, Cartoons, Crossword—33. Mind and Matter—43.

Entertainment — P.31

Controversy over the 'secret' holdings

THE ROYAL SHARES START ROW

Bunny club to sue TGWU for libel

By Robert Strange

THE LONDON Playboy Club today launched libel proceedings against the Transport and General Workers' Union and applied for a High Court injunction in the long-running dispute over union recognition for Bunny girls and other casino staff.

The legal moves follow the publication of a report today from the Government's Advisory, Conciliation and Arbitration Service which recommends that the union should be recognised by the club in Park Lane following the often bitter dispute.

As the Bunnies and other staff at the club heard the arbitration result this morning the Playboy Club issued an immediate statement.

A spokesman said: "The Playboy Club of London Ltd. has received the report of the ACAS following its examination of the application for recognition by the TGWU.

Application

"On the advice of its lawyers a writ has today been issued in the High Courtt agains both ACAS and the TGWU claiming a declaration that on various grounds the recommendation contained in this report is invalid and asking for appropriate injunctions."

The statement continued: "Proceedings for libel have also been issued against the Transport and General Workers' Union."

In today's report ACAS ruled that the TGWU should be allowed to negotiate for gaming staff at the Park Lane premises.

PLAYBOY pickets — Flashback to the early days of the dispute in 1974.

By William Kay

AT THE HEIGHT of the controversy over decision to wrap a veil of secrecy around the Queen's investments, the Evening Standard is able to reveal that she and other Heads of State have a combined share stake in British industry totalling more than £100 million.

A major row has broken out in the wake of the news that the Government has decided to make the Queen and other rulers exempt from the provisions of the new Companies Act, which otherwise gives companies the power to find out who is hiding behind nominee or disguised names among their shareholders.

But an exclusive survey of the registers of leading UK firms shows that the Queen and other heads of State own at least £90 million worth of shares.

Under the new Companies Act, which came into force this week, the investments of Heads of State are now being shown under the name of Bank of England Nominees Ltd.—a device which is intended to protect individuals like the Queer from having to reveal their own personal portfolio.

Ironically, however, the change in the law does for the first time give a fascinating profile of the type of company favoured by rulers who have money invested in this country.

Gifts from public

The overall cash figure is likely to be well over £100 million. We have uncovered more than 20 separate holdings after contacting about 50 companies.

And several Heads of State, including the Queen, are believed to hold British Government stocks—but this register is not open to the public.

Our list shows a cross-section of the most successful companies in British industry.

But some of the investors will be criticsed because of their social and political overtones.

The anti-apartheid lobby will not be pleased by the £6,900,00 0stake in Barclays Bank.

And there will be some dismay that the list includes a heavy investment in Imperial group the John

Cont. Back Page Col. 2

Troops shoot

10 dead

ISLAMABAD

AT LEAST 10 people were reported to have been shot dead today by troops enforcing martial law.

Pakistani soldiers were said to have opened fire when opposition supporters tried to stage a protest march.

Trouble also flared today in the North-West frontier capital of Peshawar when police were reported to have fired on opposition demonstrators.

Witnesses said at least four people were wounded, one critically.

The clash began when police

Cont. Back Page, Col. 4

The Queen's amazing plea

❝I cannot forget that I was crowned Queen of the United Kingdom of Great Britain and Northern Ireland❞

The Queen yesterday

MY UNITED KINGDOM

By John Warden

THE QUEEN publicly revealed yesterday her long-held anxiety that her Kingdom may be splitting up by devolution.

She took the only chance she has ever had to tell Parliament about it— in her Jubilee speech to both Houses.

Not since 1910 has a monarch risked coming so near the political firing line.

In that year George V refused Asquith a dissolution of Parliament, but gave way when the Cabinet resigned.

Last night the Queen was being praised as much as blamed for appearing to speak out against the separatists — an interpretation agreed by Nationalist critics and loyalist supporters alike.

Coinciding with Nationalist successes at the Scottish local polls, the Queen's remarks promptly set the heather ablaze.

Five well-planted paragraphs did it in her reply to loyal addresses in Westminster Hall.

She said: "The problems of progress, the complexities of modern administration, the feeling that metropolitan government is too remote from the lives of ordinary men and women — these among other things have helped to revive an awareness of historic national identities in these islands."

Casting her eyes round the historic Norman Hall she went on: "I number Kings and Queens of England and of Scotland and Princes of Wales among my ancestors, and so I can readily understand these aspirations."

A pause, quite long, then, raising her voice: "But I cannot forget that I was

Nixon confesses: I let down my friends, I let down my country

—See Page 15

Page 2 Column 3

Bianca joins the wild bunch

When Bianca and Mick Jagger attend a party it's " anything goes " as proved by yesterday's wild scenes at a New York disco. Bianca (left) and a model girl were joined by a horse. See Page 3

TV Pages 20-21 ● Weather Page 2 ● Target, Foreign Page 4 ● Hickey, Rupert Page 13 ● Large Crossword Page 14 ● Letters Page 23 ● Sport starts Page 31　　TELEPHONE : 061-236 2112

Daily  Mail

WEDNESDAY, JUNE 8, 1977

8p (CHANNEL ISLANDS 9p)

The Queen says it for all of us

IS EVERYBODY HAPPY? I AM!

THIS was the moment that really captured the spirit of the Jubilee as the Queen walked among the people packed together outside St. Paul's Cathedral. The happiness that until then had been almost visibly kept in check bubbled from her. 'Everybody quite happy?' she asked one set of cheering spectators who had suffered the indifferent weather for hours. Then before they could answer she replied for herself. And there was no doubting it : 'I am.' Then later : 'What a lovely day, we are so lucky.' The Queen's walk from the cathedral to Guildhall was scheduled to last 20 minutes. In fact it took almost twice as long. But time didn't matter—by now it really was the day for the Queen and the people. The laughing faces around her tell the story.

  INSIDE your special Jubilee Mail: Royal Walkabout 2, 3, Shaun Usher's view 6, Barbara Griggs on the Fashions 13, Photo Extra 23-26

DAILY Mirror

BRITAIN'S BIGGEST DAILY SALE   7p   Wednesday, June 8, 1977

JUBILEE PICTURE SPECIAL

1977 — THE QUEEN'S SILVER JUBILEE

Queen, Prince Philip, Captain Mark Phillips, Princess Anne, the Queen Mother, and Princess Margaret.   Picture : ALISDAIR MACDONALD

HAPPY FAMILY!

JOYOUS: The Queen framed in the crowd. Picture: BILL KENNEDY

Salute to a silver lady, riding in a coach of gold

THIS was the grand finale. The day a nation's favourite family took a bow.

The day Britain—flag-waving, chanting, cheering Britain—said a warm thank-you to its Queen.

Thank you, simply, for being a super, silver lady.

It said THANKS in the throng of happy, loyal faces that watched the Queen glide through London in her coach of gold.

THANKS from the mil-lions at home and abroad who were glued to their TV sets—and wished they could be there.

And THANKS for a pledge fulfilled. A pledge she made before her coronation to give her life to the service of her people.

The Queen recalled that vow yesterday in London's Guildhall: "It was made in my salad days," she said, "when I was green in judg-ment.

"But I do not regret one word of it."

Yet beneath all the mag-nificence and majesty, the fun and frolics, was a family occasion.

A time for one special family to celebrate 25 years of peaceful reign. A time for the nation's family to rejoice . . .

The Queen rules, UK.

JEAN ROOK Centre Pages

DAILY EXPRESS

No. 23,940   Friday June 17 1977   Weather: Dry: Sunny spells   8p

Express Exclusive

Engagement next week
Sons will be Protestant, daughters Catholic

CHARLES TO MARRY ASTRID
–Official

By JOHN WARDEN

PRINCE CHARLES is to marry Princess Marie Astrid of Luxemburg. The formal engagement will be announced from Buckingham Palace next Monday.

The couple's difference of religion — she is a Roman Catholic — will be overcome by a novel constitutional arrangement: any sons of the marriage will be brought up according to the Church of England, while daughters will be raised in the Catholic faith.

The Queen and Prince Philip have assented to this procedure, which also has the approval of Church leaders.

Prince Charles, who is 28, first met 23-year-old Astrid about a year ago.

Although their association has been kept secret by the Palace—even to the extent of denying they had ever met — a close friend said last night: "They fell for each other at that first meeting."

Astrid — who will become Princess of Wales on her marriage and should eventually be Queen, is the daughter of the Grand Duke of Luxemburg. Her mother, the former Princess Josephine Charlotte, is the daughter of the former King Leopold and Queen Astrid of the Belgians.

Princess Marie Astrid: Love at first meeting

Murder as the royal yacht sails in

OUR FRONT LINE QUEEN

British couple shot dead in France

A BRITISH couple were found murdered in Southern France last night.

They were shot dead in their car on a lonely mountain road ten miles from St. Tropez.

The couple were in a blue Ford Cortina. Each had been shot three times with a revolver.

Police believe they were asleep when they were attacked by bandits. Their passports and valuables were stolen.

The man was in his sixties and the woman, aged about 60, wore a blonde wig over grey hair. The spot where they were found is normally only used by picnickers.

Remote

It is thought the couple were from Cleveland in north-east England.

An underworld tip sent a police patrol to the remote mountain track seven miles from Grimaud.

Among those called to the scene were the British Consul Mr Michael Alan-Smith and Consular Information Officer Mr Gerald Clode. Despite missing documentation it is believed they were able to make an identification. Interpol were trying to trace relatives.

In March, 1973, school-teacher John Cartland, 60, was axed to death while on holiday in a caravan near Aix-en-Provence — about 50 miles from the latest murder spot.

Injuries

The caravan was set alight and Mr Cartland's son Jeremy, 29, received minor injuries.

An international warrant for Jeremy's arrest for the alleged murder of his father was later made void.

Twenty-five years ago former wartime British agent Sir Jack Drummond, his wife and eleven-year-old daughter Elizabeth were all murdered while they were on a camping holiday near the French Alpine village of Lurs, 60 miles North East of Marseilles.

Local farmer Gaston Dominici was convicted of the murder.

This is the city the Queen will visit today. On the tense Jubilee streets of Belfast, Army checks and alerts go on.

THE Queen sailed into the most dangerous hours of her life last night as Ulster saw yet more killing.

The royal yacht Britannia, escorted by a guided missile destroyer, anchors in Belfast Lough just after eight o'clock this morning.

From that moment on, despite every precaution that a security operation by 32,000 troops can take, the Queen will be in unprecedented physical jeopardy.

Just how much she will be in the front line was spelled out yesterday when an IRA sniper murdered a soldier in revenge for the death of a teenage petrol bomber shot dead four hours earlier by the Army. And, with even more chilling implications for royal security, a bomb exploded in the grounds of the new University of Ulster in Coleraine, which the Queen visits tomorrow.

Appalled police chiefs were trying to find out how terrorists penetrated intensive security patrols and carried their 1lb. of gelignite

Daily Mail Reporters

more than 200 yards from the perimeter fence. Then they had time to bury the bomb in a flower bed only 150 yards from the university's main buildings complex where the Queen and Prince Philip will spend six hours.

First engagement for the Queen today will be an investiture at Hillsborough Castle, the former governor's residence outside Belfast. She will fly there by helicopter, usually considered too dangerous transport for her. In Ulster is has been decided it is too dangerous for her to do anything else.

Hijacked

There will be no walkabouts, no drives past crowds. But this afternoon at Hillsborough the Queen will be host at a garden party for about 2,500 guests before returning to Britannia to give a reception for 200 people.

Britannia will sail overnight to anchor off the North Antrim coast ready for the second day's activities. Until midnight the yacht will remain floodlit and hug the coast to enable as many people to see it as possible — at a distance.

Tomorrow, the Queen flies to Coleraine. To the university where last night porter Knox Connor, yet another shocked eye witness to yet

another Ulster bomb blast, said : 'I was standing at the main entrance and the explosion lifted me off my feet. A shower of earth came down all around me.'

Forensic experts were trying to discover whether the Coleraine bomb was planted at the same time as another device which was found in a lavatory inside the university 11 days ago. That bomb had a sophisticated new timing device but the police did not know whether this could have delayed yesterday's blast for so long.

The soldier who died in West Belfast was a 20-year-old Private Lewis Harrison, of a 3rd light infantry patrol sent out to prevent women and children straying into the area around the hi-jacked lorry which was believed to contain a bomb.

The ten men of the patrol were warned by officers that they would be marked men after one of the same regiment's patrol commanders had shot dead the teenage petrol bomber earlier.

But when a hijacked tipper truck was driven to the front gate of their barracks and dumped there with a shouted bomb warning, the patrol had to go out to investigate.

Their job was to protect local women and children from the bomb they thought was on board the lorry. They were deployed as a screen 200 yards around the lorry, stopping civilians getting too close.

Turn to Page 2, Col 1

BRITAIN'S FAMILY PAPER

DAILY EXPRESS

No. 23,987   Thursday August 11 1977   Weather: Dry, sunny spells   8p

FOR VALOUR

On the day the Queen risked her safety to win the hearts of her most tormented people

By John Ley

THE QUEEN presented medals to the heroes of Ulster yesterday—while her own bravery won all hearts.

She looked tense as she arrived by helicopter for her first engagement in the war-torn Province.

But soon that old smile was back, in response to the delighted cheers of children.

The royal yacht Britannia had arrived in Belfast Lough in mist. But by the time the Queen flew the 15 miles to Hillsborough Castle the sun was shining.

At the old Government House she held an Investiture and then a garden party.

She was perhaps frustrated at not being able to walk through the streets as in the rest of her United Kingdom.

But the streets of Belfast were bloody again yesterday. First a bomb. Then a mob clash with the Army. Finally the shooting of an officer.

After the garden party the Queen and Prince Philip returned to Britannia to hold a reception for peace people.

The floodlit royal yacht sailed overnight to the north coast for another programme today on the fringes of terror.

Cummings

VICTORIA CROSS
For courage beyond the call of duty

VICTORIA REGINA 1837~1901

MEETING THE PEACE WOMEN: Page 15 HER DAY OF PEACE AND WAR: Centre Pages

---

Weather Page 2 ● TV and Radio Pages 18, 19 ● Finance Pages 22, 23 ● Sport starts Page 27 ● And don't forget your Crosswords and Target are on Page 26.   Telephone : 01-353 8000

Daily Mail

WEDNESDAY, NOVEMBER 9, 1977   8p (CHANNEL ISLANDS 9p)

48 PAGES . . . and
Money Mail too

More money to help pay the Queen's expenses

A RISE FOR THE ROYALS

By ANTHONY BEVINS, Political Correspondent

THE QUEEN has been awarded an extra £290,000 by the Treasury to meet her bills this year.

Mr Denis Healey, Chancellor of the Exchequer, revealed last night that the Queen's new annual expenses allowance for 1977 amounts to £1·9 million.

This is an increase of more than £500,000 since 1975.

But it was being stressed in Whitehall that the extra money — an 18 per cent. increase—is in no sense a pay award. It goes to meet the Queen's expenses and to cover extra wages and salaries for her staff.

Other members of the Royal Family also received increases.

The Queen Mother got an extra £15,000 putting her on £155,000. Princess Anne an extra £5,000 moving her up to £50,000 and Princess Margaret also an extra £5,000 giving her £55,000.

The extra bill for the Treasury will be £315,000.

Allowances for other members of the Royal Family come out of the Queen's purse with Princess Alexandra — Mrs Angus Ogilvie—whose expenses this year were put at £50,000, receiving an extra £10,000.

Frozen

But the allowances for Prince Philip and Princess Alice, Duchess of Gloucester, were both frozen with the Prince getting £85,000 and Princess Alice £25,000.

The Duke of Gloucester is the only one to have taken a cut—from £28,000 down to £26,000.

The Duke of Kent gets an extra £3,000, putting him on £48,000, and Princess Alice Countess of Athlone received her first increase for two years, an extra £1,000 to put her on £6,000.

The figures were given by Mr Healey in a Commons written reply to Mr Willie Hamilton the anti-monarchist Labour MP for Fife Central.

Last night he said they were 'absolutely outrageous and indefensible.'

But no title for Anne's baby

By NIGEL NELSON

PRINCESS Anne and Captain Mark Phillips have decided not to accept a title, which means the Princess's baby — fifth in line to the Throne — will be known simply as Miss or Master Phillips.

The baby, the Queen's first grandchild, is due to be born at the weekend.

It will be the first time a Sovereign has had an untitled grandchild for nearly 500 years, reflecting the fashionable notion that titles count for little.

The discreet announcement from Buckingham Palace yesterday that ended speculation over the child's possible name came as Princess Anne, 27 last August, was spending the last few days before the birth relaxing in her private suite of rooms at the Palace.

Clothes for the baby, including knitted booties, have been pouring in from wellwishers.

She will have the baby in hospital, although which one she is presently engaged in frantic preparations for the royal

Turn to Page 11 Col 1

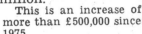

The Queen
Expenses reach £1·9m

Princess Anne
She gets an extra £5,000

Princess Alexandra
£10,000 more from the Queen

New blackout threat

By ROBERT PORTER Industrial Correspondent

THE Premier last night stepped into the power workers' row with a ruling that the rebels should not receive one of their demands — pay during their work-to-rule.

A similar tough line was taken by the Home Secretary, Mr Merlyn Rees, who refused to meet the pay demands of the firemen, who are planning to strike from Monday.

The uncompromising Downing Street line which is likely to plunge the country into more blackout chaos this week brings Mr Callaghan into outright conflict with Energy Secretary Mr Anthony Wedgwood Benn, who spent yesterday striving for a low-key solution to the power dispute.

Mr Benn said earlier that payments to the rebels during work-to-rule would not present a problem.

But then the power engineers, who have worked around the clock to minimise the actions of rebel manual workers, stepped in.

Mr John Lyons, secretary of the Electrical Power Engineers' Association, launched a scathing attack on Mr Benn for giving no support to official union opposition to the rebels.

He warned of total and bitter resentment from his members if the rebels were paid: 'There would be an explosion of anger if that took place.'

Then at 5 p.m. the Electricity Council, fortified by Downing Street approval, announced flatly that no one would be paid from the time of their 'no pay' ultimatum last Friday.

Mr Callaghan is prepared to risk two or three more days of anger and disruption in the deliberate calculation that public opinion will finally force the rebels back.

Risk

It is a policy fraught with danger. Last night Mr Cliff Hoyle, a rebel leader at the militant Eggborough power station, said : 'Unless assurances are given on our three points, we will not accept normal working.'

Yesterday there were no power cuts until the peak evening period. These lasted for about an hour and a half throughout the country. The Electricity Council warned that there was a risk for the lunch-time and early-evening peak today.

In the firemen's dispute, a two-hour meeting between Mr Rees and the executive council of the Fire Brigades Union ended in deadlock.

The firemen's representatives said that Mr Rees had failed to come up with any pay proposals that they could put to their members in hope of averting the strike.

Although the Services will be on call to fight fires there will be few of them who are trained, and they will operate from their own barracks, which is likely to lead to considerable delays.

Bomb blitz warning : Page 2 John Edwards—Page SIX.

He's doing fine… a 7lb 9oz boy for Anne and Mark and his first visitor is his grandmother

THE QUEEN'S PRIDE AND JOY

By NIGEL NELSON

The happy grandmother : The Queen arrives to see Princess Anne's baby

THE smile said it all about how the Queen felt to be a grandmother.

A crowd cheered as she arrived at St Mary's Hospital, Paddington, to see Princess Anne's son for the first time last night.

The Queen gave a short wave and a long smile before she went inside.

The baby—7lb. 9oz., with a lot of dark hair and his mother's blue eyes—was asleep during the visit, which lasted about 35 minutes.

Around his left wrist was a plastic tag enscribed 'Baby Phillips.' He is to have no title, at his parents' wish, and no name has yet been announced.

The child is fifth in line to the throne, though he will be overtaken by any children that Prince Charles, Prince Andrew or Prince Edward have.

Captain Mark Phillips, who was with

Princess Anne for the birth yesterday morning, was back at the hospital before the Queen arrived.

The occasion was 'quite delightful', said a nurse. 'They were like an ordinary family sitting round the cot.'

Captain Phillips left after spending two hours with Princess Anne and said: 'I'm absolutely thrilled.' Being present at the birth was 'very exciting.'

He went on: 'I enjoyed the experience. It was a perfectly normal delivery,

Trust a baby to get them up—Page 2

The bells peal out—Page 4

as far as I could see. The Queen is also very pleased.'

Capt. Phillips was dressed in a green robe and white mask as he watched the birth of his son.

He did an afternoon's work at the Ministry of Defence before returning to the hospital for the evening visit.

It had been quite a day. And as Mark left again, he brushed back a lock of windblown hair and remarked that he was tired and wanted some rest.

INSIDE: Lynda Lee-Potter 7, World Wide 9, Femail 12-13, Diary 17, Money Mail 19-30, Prize Crossword 31, TV 32-33, Classified Adverts 39-43

Kensington Palace announce the end of a royal marriage

MARGARET: A DIVORCE

PRINCESS MARGARET and Lord Snowdon are to seek a divorce. The news came in an announcement from Kensington Palace this afternoon.

It said: "Her Royal Highness The Princess Margaret, Countess of Snowdon, and the Earl of Snowdon, after two years of separation have agreed that their marriage should formally be ended. Accordingly Her Royal Highness will start the necessary legal proceedings."

The Princess is confined to bed in hospital, suffering from suspected gastro enteritis. Lord Snowdon, according to his secretary, was this afternoon "on a photo assignment in London, working hard as he normally does."

Married 18 years

A Kensington Palace spokesman said the Princess had "no plans for re-marriage."

He added: " Of course, we are not in a position to comment about Lord Snowdon."

Proceedings were already under way and the 47-year-old Princess will be represented by the Queen's solicitor, Mr. Matthew Farrer.

He said: "The Princess is suing for divorce. This is a technicality, one party has to start the proceedings.

"The marriage has broken down and the couple have lived apart for two years. These are obviously the grounds for divorce."

The spokesman said that the Princess was "making progress" in hospital and he added: "The result of tests taken by the doctors will not be known until Friday."

The Queen, who is at Buckingham Palace this afternoon, has been kept informed. But no constitutional consent is needed in matters of this sort, said the spokesman.

Custody of children

The couple, who separated in March, 1976, after 18 years of marriage, have two children, Viscount Linley, aged 16, and Lady Sarah Armstrong-Jones 13, and the Princess will continue to have custody of them.

The Kensington Palace spokesman made it clear that the couple will continue to be friends. "Naturally Princess Margaret and Lord Snowdon

Before the break .. Princess Margaret and Lord Snowdon with Lord Linley and Lady Sarah Armstrong-Jones.

will continue to see each other on the same friendly basis as they have with each other over the last two years."

Since the separation Lord Snowden has become a close friend of Lucy Lindsay-Hogg, daughter of the clothing manufacturer Donald Davies. She was not at her Kensington home this afternoon.

Roddy Llewellyn, Princess Margaret's friend is on holiday in Marrakesh, Morrocco.

Divorce will not alter the Princess's position. She will keep her title and her position in Royal circles, and, said the spokesman: "She will continue her Royal duties as soon as she is fit enough. It is purely coincidental that Princess Margaret is in hospital. These arrangements were well under way before she became ill and her illness has nothing to do with the pending proceedings."

Financial arrangements between the Princess and her husband will also continue to be the same, but these are not being made public.

Solicitors of both the Princess and Lord Snowdon have been in close touch for some time and " Formal proceedings will begin within days."

DAILY Mirror

PHOTO FINISH!

Thursday, June 8, 1978

WHAT A THRILLER ! The Queen and Lord Porchester, her racing manager, watch the nail-biting Derby finish.　Picture: MIKE MALONEY.

Fans pelt the Scots

From ALASDAIR BUCHAN in Cordoba

FURIOUS Scottish fans threw stones and tried to break into their team's coach as it left the scene of a dismal World Cup effort last night.

Ally MacLeod's "Tartan Army" had just managed to scrape a 1—1 draw with no-hopers Iran.

Only an own-goal by an Iranian defender saved the Scots from defeat.

The worst abuse was reserved for manager Ally when he left the dressing room at the Cordoba stadium last of all.

One angry fan shouted : "We walked a million miles for you!"

And another group of fans chanted : "It's all for the money !"

Supporters making the V-sign chanted : "Ally out—Ally out !"

A wailing police car and heavy police guard failed to keep the angry Scottish fans at bay.

Earlier, a dozen were taken into police custody after police spotted an obscene banner in a nearby cafe.

Following Holland's 0-0 draw with Peru last night, Scotland must now beat Holland by three clear goals to get into the next round.

After last night's results, bookies were quoting Scotland at a staggering 5,000-1 to win the Cup.

● World Cup Special — Page 31 and Back Page.

Derby picture to remember

IT'S the greatest Royal picture of the year.

It was taken by Mirror cameraman Mike Maloney at the finish of the greatest race of the year, the Epsom Derby.

And it uniquely captured the Queen's bubbling excitement as her favourite sport of horse-racing turned on a majestic show.

The Queen's own runner, English Harbour, which trailed in eighteenth of the 25 starters, might have given her little to cheer about. But she was on her feet with everyone else as Shirley Heights beat Hawaiian Sound in a dramatic photo finish.

Just the length of a horse's head robbed 46-year-old American Willie Shoemaker, on Hawaiian Sound of a fairytale success in his first Epsom Derby ride. But like the Queen, Willie shrugged off the disappointment of losing. "A brilliant ride." said one consoling chap. "Nearly brilliant," replied Willie.

● Portrait of a royal punter—Page 3
● Racing Mirror—Pages 28 and 29

National Insurance Services

Bahrain 252452

GULF MIRROR

Bahrain : 250 fils   Qatar : QR 2.5   Kuwait : 200 fils   Saudi Arabia: SR 2.5   UK : 40p

SATURDAY, FEBRUARY 17 TO FRIDAY, FEBRUARY 23, 1979 NO. 418 N.

THE ROYAL HONOURS GO BOTH WAYS

A double triumph

By Gulf Mirror Reporters

A SMILING Queen Elizabeth was ending the Bahrain leg of her Gulf tour on Saturday, carrying the Star of Al Khalifa and a surprise gift in her baggage — and cheers of the island still ringing in her ears.

During her rigorously-scheduled 53-hours in Bahrain, she drew crowds by the thousand and saw just about everything — from banquets to burial mounds, dhows to dancers and horses to handicrafts. And she also saw — and received — flowers, bouquets of them.

Along every route her motorcade sped, there were people and flags and honking cars, applauding the Queen and Prince Philip — and the Amir, His Highness, Shaikh Isa bin Sulman Al Khalifa.

For it was a double triumph for host and guests, for Bahrainis and Britons, and indeed for all nationalities.

It followed in the wake of an enthusiastic opening to the tour in Kuwait. But the Royal arrival by sea in Britannia set the scene for that little something extra.

Bahrain was looking its best, its pavements polished, its trees in full green — and the flags fluttering jauntily.

It was joyous, it was regal, it was calm and though security was there, it was hardly ever in evidence, a tribute to peaceful Bahrain, to its people and to the popularity of the Royal visitors.

No where was the calm more evident than at the Sulman Falcon Centre near Zallaq.

The Duke was not keen to hold one of the magnificent birds, and when it was suggested he should let one of the falcons perch on his arm, he said: "Well. Can't I just look at it."

But the Royal tour had its more serious moments.

On Thursday evening, the Queen appointed the Amir, Knight Grand Cross of the Most Distinguished

In an unprecedented goodwill gesture, King Khalid has granted an amnesty to 25 Britons in jail in Saudi Arabia. The Queen was said to be delighted when told the news minutes before disembarking from Britannia in Bahrain.

Order of St Michael and St George — one of Britain's highest orders of chivalry.

And at the same ceremony at Gudaibiya Palace, she made the Heir Apparent, Shaikh Hamad, a Knight Commander (KCMG).

In return the British sovereign was awarded Bahrain's highest decoration when the Amir presented her with the Star of Al Khalifa.

On the eve of her departure, the Queen and the Duke of Edinburgh hosted a return banquet for the Amir, the Prime Minister and Heir Apparent on board the Britannia. Later, 250 guests came on board to be presented to the Royal couple and then watch a spectacular floodlit Beating of the Retreat by the Royal Marines.

MURDER OF LORD LOUIS

Mountbatten and 15 soldiers killed by IRA

Earl Mountbatten, victim of Ireland's Murderous Monday

Daily Mail Reporters

IN a day of unparalleled horror in Ireland, Lord Mountbatten of Burma, the Queen's cousin, and 15 British paratroopers were murdered by the IRA.

The killings were cowardly and callous.

Lord Mountbatten died when a bomb planted on his converted fishing boat exploded half a mile off Co. Sligo on the West coast of the Irish Republic.

His 15-year-old grandson, the Hon Nicholas Brabourne, also died in the blast and so did his boatman, Paul Maxwell, also 15.

Lord Mountbatten's daughter, Lady Patricia Brabourne, 55, her husband Lord Brabourne, 54, the Dowager Lady Brabourne, 82, and Nicholas's twin brother, Timothy, also were on board and were taken to hospital.

Last night the two women and Timothy were seriously ill in a hospital intensive care unit. Timothy was believed to be in danger of losing an eye. Lord Brabourne was said to be badly hurt and in a general surgical ward.

The Provisional IRA said similar radio-controlled bombs were used to

Turn to Page Two Col. 1

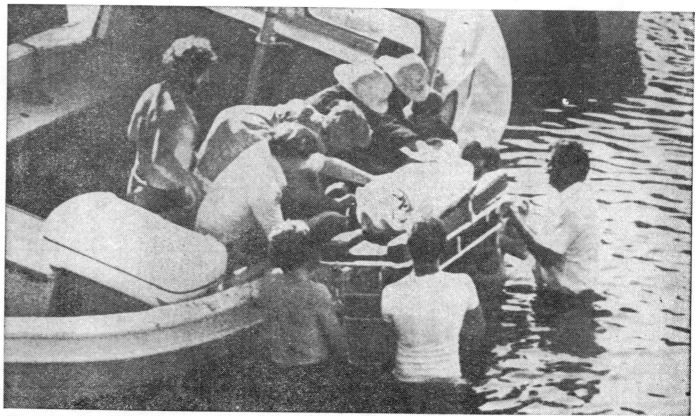

End of a legend: Mountbatten's body is taken from the boat which brought it to shore

Picture album of a royal life—a four-page tribute to 'Uncle Dickie' starts in Page 15

The Queen's adviser named as fourth man in Burgess and Maclean spy scandal

The Express says

THERE CAN be no immunity for traitors out to destroy this country, whatever their station in life. Those politicians or officials who gave Blunt immunity in 1964 must be called to account, wherever they are today ... and the Government must act to relieve our fears. How many others still combine high office with that of mole for Soviet Russia ?

See Opinion : Page 8

TRAITOR!

Mole flees: How many more spies are there?

THE QUEEN AND THE SPY : Blunt and the Queen in 1959, before his confession

THE spy who was exposed as the Fourth Man vanished last night.

To a stunned Commons, the Prime Minister named Sir Anthony Blunt, pillar of the Establishment, as a self-confessed Russian spy, ending 15 years of cover-up.

As Mrs Thatcher made the revelations, the "Royal Mole" was already out of

By Alan Cochrane and Gordon Ogilvie

the country — tipped off officially 24 hours earlier.

He was no longer Sir Anthony. Buckingham Palace announced immediately t h a t the Queen had stripped him of his knighthood — her personal gift, Knight Commander of the Royal Victorian Order, in 1956.

The Palace referred to him simply as "Blunt". It is the first time in the history of the order that a recipient has been disgraced in this way.

The Queen knew he was a spy 15 years ago and he would have lost the knighthood then but for the intervention of the Secret Service.

It was in 1964 that Blunt, former MI5 man, confessed to having

passed secrets to the Russians and to have helped in the defection of Foreign Office officials Guy Burgess and Donald Maclean. He had first been suspected 28 years ago, in 1951.

Blunt, now 72, was well known in Palace circles. An art historian, he was adviser on paintings to George VI and the present Queen for 33 years.

Last night there were indications of more startling developments in the spy scandal.

Author Andrew Boyle, whose recently-published book "Climate of Treason" led to the naming of Blunt, said he knew of at least 25 other people involved in espionage.

At least half a dozen he said were still active. "And I know their names."

In a dramatic twist, Left-wing

Labour MP Mr Bob Cryer last night tabled a Commons question concerning a fifth man. It must be answered on Monday.

Mr Cryer's question to the Attorney - General, Sir Michael Havers, asks : " If he will refer to the Director of Public Prosecutions with a view to prosecution for breaches of the Official Secrets Act the conduct of Dr Wilfred Mann in connection with the defection of Burgess and Maclean."

DENIED

Dr Mann is a former British physicist now living in California. He denied to the Daily Express last night that he was the Fifth Man.

It was in 1964 that Blunt came to a squealer-dealer arrangement that gave him immunity from prosecution in return for his co-operation with the counter-

intelligence service. He was protected from exposure by a succession of Governments.

In a Commons reply, Mrs Thatcher disclosed that he had been a recruiting agent for the Russians as a don at Cambridge in the 'thirties.

During the war he regularly passed on secrets.

At the end of the war Blunt resumed his career as an art historian, but in 1951 he used his old contacts with the KGB " to assist in the arrangements for the defection of Burgess and Maclean." He was also an associate of the Third Man, Kim Philby.

The row over why Blunt was allowed to leave Britain intensified last night.

Tory MP Mr Tony Marlow has tabled a question asking the Home

Page 2 Column 4

DAILY Mirror

BUDGET SPECIAL

Thursday, March 27, 1980   9p

GOOD DAY FOR THE ROYALS

£10,500 UP

£19,600 UP

£435,000 UP

MEAN DAY FOR THE REST

By JOHN DESBOROUGH, Chief Political Correspondent

● A MASSIVE pay rise for the Royal Family was announced yesterday — just as Britain was hit by a grim Budget.

● For the Royals, Chancellor Sir Geoffrey Howe handed out an extra half a million pounds.

● For the rest of Britain, the Chancellor presented a Budget described by Labour leader Jim Callaghan as the meanest since 1931.

● He pushed up prescription charges to £1 next December and slapped 2p on a pint of beer, 50p on a bottle of whisky and 5p on twenty cigarettes.

● The Government also revealed its plans to chop £3,700 million off its annual spending by 1984.

● Under the Royal rises, the taxpayer will provide an extra £435,000 for the Queen, £19,600 more for Princess Anne and £10,500 more for Princess Margaret.

Mirror Comment—Page 2.. Your Budget Guide—Pages 2, 3, 16 and 17

HIGHEST MORNING SALE IN N.S.W. (ABC AUDIT)

The Daily Telegraph

Phone 2 0924   SYDNEY, WEDNESDAY, MAY 28, 1980   Price 20c*   (Interstate freight extra)

INSIDE

FOUR PAGE TURF GUIDE

You and your rights
— Page 6

Kangaroo squad named
— Back Page

Sydney welcome crowns the tour

The people of Bankstown turned out in their thousands yesterday to welcome the Queen to their city. This was yesterday morning's scene at the airport.

Nearly a quarter of a million Sydneysiders gave the Queen a roaring, flag-waving, welcome yesterday.

The size of the crowds which turned out to welcome the Queen and the Duke of Edinburgh everywhere they went astonished tour organisers and

By BUZZ KENNEDY

delighted the royal couple.

The Queen was said to have been disappointed by the lukewarm reception she received in Canberra, which she visited on Sunday and Monday to perform her main duty of the tour — the official opening of the High Court of Australia Building.

Canberra crowds were small and spiritless. Demonstrators tried to break up the crowd at the High Court opening and fighting broke out. Three were arrested.

The Duke is reported to have expressed strong disappointment

over the Queen's reception in the national capital.

But all that was washed away by the flood of warmth and enthusiasm in Sydney yesterday.

In Martin Place, packed from end to end with cheering thousands, a beaming Duke turned to me and said, "It's great!"

The fervor and size

of the crowds amazed even the most optimistic among the tour organisers.

It began when the royal couple arrived at Sydney's real front door — in the western suburbs, centre of Sydney's population. (Report, Page 3).

From Bankstown the royal couple travelled by train — made up of all-new, gleaming car-

riages — to Martin Place.

The Bankstown stationmaster, Mr Frank Ryan, was presented to the Queen. What did she say to him?

"I can't remember," he said. "It was too much for me."

Crowds were 10 and 12 deep along the fences on both sides of the railway station as the train drew out — and

continued almost all the way into the city.

Groups of schoolchildren were dotted along the way, thousands of people who had obviously knocked off work while the train passed stood on vantage points, on piles of dirt and stacks of lumber and on boxes in backyards to wave and cheer as the train went by.

Contd. Page 3

STATE: Showers. **CITY:** Fog, showers. Top temps: City, L'po ol 21 (details, map P39). TV P14. J'pot Lottery 1722 P38. Finance P14. TAB: 11 am-6.30 pm. Tele-Trading 2 0924

Queen Mother shows 'the human face of royalty'

THAT SMILE!

And a royal wave to the joyful crowd

By BRIAN JAMES

SHE turned on the steps of St Paul's and in the wind the loose chiffon shoulders of her lilac dress flew free like a cape ... the Wonder Woman of the Royal set.

Queen Elizabeth the Queen Mother yesterday put on a smile undamaged by a million outings and listened to London's greeting for her 80th birthday.

Then she turned and went inside the cathedral, there to hear Archbishop Runcie get it right, absolutely right, when he declared she has shown 'the human face of royalty'.

That was why, as the sun filled the skies, the capital had filled its streets to wave at and wonder at the endless warmth of this, the ultimate Grannie.

It was a day of pomp, naturally, on the famous route from Buckingham Palace to St Paul's, two miles along which the courts and corteges have rumbled for centuries,

Turn to Page 2 Col. 1

For the mother A loving smile from the Queen during yesterday's service at St Paul's Cathedral

For the crowd A classic wave from the day's heroine as she stands on the steps of St Paul's to salute those who have lined the route to cheer her

THE Sun

WE SCOOP THE POOLS AGAIN!

See Page Five

Thursday, September 18, 1980   12p   TODAY'S TV: PAGES 14 and 15

Killer bug hits holiday Britons

● ONE Briton has died and five more are seriously ill in hospital with Legionnaires Disease.

● All six recently returned from holidays at the Rio Park Hotel at Benidorm, Spain, the source of previous outbreaks of the disease.

● Last night an alert went out to health authorities all over Britain.

Full story—Page 7

Dock strike peace deal

● DOCK leaders last night worked out a peace plan to avoid the crippling national strike threatened for Monday. Employment Secretary Jim Prior earlier offered extra cash to 178 dockers who faced the sack.

Full story—Page 2

West Ham fans on rampage

● WEST HAM soccer fans rioted as the London team went down 3-1 to Castilla in Spain last night. It was a bitter disappointment to the second Division club, who had written to every supporter on the trip to Madrid asking for good behaviour.

Full story—Back Page

CHARLIE'S GIRL!

'You know I can't say anything about the Prince or my feelings for him'

REVEALED . . . Lady Diana poses with pupils Louise and Scarlett
Picture by ARTHUR EDWARDS

THE bubbly blonde teenager tipped as the next Queen of England stepped regally into the limelight for the first time yesterday.

Prince Charles's new girl, vivacious 19-year-old Lady Diana Spencer, posed for photographers outside the kindergarten where she teaches.

But she refused to speak about her romance with the Prince. And that silence improved her chances of making the marriage of the century.

SERIOUS

For the youngest daughter of the Earl Spencer is the first serious girlfriend of the Prince who has kept mum.

As I strolled with her through the grounds of the Young England kindergarten, attached to St. Saviour's Church in London's Pimlico, Lady

By HARRY ARNOLD

Diana said: "You know I cannot say anything about the Prince or my feelings for him.

"I am saying that off my own bat. No one has told me to stay quiet."

But later she could not stay quiet when she was shown the pictures that were taken.

She was mildly embarrassed by the one which showed she was not wearing a slip under her cotton skirt, patterned with floral hearts.

"I was so nervous
Continued on Page Two

IN LOVE AGAIN!

Lady Di is the new girl for Charles

How The Sun broke the news on September 8

THE Sun

Saturday, October 18, 1980   12p   **TODAY'S SPORT STARTS ON PAGE 25**

BLACK MAGIC

Velvet Queen wows them at the Vatican!

Reigning in Rome . . . the Queen in velvet splendour with the Pope at the Vatican

From JAMES LEWTHWAITE in Rome

THE QUEEN wore black to go to the Vatican yesterday . . . and the effect was magical.

She looked magnificent for her private audience with Pope John-Paul II.

Even fashion-conscious Rome was wowed by her beautiful full-length velvet-and-taffeta gown.

Because of Papal protocol the Queen had to wear black — a colour many women try to avoid. But she turned it into a royal triumph.

Fashion experts who have seen her on numerous tours could not remember when she looked so regal.

Her black cascade veil was held in place by a superb diamond tiara. H gown sparkled with more jewels, cluding the diamond of the Garter her sleeves.

Around her neck were double-che pearls, and a tiny diamond glister on her wrist.

CHEERED

As she swept along the norma quiet corridors of the Vatican, you trainee priests cheered their hea off

It was a great triumph for Queen's youngest and latest dr designer, Ian Thomas.

Royal favourite Hardy Amies designed a dress in black lace, the Queen preferred Thomas's cr tion.

The audience—the fi State visit to the Vati by a British monarch was also a great succe

The Queen and Pri Philip talked with Po John Paul for 42 minu 17 minutes longer th scheduled.

They spoke in Engl one of the Pop favourite languages, afterwards they swap gifts.

The Pope presented Queen with a set leather-bound volume The Divine Comedy,

Continued on Page Two

NEXT WEEK IS EXTRA-SPECIAL IN YOUR EXCITING SUN

DAILY Mirror

ednesday, October 29, 1980   12p

FACE TO FACE: The Queen and King Hassan exchange sharp words.

Snubbed again by the King of Morocco

EDWARD VALE reports from Marrakesh

THE QUEEN waged a bizarre desert war with the King of Morocco yesterday.

She made no attempt to hide her anger over the latest in a series of four mix-ups.

Throwing her hands in the air, she seemed to say: "What the blazes is going on?"

Hostilities broke out when Prince Philip refused to sit where the unpredictable King Hassan directed him, and moved beside the Queen instead.

The King, stumped over what to do next, stormed off into an air-conditioned coach — leaving his guests sweltering under a tent.

At the end of it all, according to one source, the Queen said: "I give up."

The amazing confusion came on the second day of a three-day official visit to Morocco, and followed other mix-ups on day one.

Forgot

The King made a number of last-minute changes in the programme and forgot to tell the Queen.

Yesterday the royal parties drove out to a camp of tents pitched in the foothills of the Atlas Mountains.

The plan was to watch dancing displays and a charge by 1,500 horsemen.

All three royals walked into a tent to watch the show and had been there only a few minutes when the King vanished.

For five minutes the Queen and Prince Philip stood chatting together. At one stage the Queen put her hand inside the belt of her red-and-white check dress—a sure sign of a royal bad mood.

The first skirmishes followed. It appeared that the Queen was angry at being kept waiting.

The King then reappeared briefly, puffing on a cigarette. He kept putting up his hands as if to say: "What can I do?"

The Queen, apparently not satisfied, stretched out her arms. Prince Philip said something to her and she put up her hands again.

Cigarette still in hand, the King then showed the Queen to an arm-

● Turn to Page Two

BACK TO FRONT: The Queen is furious as she is snubbed by King Hassan.

Pictures by RON BURTON

NO WAY TO TREAT A LADY!

DAILY Mirror

Wednesday, February 25, 1981   12p

HIS ROYAL HIGHNESS THE PRINCE OF WALES PRESENTS:

MY DI

SOUVENIR ISSUE
PLEASE TURN TO BACK PAGE
ALSO PAGES 2, 3, 7, 15, 16 AND 17

Printed by West of England Newspapers Ltd, Burrington Way, Plymouth, England.

DAILY STAR

THURSDAY, FEBRUARY 26th, 1981   10p (12p C.I.s, Eire)   Printed in London

STING
PICTURE
SOUVENIR
SEE PAGE 5

10p

Watermen: Maggie does a U-bend

By CHARLES RAE
Industrial Reporter

WATER Authority bosses last night gave in and offered 33,000 workers a new pay deal only hours before a strike deadline ran out.

The 12.3 per cent rise was immediately rejected by union leaders.

They will recommend their 33,000 members to accept the deal, giving them a weekly rise of between £11.60 and £13.36, in a nationwide ballot.

It was as Maggie Thatcher was arriving in America for talks with President Reagan, looked like yet another U-turn by the Government.

But Sir Robert Marshall, national Water Council chief, admitted he had been in touch with Environment Minister Tom King three times in the last 24 hours.

Anxious

"I kept the Government informed because they were as anxious as I," said Sir Robert.

He said bosses were prepared to offer more money because the most worrying thing that had occurred was the coal miners situation.

Said Sir Robert: "Our men have tended to concentrate on the 13 per cent miners pay settlement.

"They also obviously saw the settlement of the pit closure problem and the reinforcement of mining power . . . muscle if you like."

Misery

He added "We saw ourselves moving into an area of very heavy industrial action.

"It would be difficult in our view to justify the great misery which would occur if we went into a strike situation."

They have urged an unofficial action return to normal working.

Mr Keating, assistant general Secretary of NALGO—one of the four unions involved—said: "This clearly means the watermen are in the big league."

QUEEN ACTS IN BRITANNIA SCANDAL

EXCLUSIVE

By ANTHONY SMITH

THE QUEEN has ordered a thorough inquiry into the sex scandal aboard the Royal Yacht Britannia.

Eleven junior ratings are understood to have been charged with sex offences, and the affair is blowing up into a major embarrassment for the Royal Family.

Details of the alleged homosexual vice ring below decks were given to Prince Philip when he visited the Royal Yacht in Portsmouth last Friday.

The Queen is especially anxious that any whiff of scandal should be cleared up quickly in case Prince Charles decides to spend his July honeymoon on the vessel.

A senior officer confirmed last night that Prince Philip had spoken to the Britannia's commanding officer.

Curious

"His discussions on board were private," he said. "But we understand that the Duke was naturally curious and asked what was going on.

"In that event he would be told everything."

Detailed reports of the investigations have been sent to the Queen's Press secretary at Buckingham Palace.

The men charged under the Naval Discipline Act could face jail sentences and dismissed from the Service.

And the Royal Family is faced with the detailed exposure of sordid activities when the allegations are made public at a court martial.

TO THE MANNER BORN . . .

LADY DIANA is learning fast. After just one night at Clarence House — where she is staying with the Queen Mother — she has got the Royal wave almost right.

The future Princess of Wales gave her first, near-perfect Royal wave as she was being driven from Buckingham Palace yesterday.

But Prince Charles's bride-to-be added her own touch. Instead of the customary Royal wave with the back of the hand inclined towards the crowd, she did it with her palm facing outwards.

Congratulations

Colin Macer, the Press Association's chief photographer who has snapped many Royal waves said: "It summed up her character — open, outward-going and friendly."

The Queen Mother was all smiles yesterday as she celebrated her grandson's engagement with East Enders in London.

"It's lovely, isn't it?" she told a crowd who shouted their congratulations.

It has not been decided how long Lady Diana will stay at Clarence House.

Di's shadow—Page 4

Trying it the Royal way: Lady Diana waves to well-wishers yesterday . . . but the hand action isn't quite right yet

Threat to England Test tour—Back Page

Sunday Mirror

22p June 14, 1981 No. 943

Six pistol cracks ring out—then the sudden fear.. 'Has the Queen been shot?

THE AWFUL MOMENT

■ THIS was the awful moment in London yesterday when six shots rang out as the Queen rode past.

■ A MOUNTED police officer still has his hand raised to salute Her Majesty on her way to the Trooping the Colour ceremony.

■ SIX pistol cracks sounded and the sudden fear was: "Has the Queen been shot?"

■ BUT even before the echoes of the shots died away a policeman, shirt-tail showing, pictured dashing to grab a youth.

■ THE PC was half way across The Mall before many in the crowd had time to turn their heads to see where the shots came from.

■ POLICE, an ambulanceman, and even members of the public pounced on the gunman — who fired a starting pistol using blanks.

■ LATER a 17-year-old youth was charged under the Treason Act.

TREASON CHARGE
—Back Page

Full story
—Centre Pages

The Queen reins back to control her frightened horse as a policeman runs towards the gunman. Picture: DAVID KILBURN

DAILY EXPRESS

Monday June 15 1981 ● 12p ● Weather : Bright periods THE VOICE OF BRITAIN ★★★

Marksman, 17, who won trophies for shooting

GUN BOY

Youth is accused of firing a pistol near the Queen

By COLIN BELL and DANNY McGRORY

THE BOY accused of firing a blank pistol at the Queen is an ace marksman and has won cups for shooting, it was revealed last night.

Marcus Sarjeant, 17, who has pin-up pictures of Prince Charles and Lady Diana in his bedroom, will appear in court today charged under the Treason Act.

The quiet, strapping young man who was arrested at the Trooping the Colour on Saturday was once in the Air Training Corps.

The officer who ran his squadron said: "As a leading cadet he would have had tuition in the safe handling of firearms and would know quite a bit about them."

A LONER

Sarjeant, of Capel le Ferne, near Folkestone, Kent, is described by his friends as a bit of a loner, but always pleasant.

They said he has no girlfriends and loves fishing and collecting butterflies and stamps.

He joined the Marines last year but left after only three months, telling people he did not like "the bullying."

His 70-year-old grandmother Mrs Sylvia Sarjeant, of Church Hougham, near Dover, wept as she talked of her shock at his arrest.

"Marcus has a darn good happy home and family," she said. "The family have done really well. They are very comfortably off.

"He is unemployed and has

Page 2, Column One

NOT a care in the world —the Queen watching Prince Charles play polo yesterday. Saturday's six-shot drama seems not to have affected her at all. Certainly it hasn't altered any of her plans or her "Queen of the People" way of life. —Full story Pages 2 and 3.

Laughing off a day of danger

Air Cadet Marcus with some of his shooting trophies

PLUCK THAT WON A NATION'S HEARTS: PAGES 8 & 9

V Guide Pages 18, 19 • Weather Page 2 • Hickey Page 13 • Express Woman Pages 16, 17 • Motoring Page 22 • Letters Page 24 • Stars Page 26 • Sport starts Page 27

PERFECT!

**Balcony scene at Buckingham Palace : To huge cheers from the crowd, Prince Charles kisses his beautiful bride.
One little bridesmaid watches, two others clinging to Princess Diana are too tired after their long day**

INSIDE : More news and pictures 2; 3, 4, 7, 9, 10, 11; Femail—The Dress 13-15; Party Time 16-17; The TV Battle 19; Nigel Dempster 23; Going Away 24-25

DAILY Mirror

Friday, February 5, 1982   14p   *

After 30 glorious years as Queen

THEN: The young Queen after her Coronation.

LONG MAY SHE REIGN

BY TOMORROW, the Queen will have reigned for 30 years, more than any other monarch this century. While all else has changed, she has been unchanging.

In those years the influence of Britain has been diminished. Hers has grown.

This nation is no longer renowned as a great power. She remains the most famous woman in the world.

When she came to the throne in 1952 she was a young wife and mother. Today she is in her middle age and a grandmother. Churchill was her first Prime Minister. He and his successor, Eden, are long dead. Those who followed—Macmillan, Home, Wilson, Heath and Callaghan—have passed from power.

She is still there.

She has lived a life of great privilege, but has never known the privilege of privacy which most of us enjoy.

The tinsel of public life—its sporting heroes, its film stars, its politicians and their scandals—has glittered briefly and gone. The Queen has endured.

While foreign monarchies have tumbled, Britain's has grown stronger. There

MirrorComment

is less republicanism today than there was 50 or 100 years ago.

Instead of being undemocratic, the monarchy has become part of the rock on which British democracy rests.

The credit for that belongs to the Queen. It is the achievement of her 30 years.

● What do you know about the Queen? See Centre Pages.

TODAY: Britain's strength and most famous woman in the world.

Air girl Roz takes off for TV

By ALISTER MARTIN

HER face is world famous, yet you probably don't even know her name.

But Roz Hanby plans to take good care of that. The girl from the British Airways ads is quitting the air to go on TV.

Roz, who has assured millions "We'll take good care of you," will present a Monday night chat show for TVS in Southampton.

After a champagne celebration yesterday, 30-year-old Roz said: "I'm delighted and very happy.

"I never dreamed that when I became a stewardess it would lead to this."

Roz's show, which starts in April, will be called Watch This Space... That Monday Evening Feeling.

A TVS spokesman said: "It's designed to get rid of everybody's Monday blues.

Roz is just the girl for that."

British Airways were less happy. Their spokesman said: "We'll never replace her. She's an impossible act to follow—one in a million.

"We wish her well. She will still appear in our adverts all over the world.

"She is even better known in most other

countries than she is here."

Roz, whose boyfriend is BBC presenter John Tidmarsh, explained: "I just love talking to people. It's why I became a stewardess.

"I'll enjoy cheering people up and I hope my TV career will go on from there.

"I just hope it will be as much fun as my time at British Airways."

Roz plans to go out in style. She made arrangements yesterday to make her last flight as a stewardess in Concorde.

ROZ: A high-flier for TV

THATCHER PICKS A NEW HARD MAN

SEE PAGE 2

The Citizen

Friday,
April 16, 1982
Ottawa

Final Edition
$1.25 weekly
home delivered
25¢ per copy

Warm welcome greets Queen

— Chris Mikula, Citizen

Nervous Kelly Davison, 9, welcomes Queen Elizabeth with traditional bouquet

tgif

It's a jungle out there in the wine stores on both sides of the Ottawa River, so our expert Peter Ward has compiled a comprehensive guide to some of the best values.

TV Tip

NHL Hockey: Quebec Nordiques meet the Boston Bruins in game two of the division finals. Channels 4, 5, 6M, 9 and 11 at 7:30 p.m.

A Queen at ease charms spectators

By Don Collins
Citizen staff writer

They were all there Thursday — the nervous little flower girl with the trembling lower lip, the well-scrubbed dignitaries, the excited young Inuit, two lonely demonstrators and possibly 5,000 others — as Queen Elizabeth arrived on a warm spring afternoon to begin her 12th visit to Canada.

From an historic point of view, it is the most significant visit of all. Saturday, the day before her return to England, she will proclaim Canada's new constitution.

But for a while Thursday, with the temperature soaring to almost 14 degrees and flags snapping in a 10-to 15-kilometre wind, all thought seemed to be focused on the charming 55-year-old monarch and not the job that awaited her.

There was the familiar smile, the nod, the gentle wave of the hand as she stepped from the Canadian Forces Boeing 707 at CFB Uplands airport at 3:11 p.m., just a minute behind schedule.

Prince Philip, who remained in England to attend a special dinner Thursday, was due arrive at Uplands at 11:30 a.m. today.

Most of the Queen's initial encounters were with people of high public profile, like Prime Minister Pierre Trudeau and Gov. Gen. Edward Schreyer.

But it was the reaction of the little people that really told the story of what both she and the constitution mean to the country.

Inside the cavernous Hangar 11, where about 500 adults and children awaited her arrival for as long as an hour, Girl Guides from the Second Carp Company were asked by a reporter why they thought the Queen was coming.

"She's going to sign this piece of paper so we don't have British rules anymore, and we'll make up our own laws," said 11-year-old Krista Wilson.

Added Jennifer Rothwell, 10: "She's going to give us the constitution so we can make up our own laws and not have the governor general approve them."

The thin lines of people that covered many parts of the route to Rideau Hall, official residence of the governor general, seemed pleased with the fleeting glimpses they got of the Queen.

(They, page 43)

CLEARING ... MAYBE

The Uplands weather office says showers predicted for early Saturday may end shortly before the 11 a.m. start of the proclamation ceremonies on Parliament Hill. The temperature is expected to rise to a high of 17 degrees, with the prospect of some afternoon sunny breaks.

— Wayne Cuddington, Citizen

Prime Minister Trudeau escorts Queen Elizabeth upon her arrival Thursday

Lévesque's plea: 'Quebec must belong to us'

By Duart Farquharson
Southam News

MONTREAL — Premier René Lévesque told "the French nation of Quebec" Thursday its unprecedented constitutional isolation meant it is time to form "a country where we will be truly at home."

In the most separatist-sounding speech he has made to the province in years, Lévesque, who usually reserves outright appeals for independence for gatherings of his own followers, said Quebecers should "decide soon, before it it too late, that Quebec must belong to us."

Blackboard pointer in hand, props assembled, Lévesque was at his best in his old professional role of television communicator as he argued on the province-wide TVA network that the new Canadian constitution had been drawn up "not only without French Quebec, but specifically against French Quebec."

He said the "totally unacceptable" result should serve, "as nothing has before, to open our eyes to the only valid direction that we can take as a nation — the nation that we are."

Lévesque said the new Canada Act was really the same old BNA Act of 1867, "a law placed upon us by a foreign power," now proclaimed "as yet another British act because they couldn't finish the job in Canada."

Noting Prime Minister Trudeau had said it was the job of British parliamentarians, if necessary, to "hold their noses and pass" the Canadian legislation, he suggested "Her Majesty the Queen is perhaps also holding her nose" as she prepares to proclaim the new law Saturday.

The federal government has asked the privately-owned TVA network for equal broadcast time following Lévesque's address. A network spokesman said a decision will be made Monday.

(Federal, page 55)

Half region's doctors join OHIP-fee protest

By Denise Harrington
Citizen staff writer

Slightly more than half Ottawa-Carleton's doctors closed ranks behind the Ontario Medical Association Thursday and withdrew all but emergency services to protest medicare fees, a Citizen survey found.

A telephone survey of the offices of 550 doctors in the region Wednesday and Thursday showed 314 doctors, 57 per cent of those contacted, closed their offices, and 236 were working.

About 700 doctors belong to the Ottawa Academy of Medicine, although academy president Dr. Gordon Liberty estimates about 900 doctors work in the region.

Liberty disputed The Citizen survey based on doctors' telephone listings, saying three doctors had complained their receptionists were asked if their offices were open, but were not asked if doctors were seeing patients.

He estimated about 75 per cent of doctors had closed their offices or withdrawn services, basing his figures on reports from various doctors' offices. The academy did not conduct any formal survey to find out how many doctors took part in the walkout.

Citizen surveyers asked doctors or their receptionists whether they were supporting the OMA action and closing their offices. If the answer was no, they were then asked whether they were seeing patients.

(Doctors, page 3)

British cabinet on war footing

Citizen news services

The British cabinet was put on war footing today to deal with the Falklands crisis and U.S. Secretary of State Alexander Haig delivered a message from President Reagan to Argentine President Leopoldo Galtieri in Buenos Aires.

The British move came after Argentine warships put to sea Thursday in a possible challenge to the British blockade of the islands, seized by Argentina April 2.

The British naval task force was due to arrive at Ascension Island in mid-Atlantic anytime but the defence ministry declined to comment on the fleet's location.

"It is clear tonight that the task will not be easy," Haig said when he arrived for another round of his peace-shuttle. "The stakes are so high that they demand the ultimate effort of all participants in these discussions."

Haig, accompanied by special envoy Vernon Walters and U.S. Ambassador Harry Shlaudeman, met for 30 minutes at Government House with Galtieri and Foreign Minister Nicanor Costa Mendez, then drove to the foreign ministry for more talks with Costa Mendez.

Haig made no comment to reporters waiting at Government House and the Foreign Ministry, but a high-ranking Argentine diplomat remarked to a local radio station that "yesterday I was pessimistic, but today I'm optimistic" about the outcome of the talks.

In London, government officials said Prime Minister Margaret Thatcher ordered her key ministers — including Foreign Secretary Francis Pym and Defence Secretary John Nott, to remain in the capital this weekend.

Government ministries were ordered to keep key officials permanently in touch. Officials said the orders amounted to war footing.

The last time such emergency measures were taken was during the 1973 Middle East war when the Soviet Union threatened to intervene and former president Richard Nixon ordered U.S. forces on a worldwide alert.

(More stories page 6)

THE STANDARD

Tuesday, June 8, 1982. 15p. *Incorporating the* Evening News

LATE PRICES STOP PRESS

Reagan's historic message to MPs

'Your young men fight for a cause...for the belief that aggression must not pay'

PARTNERS!

by David Meilton

PRESIDENT REAGAN, in an historic address to both Houses of Parliament, today placed himself four-square behind Britain's forces in the Falklands.

He told the assembled Peers and MPs that Britain's young men were fighting for a cause, not "for mere real estate".

Speaking from the Royal Gallery at Westminster, the President said: "On distant islands in the South Atlantic young men are fighting for Britain.

"And yes, voices have been raised protesting their sacrifices for lumps of rock and earth so far away. But these young men are not fighting for mere real estate.

"They fight for a cause, for the belief that armed aggression must not be allowed to succeed and that people must participate in the decision of government under the rule of law.

"If there had been firmer support for that principle some 45 years ago perhaps our generation would not have suffered the blood-letting of World War Two."

HOME ON THE ROYAL RANGE

Reagan's morning at Windsor, Pictures Page Three

When, after nearly 20 minutes, President Reagan said Britain's forces were "fighting for a cause" there was spontaneous applause, led by Mrs Thatcher.

The President also made a brief reference to the Middle East. He said: "In the Middle East the guns sound once more, this time in Lebanon, a country that for too long has had to endure the tragedy of civil war, terrorism, and foreign intervention and occupation."

On arrival at the Royal Gallery Mr Reagan had been greeted by Mrs Thatcher, who wore a navy blue dress with silver spots.

Mrs Nancy Reagan accompanied her husband on the drive to Westminster, and preceded him into the gallery to listen to the address, seated next to Mrs Thatcher.

Mr Reagan, was introduced by the Lord Chancellor, Lord Hailsham.

The President began his address by saying that the world was at a turning point in the battle against totalitarianism. "The emergency is upon us," he said.

He hoped for a global crusade, led by Britain and America, for freedom and democracy "which will leave Marxism-Leninism on the ash-heap of history as it has left other tyrannies which stifle the freedom and muzzle the self-expression of the people."

Several times he quoted Sir Winston Churchill

RELAXING the reins of power ... President Reagan joins the Queen in Windsor Park.

as the epitome of British courage in the face of adversity.

"He left us a message of hope for the future, as timely now as when he first uttered it as Opposition Leader in the Commons nearly 27 years ago," Mr Reagan said.

"When we look back on all the perils through which we have passed and at the mighty foes we have laid low and all the dark and deadly designs we have frustrated, why should we fear for our future? We have,' said Sir Winston, 'come safely through the worst.'

"'The task I have set forth will long outlive our own generation. But together, we, too, have come through the worst.

"Let us now begin a major effort to secure the best—a crusade for freedom that will engage the faith and fortitude of the next generation.

Repeatedly President Reagan returned to the theme of the

Continued Page 2, Col 6

MAX HASTINGS ON BRITAIN'S CAPTIVES

PAGE TWO

QUEEN MOTHER IN HELICOPTER DRAMA

PAGE FIVE

WAGNER TO WED AGAIN

Robert Wagner... in love again

See Centre Pages

Jill St John... his next bride

QUEEN SPOKE TO PROWLER AT HER BEDSIDE

The Queen... cool courage with intruder

Prince Philip... he was in another bedroom

Ten-minute chat.. then she escaped from room

By HARRY ARNOLD and SHAN LANCASTER

THE QUEEN had an amazing face-to-face meeting with a prowler in her bedroom, it was revealed last night.

The intruder sat on her bed and chatted to her for 10 minutes before a footman came to her rescue.

The drama began after the prowler got into the Queen's bed-chamber at Buckingham Palace—an unprecedented breach of security.

As he sat on the Queen's bed, she woke up ... and calmly started to talk to him.

Then he asked for a cigarette and the Queen saw her chance to escape. She stepped into the corridor and alerted her footman.

The footman walked quickly into the bedchamber and calmly overpowered the intruder.

But a North Country chambermaid who saw him being taken away let slip a horrified remark.

The Queen, greatly amused, later mimicked her terrified squeak of: "Bloody hell, ma'am, what's he doing in there?" Last night, a senior detective paid tribute to Her Majesty's quick thinking and courage:

"The Queen was very brave. By being calm she did not alarm the man," he said.

"He might have panicked and it could have been a very different story.

"It is the most incredible story of how someone can walk in off the street and end up in the Queen's bedroom."

At the time of the incident last Friday, Prince Philip was sleeping in a *Continued on Page Four*

EXCLUSIVE: Security scare at Di's home—See Page 4

DAILY Mirror

Fury over Royal security

Tuesday, July 13, 1982   16p   *

HOW could a man break into the Palace . . . TWICE?

WHY did police take thirty minutes to arrive?

The questions facing Home Secretary Whitelaw and Yard chief McNee

SEE PAGES TWO, THREE, THIRTEEN, FOURTEEN and FIFTEEN

DAILY Mirror

Tuesday, July 20, 1982   16p   *

SHAME OF THE QUEEN'S POLICE CHIEF

ON GUARD: Commander Trestrail at the Queen's elbow at a function in 1980. He was her close and trusted bodyguard for nearly ten years, a companion as well as policeman.

❛ He has confessed to a homosexual relationship with a male prostitute ❜

—Home Secretary William Whitelaw yesterday

BUCKINGHAM Palace was rocked and the Government sent reeling by yesterday's revelation that the Queen's personal policeman had been having an affair over many years with a male prostitute.

Commander Michael Trestrail, 51-year-old head of the Royal Protection Squad and bodyguard of the Queen, admitted the scandal

By TERENCE LANCASTER, Political Editor

on Saturday and promptly resigned from the police force.

Scandal? Yes.

It is not a scandal to be a homosexual. Homosexuality is legal. But even today homosexuals are still liable to blackmail.

It is a SCANDAL that a homosexual should be in a sensi-

tive position inside the Palace. It is a SCANDAL that his homosexuality was not revealed in the positive vetting he had to undergo before he took up his post.

It is a SCANDAL that he confessed on Saturday and the Home Secretary was not informed until yesterday morning. It is a SCAN-

DAL that follows on two others:

● The intrusion by Michael Fagan into the Queen's bedroom.

● The revelation that the Government's top-secret communications centre at Cheltenham has been infiltrated by enemy agents.

Home Secretary Willie

Whitelaw, already under attack after evidence of repeated break-ins at Buckingham Palace, told the Commons:

❛ Commander Trestrail, the Queen's police officer, has confessed to having a homosexual relationship over a number of years with a male prostitute. He has resigned from the Metropolitan Police. ❜

MPs were not so much surprised

TURN TO PAGE THREE

The first official portrait of William – by Snowdon

DIANA AND HER BABY PRINCE

Daily Mail Reporter

INTRODUCING the most famous face of the 21st Century : Prince William of Wales, at 29 days old.

One day, as King, he will be on the coins, the stamps and the banknotes that our grandchildren and their children will use.

Already, he is the best-known baby in the world.

This first delightful official portrait of him with his mother the Princess of Wales is released today, his parents' first wedding anniversary.

It was taken nine days ago at Kensington Palace by William's great-uncle, Lord Snowdon, as was another on the centre pages. He said : 'I think the pictures speak for themselves if you want to know how the mother and baby are feeling. It was a great honour and a pleasure to be asked to take them.'

Prince Charles said when his son was born that William had the 'good fortune' not to look like him. The baby has blue eyes and fair hair like his mother, but then most babies have blue eyes at first and there does not seem to be enough hair yet to be significant.

So who does he take after? Is there, perhaps, a look of his royal grandmother ? Or even great-great-grandfather George V ? Within the family and now across the nation, the debate on such questions is, no doubt, only just beginning.

For the photo session, Prince William was in a long gown with lace edging and was posed on a cream lace cushion. Princess Diana, looking stunning, wore a cream silk dress with a necklace of cultured pearls set in diamonds with matching heart-shaped diamond earrings.

MOTHER, FATHER AND BABY PICTURE—CENTRE PAGES

DAILY Mirror HOME

Saturday, September 18, 1982   16p   ★   Portsmouth

DATELINE:

"There were times when I was really terrified. But I would say to myself, I'm going to survive come hell or high water"

See Pages 2, 3 and 7

HIS ROYAL HAPPINESS: Jubilant Prince Andrew, ashore with proud Prince Philip after the carrier Invincible sailed home from the Falklands to a tumultuous welcome at Portsmouth yesterday.   **Picture: KENT GAVIN**

BINGO £1,000,000

Play it once, play it twice
See Page 12

DAILY STAR

FRIDAY, SEPTEMBER 24, 1982   15p   (C.I.s)   Printed in London

I DONE THE QUEEN A FAVOUR

The Queen: told of verdict

THE ROYAL INTRUDER

Michael Fagan, found not guilty yesterday of stealing wine at Buckingham Palace, is pictured earlier this year with his dog. Fagan is still in custody on other charges, but when his family visited him last night he told them: "I'll soon be home."

THE man cleared of burglary at Buckingham Palace claimed yesterday: "I done the Queen a favour."

Michael Fagan, 32, said he had exposed the Palace's weak security.

Fagan told an Old Bailey jury: "I had been around it with the children and I knew the security was a bit lax.

"So I decided to show how easy it was to go in. I wanted to prove that the Queen wasn't in a very safe position so I walked

By JAMES NICHOLSON, TOM ROCHE and BARRY GARDNER

round and disturbed this young lady and I didn't know what to do then.

"I went in through the window. I startled her and she ran off. I just walked straight in like I was surprised I wasn't captured straight away after disturbing the young lady. I could have been a rapist or something.

"I stayed there for about half an hour. I even had a chance to have a drink because I was thirsty, you know what I mean?"

Londoner Fagan, an unemployed labourer, was found not guilty of burglary and stealing a quantity of wine belonging to Prince Charles.

The Queen, who is staying at Balmoral with Prince Charles and Princess Diana, was told of the verdict by her private secretary Sir Philip Moore.

Father-of-four Fagan went into the witness box yesterday to tell of his amazing escapades inside the Palace. He said:

"I walked past a lot of rooms. One had Princess Anne on the door and another had Mark Phillips, you know, so I thought they might be asleep, I didn't want to disturb them.

"I looked in one bedroom which had Prince Philip on it but they was out visiting Reagan, you know.

"I expected to get captured. I was waiting to be captured. I drank it because I was waiting for someone to come.

"I don't remember everything. I was thinking I'm thirsty. I was waiting to get pinched. I waited about half an hour until I realised nobody was going to pinch me.

"I didn't try and conceal the fact I went into the palace. In my opinion I done the Queen a favour by proving that her security wasn't one up. I was thirsty and I couldn't find a tap I thought I'd earned it."

Prosecuting counsel Mrs. Barbara Mills asked Fagan: "It wasn't yours to drink was it?"

Fagan replied: "It wasn't my Palace to get into, was it? I was very thirsty.

"I thought I'd done a hard day's work for the Queen, breaking her security. I even sat on the Throne."

Mrs. Mills told the jury: "It's no defence to say, 'I thought the

Turn to Page 4

Telly guide: Pages 18, 19 ● £40,000 Bingo: Page 26

The Times

OF SWAZILAND

Price 15 cents   Tuesday, October 26, 1982   Vol. 80 No. 194

WHIRLWIND TOUR A REAL 'SMILING SAFARI'

PRINCESS MEETS HER 'CHILDREN'

A RADIANT Princess Anne yesterday met the children of Swaziland ... and they loved her.

The Princess's whirlwind three-day visit to the kingdom was a real "smiling safari" as she visited three separate children's projects in the Hhohho District.

Wherever she stopped on her tour, Princess Anne was surrounded by happy, smiling children and she responded to their warm welcome by spending long periods chatting to them.

By JAMES DLAMINI

In fact the Princess was so at home chatting to the kids that at times her tight schedule was threatened and officials with her were left anxiously checking their watches.

The Princess, who is president of the Save the Children Fund, arrived in Swaziland on Sunday to visit the Fund's projects here.

Princess Anne drove by car from the Royal Guest lodge just outside Lobamba to Ntfonjeni, deep inside the bundu.

The tour party was temporarily joined by Prince Gabheni at Ntfonjeni. She was greeted by a long line of children who had been anxiously waiting for her arrival.

They cheered and stampeded into a hall where the function was to be conducted. In the hall, the children met her with a hymn.

After hymns, schools choirs performances were conducted. Two children then provided her with gifts and flowers.

There is a Save the Children Fund feeding project at Ntfonjeni school. "We feel we're the luckiest school in Swaziland," said an official when the Princess departed amid more cheers from the children.

From Ntfonjeni she proceeded to Emkhuzweni Rural health centre. From Ntfonjeni to Emkhuzweni, it is a long dusty drive through scrubland. The centre is run by the Holiness

PICTURES ON PAGES 6 AND 7

Union Mission which has some immunisation equipment purchased by Save the Children Fund.

"Its like a mini hospital. We do all sorts of things, including operations here," one of the staff members was heard telling the Princess during the tour of the centre.

In the centre, she visited the outpatients department where she occasionally stopped and chatted with patients. She also visited the wards, where she would also stop and chat with patients lightheartedly for some time.

The management of the clinic provided her with a light lunch before she proceeded to the Nkamanzi Rural Immunisation Centre.

The Nkamanzi is a joint Swaziland government and Save the Children Fund project.

She watched as a children's mass immunisation was being conducted under a tree for lack of accomodation. The

(Back Page Col.3)

Her Royal Highness, Princess Anne chatting to Prince Gabheni, Minister for Home Affairs at Ntfonjeni yesterday.

MOURNING: 57 FINED

A TOTAL of 57 people have been fined for refusing to honour the mourning directive.

Twenty-nine of them were fined a total of E1,740 by the Nhlangano National Court last week.

Others have been fined by the Manzini and Bhunya National Courts.

Almost all the accused told the courts they could not cut their hair because it

By MASHUMI TWALA

was against their religious beliefs.

At the Nhlangano National Court, the court president called for order when seven accused, calling themselves Jehova's Witnesses, started preaching to the court.

They opened their bibles and quoted several verses to support their defence.

Chief Jeremiah Dlamini of the Vusweni area, where the seven "Witnesses" stay, told the court that when the Royal Directive for mourning was issued, he summoned all his subjects and notified them.

He said: "These seven pointed out blankly that they could not afford to do that as it is against their religion. I warned them that they could be prosecuted if they refused."

"A few days later, I was notified that these people were determined not to cut their hair because, it would not be proper for them. That is when I decided to take action and brought them to the police."

In their defence, the Witnesses said: "We heard the

(Back Page Col.6)

DAILY Mirror

Saturday, March 5, 1983   16p

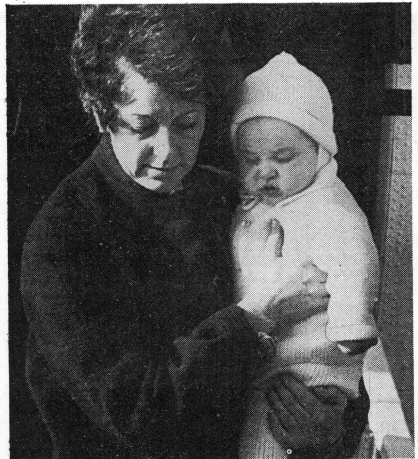

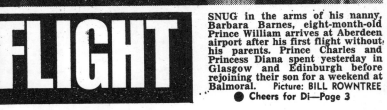

FLIGHT

SNUG in the arms of his nanny, Barbara Barnes, eight-month-old Prince William arrives at Aberdeen airport after his first flight without his parents. Prince Charles and Princess Diana spent yesterday in Glasgow and Edinburgh before rejoining their son for a weekend at Balmoral.   Picture: BILL ROWNTREE
● Cheers for Di—Page 3

and FANCY!

AN extravagant dress worn by the Queen was the talk of surprised guests at a formal State banquet in San Francisco. The dress was made of champagne silk taffeta and featured two huge shoulder bows. Topped with a tiara, necklace and earrings it was in complete contrast to the Queen's normal understated style.
● Royal joker—Page 3.

BBC HALTS SALE OF ROYAL LETTERS

FIVE personal notes written by Prince Charles were withdrawn from auction yesterday after legal threats from the BBC.

In the notes Charles complains about public appearances and jokingly refers to ending up in a "lunatic asylum."

The notes, written to the BBC's former "Royal producer", Anthony Craxton, were due to be auctioned by New York dealer Charles Hamilton.

But minutes before they went on sale, with advance bids already standing at £3,300, the BBC threatened legal action.

Lawyers claimed the notes were BBC property because Mr. Craxton was

From PAUL CONNEW in New York

working for the corporation when the letters were exchanged. Last night Mr. Hamilton pledged: "I shall fight this spurious case. I mean to hang on to the letters and no-one will stop the sale from going ahead.

"The BBC should admit the truth. It's pressure from the Royal family that has led to this.

"The real story is that the Queen doesn't like the idea of Prince Charles's letters being sold like those of Abraham Lincoln or George Washington at a common public auction."

All five of the letters to Mr. Craxton, who was

friendly with the Royal family, were written six years ago. They concern future dates with the media.

In one Charles writes: "I've been persuaded to subject myself to yet another confrontation with commercial radio.

"I still think it's a waste of time. I trust you are surviving the strain of all these preparations.

"Perhaps we shall end up in the insane asylum next year when it is all over."

Mr. Hamilton said Mr. Craxton supplied him with the letters.

Last night the BBC said: "Buckingham Palace was not involved in this action. It is entirely down to us."

Mr. Craxton no longer works for the BBC.

DAILY STAR

WEDNESDAY, AUGUST 10, 1983   15p (16p C.ls)   Printed in London

BLOODY PEEPING TOMS!

Charles shouts at photographers after a hot day in the saddle

PRINCE Charles rode off into the sunset yesterday after shooting from the hip at photographers.

After an exhausting game of polo, watched by the Princess of Wales, Charles charged up to the photographers and said:

"Bloody people. Get these people out of the way. Bloody peeping toms.

"Why can't you leave my wife alone for one bloody second? Leave her alone, for God's sake."

In fact, the Princess was 150 yards away on the other side of the polo field.

Immediately after his outburst, Charles rode off leaving police and photographers baffled. They stood and watched as he rejoined his team which

By DICK DURHAM

had just won a match at Cirencester, Gloucestershire, by 7 to 5.

Police took no action against the photographers because they considered it to be an outburst just in the heat of the moment.

There were about 20 photographers together in a group on the edge of the playing area. Some were professional Pressmen and others holidaymakers.

The Princess of Wales sat in a car in isolation happily watching the game with her bodyguard detective Alan Peters.

The Daily Star's royal photographer Ken Lennox, who was covering the match, said: "Diana looked relaxed and happy sitting in her car with the doors open.

"She arrived after Charles and

Turn to Page Two

Charles . . . "Can't you leave my wife alone?"

A few soothing words from Princess Diana . . . and he calms down

But it all ends in peace as Star photographer Ken Lennox says: 'Even in a rage, Charles is a gentleman'

Jockeys quizzed in race fixing probe

By BARRY GARDNER MICK SEAMARK and HARRY PUGH

SOME of Britain's top jockeys are being quizzed following allegations of a massive race-fixing racket.

Jockey Club officials are investigating claims that thousands of pounds have been paid to 15 riders—many of them household names—to rig races.

Peter Smiles, director of Racecourse Security Services, the Jockey Clb's police force, launched the probe yesterday after the alleged bribes ring, said to be masterminded by a Derbyshire gambler, was reported to him.

It is claimed one jockey was paid £6,000 to take part in rigged races and others received £1,000 a time.

Backhanders

Another top jockey is said to have been given £1,200 worth of garden machinery, while a fellow rider allegedly received cash gifts for his daughter.

A promising young jockey is also said to have regularly taken backhanders.

Mr. Smiles said yesterday: "The investigation is progressing, but we are certain there is a lot in it.

"At the moment we are treating each case individually."

Later, in a statement, he added: "The proper authorities will be informed of any suspected offence, either of a criminal nature or a breach of the rules of racing."

One leading jockey is already believed to have been cleared after being questioned at length about an alleged £10,000 bribe.

Yesterday, a young

Turn to Page 2

DAILY STAR

Daily Star —the paper in the know

TUESDAY, NOVEMBER 1, 1983   15p   (16p C.Is)   Printed in London

THE QUEEN IN TORMENT

Escaped ... Fox

Escaped ... Scofield

Stars in film crash drama

THREE film stars had an amazing escape yesterday when two horses pulling a stagecoach bolted during filming.

The driver fell off, leaving Edward Fox, Robert Hardy and Paul Scofield hanging on for their lives.

After a desperate race across a field, the stagecoach hit a wall and overturned. "It's amazing we escaped," said Robert Hardy last night.

He and Edward Fox were allowed to leave hospital later, but Paul Scofield was detained with leg injuries.

Full story: Page Three

So worried ... the Queen

She fears U.S. invasion may split up the Commonwealth

Mrs. Thatcher: Audience

EXCLUSIVE by DAVID BUCHAN

THE QUEEN is deeply concerned about the future of the Commonwealth following the astonishing breakdown of communications over Grenada.

She is so worried that the subject is likely to completely dominate tonight's Buckingham Palace audience with Prime Minister Margaret Thatcher.

The Queen fears that the United States invasion of the island of which she is Head of State could permanently damage the delicate internal relationships between Commonwealth states.

Her initial anger at not being kept informed of the American plans has given way to a heartfelt determination that she must do everything in her power to heal the wounds.

The Daily Star has learned of the Queen's torment in a remarkable way.

Firstly, the depth of her feelings has struck other members of the Royal Family so forcibly that they have privately remarked on it.

Secondly, it has become apparent in political circles that the Queen's own counsel to the Prime Minister has helped to clarify Mrs. Thatcher's mind about the American invasion and the threat it presents to the Commonwealth.

This new and vigorous viewpoint was aired over the weekend when the Prime Minister and Foreign Secretary Sir Geoffrey Howe, for the first time in the crisis, publicly rebuked President Reagan for his military adventure.

This is believed by Tory MPs to accord exactly with the Queen's views.

Both women are also now said to be united in their view that the Commonwealth is just as important as any special friendship with President Reagan—if not more so.

It is unprecedented for the Queen to let her views be known in such a frank manner, particularly on a sensitive subject.

But she is known to take her role as head of the Commonwealth very seriously—and to guard it jealously.

In conversations at the end of last week and over the weekend, members of the Royal Family felt they need make no bones about airing her concern.

A guest at one private party said : " I have never heard the Queen's

Turn to Page 2

THE Londoner

April, 1984   No 15   ISSN 0262 2521

London pride

THE GLC's giant Thames Barrier, already hailed as the eighth wonder of the world, receives its crowning glory on Tuesday, May 8, when it is opened by the Queen who will press a button to operate the immense steel gates and halt the tide.

A flotilla of small boats — 18 specially chartered by the GLC and packed with over 2,000 schoolchildren, senior citizens and disabled people, as well as scores of private vessels — are expected to converge on the barrier before the royal party leaves from the Festival pier (Royal Festival Hall) at 2.45pm

Already in position in Woolwich Reach will be historic craft from the Maritime Trust, London Fire Brigade boats giving a water display, Royal Navy minesweepers and numerous yachts and other craft.

DIGNITARIES

The Queen and Prince Philip will be met at the pier by Mr Harvey Hinds, chairman of the GLC, who will be chief host for the afternoon. Together with other VIPs, expected to include Agriculture Minister Michael Joplin, the party will sail downriver on the PLA vessel Royal Nore.

The journey to Woolwich should take 45 minutes, the boat sailing through the bar-

rier and the party disembarking at the Barrier Gardens pier where they will be met by GLC Leader Ken Livingstone and other GLC politicians, civic dignitaries and senior officials involved with the barrier and its construction.

MASSIVE

At a short ceremony before 3,000 invited guests, including 1,200 of the barrier workforce and their wives, the Queen will press a button to activate the massive gates and stop the incoming tide. It will take 15 minutes for the gates to rise into position from their concrete sills on the river bed.

While this is happening, the royal party will visit the seventh-floor control room **(Continued on Page FOUR).**

YOUR VOTE ABOLISHED!

THE GLC election due to be held in May next year will be cancelled if the Government's Local Government (Interim Provisions) Bill becomes law.

Instead of a directly-elected local authority democratically chosen to run London-wide services, from May 1985 Londoners will have imposed upon them representatives from borough councils elected for a completely different purpose.

You, the voter, will lose your vote and be denied the right to say through the ballot box whether or not you want the policies of the present administration to continue.

The Bill says that the boroughs should appoint

representatives to serve on the GLC in the transitional period before the GLC is abolished and these appointments should reflect the balance of the parties in the constituent councils. It lists how many representatives will come from each borough. They total 84, the number of parliamentary constituencies in London.

Frightening

At present 17 boroughs are Conservative-controlled, three are joint Conservative and Liberal, one Liberal and 12 Labour.

The interim GLC could therefore be composed of 56 Conservatives and 28 Labour and Alliance Members. At present there are 48 Labour, 41 Conservatives, two SDP and one Liberal.

Ken Livingstone GLC

Leader, described the Bill as "an affront to democracy".

He said: "For the first time in the peacetime history of this country we are faced with the frightening prospect of a British election being cancelled.

"Londoners are to be denied one of their most precious liberties — the right to elect and sack the people who govern them.

"For 11 months London would be ruled by a body of nominated borough councillors with absolutely no mandate from the people. The running of London will pass from Labour to Conservative control without the voters deciding.

"I appeal to all Londoners, whatever their political views, whatever they think about the GLC, to unite and fight for their basic democratic right to vote."

DAILY STAR

THURSDAY, JUNE 7, 1984   **16p**   (17p C.I.s)   . Printed in London

DAILY STAR TRIBUTE TO THE FALLEN HEROES

THE PROUDEST DAY

● TWO PICTURES yesterday summed up the sacrifice of the men who died winning the battle of Normandy. FOR AMERICA, President Reagan and his wife Nancy walk gently among the tombstones of their country's fallen heroes.

FOR BRITAIN, the Queen shares the pride of the D-Day widows, 53 of whom were flown over to Bayeux for the ceremony honouring the dead. Among them was Elsie Johnson, 63, a childless widow whose husband died at the age of 27, just a month after the landings.

Like all the widows, Mrs. Johnson has never remarried. She spoke for them all when she said: "I never found anyone as lovely as him."

D-Day Special : Pages 13, 14, 15 and 16

Homage . . . Reagan and Nancy among the tombstones

Honour . . . the Queen chats with D-Day widows with happy memories of Britain's heroes

WELL DONE MY SON! DERBY SPECIAL: PAGE 3

TV star Rossiter is dead
—see Page 3

OUR GRACIOUS QUEEN: Insulted by Canadian papers

DON'T BE SO BLOODY RUDE!

Daily Mirror MR. K!

(If you will pardon an olde English phrase)

DON'T BE SO BLOODY RUDE!

FIRST: Message to Krushchev

WE have a message today for those Canadian newspapers which insulted our Queen: DON'T BE SO BLOODY RUDE!

In astonishingly personal attacks, they accused the Queen, who is visiting their country, of being dowdy and boring.

They said her make-up was too heavy, her hats were too awful . . . and her legs "had visible veins."

HOW DARE THEY?

Already the attacks have outraged many Canadians.

Once before we had to remind someone not to be rude.

That was in 1960, when Mr Krushchev, then the Soviet leader, made a threatening outburst against the United States at a Summit meeting in Paris.

Today for a very different reason we are proud to do it again.

Marje's message to our Queen's Canadian critics — see Page 5

Daily Mail

TUESDAY, APRIL 22, 1986 — 20p

Royal Birthday Souvenir

6,000 children greet the Queen with daffodils

WHAT A BLOOMING BIRTHDAY!

More pictures on Pages 2, 3, 5 and Centre Pages

THE smile that says it all... the Queen collects daffodils from some of the 6,000 children who gathered at Buckingham Palace yesterday to deliver — in song — the nation's greetings on her 60th birthday.

Daily Mail

THURSDAY, JULY 24, 1986

20p

THE KISS

Picture : MIKE FORSTER

THEY knew what the people wanted, all right. Andrew cupped a hand to his ear and Sarah smiled when the words washed up to her.

A huge crowd, a quarter of a million, saw them on the balcony and then the chant rushed down the Mall and burst in all the space by Buckingham Palace. 'We want a kiss, we want a kiss'.

By JOHN EDWARDS

Now there was a look in the couple's eyes, a happy look, and he reached to her and their lips got closer and then they kissed.

They kissed for 500 million people in front of television sets all over the world. They kissed because now it is a convention of the Royal Wedding. And the balcony of Buckingham Palace, where the Royals have rejoiced to victories in far away places and celebrated momentous events in our history is now a place for kissing.

They could not have got away without it. There

was a roar, a giant swell of noise, cheers mixed with clapping, shouts with squeals. Andrew and Sarah had sealed it with a kiss.

The flutter of the crowd's hearts steadied. There was a gush of tears. And there was a brightness in the eyes of the couple on the balcony and then a laugh because they had played their happy part in the day of fun.

Balloons, heart-shaped balloons, drifted free and passed them on their way to the sky.

The Queen turned and her unmoved face opened briefly and she smiled, too. The Princess of Wales, Harry nearly two, a scene-stealer already, squirming in her arms, laughed shyly. Harry reached for Sarah.

On the balcony yesterday, at 2 p.m. between the showers, the sun drove down at the Royal Family and they all turned to see the kiss that confirmed the

Turn to Page 3, Col 2

Turn to Page 3, Col 2

SUNDAY Mirror

October 26, 1986   FORWARD WITH BRITAIN   ★ 28p

What do we want THE MONARCHY OR SOAP OPERA ??

TURN TO PAGE TWO

DAILY EXPRESS

Tuesday December 23 1986   20p   ★★★   THE VOICE OF BRITAIN

My wonderful memories of David

Widow of death-crash MP opens her heart

THE WIDOW of Liberal MP David Penhaligon told yesterday of her "wonderful memories".

Hours after learning her husband had been killed in a car crash near their home at Truro, Cornwall, Mrs Annette Penhaligon said:

"I have got some lovely memories. We were lucky that we were able to spend some time together last week, when we went to London for the Alliance ball with David Steel and his wife.

"He would want to be remembered as a Cornishman who wanted to do something for Cornwall.

Lovely

"His proudest achievement was to be able to get aid which helped to save something of the tin industry in Cornwall."

Mrs Penhaligon was being comforted at her home by her children, Matthew, 14, and Anna, nine.

She said she used to tease her husband about not being serious enough.

But she went on: "What he managed to do was to make a person who had no interest in politics take notice of what was happening. He was always realistic and he knew exactly how he was doing and what he was doing.

"He was a lovely father, and at least we have wonderful memories of him."

Mrs Panhaligon said her husband recently recorded an edition of Desert Island Discs with Michael Parkinson of which he was "very proud".

The BBC will wait until the new year to decide whether to broadcast the programme.

Mr Penhaligon's car was hit by a van out of control on an icy hill.

People's politician: Page 5
Express Opinion: Page 8

David Penhaligon with his wife Annette

Queen: I will not ride again

Linda walking out with her toy boy Didier

THE QUEEN has vowed never to ride a horse in public again—and that means the end of one of the most popular and traditional aspects of royal pageantry.

For no longer will the Queen be seen riding side-saddle during the annual Trooping the Colour ceremony.

Instead she will make the journey from Buckingham Palace to Horse Guards Parade by carriage.

An era has come to an end because the Queen has decided it is time for her faithful mount, the black mare Burmese, to take a well-earned retirement.

Burmese is still fit but is now nearly 24—which is 90 in human terms.

There is a danger the horse could collapse and this may have

By ASHLEY WALTON

caused concern over the Queen's security.

But Buckingham Palace said yesterday that the decision had not been made on security grounds.

A spokesman explained that the monarch simply did not want to start again with a new horse.

FOND

It takes at least four years to train a side-saddle horse and this would mean much time-consuming practice for a ceremony which is conducted just once a year.

The Queen, who will be 61 in April, has been riding Burmese for the last 18 years and is known to be extremely fond of her. The horse

Page 2 Column 5

The Queen on Burmese

Ooh, la, la! Linda's toy boy

DALLAS star Linda Gray, looking like a love-struck teenager, enjoys a night out with her new "toy boy."

He is 25-year-old Frenchman Didier Fitoussi.

The couple, who plan to spend Christmas in France, had eyes only for each other as they walked hand-in-hand, embraced and laughed the night away at a club.

A young-looking 45, Linda seems to have no worries about dating a playboy only a few years older than her son.

Since her marriage to artist Ed Thrasher broke up recently after 21 years, she has talked about the advantages of being an older woman.

She told the Express:

"Younger men are much more supportive, they're encouraging, and they're fascinated by older women."

Her son, Jeff, is 21, and her daughter, Kelly, is 19.

Dallas fashion: Page 13
Jean Rook: Page 9

Worried Queen blocks move to privatise historic Royal homes

'LEAVE MY PALACES ALONE'

HAMPTON COURT PALACE . . . to remain a "place of dignity".

by Lesley Yarranton

A PROPOSAL to hand over the running of London's Royal palaces and parks to commercial organisations under the new Civil Service structure has been vet oed by the Royal family, it was revealed today.

The Department of the Environment said that an original proposal to hive off Royal palaces, such as Hampton Court, and parks to independent commercial organisations was rejected after the Queen made it known that the Royal family wished to maintain its links with them through her ministers.

It is understood that the Queen made her wishes known to the Parliamentary committee set up to propose the list of Whitehall reforms after fears that too much commercialism could lead to exploitation of the Royal sites and buildings, many of which date back to medieval times.

Commercial ventures aimed at making the landmarks more profitable, introduced by Whitehall, will now be checked closely by ministers to ensure they are maintained as "places of dignity and respect".

The reforms could mean increased charges for visitors, more intensive marketing and moves to make more profit from restaurants, kiosks and other park facilities.

But entrance tickets to palaces would remain at an affordable price. There were no plans to introduce charges on entry to any Royal park and every effort would be made to ensure that any new venture would not result in the sites becoming too commercialised.

Mr Nicholas Ridley, Secretary of State for the Environment, announced within hours of Mrs Thatcher's statement on the Whitehall reforms that he hoped to have the Royal palaces under agency management by April next year.

The 900 staff at the Department of Environment who currently deal with the palaces and parks are to be transferred to the new agency.

Jobs switch

Buildings which will be affected include Hampton Court and its gardens and park, the Tower of London, the State apartments and court dress collection at Kensington Palace, the Banqueting House and Kew Palace.

Another agency will run all the parks—Hyde Park, Kensington Gardens, St James's Park, Green Park, Regent's Park, Primrose Hill, Richmond Park, Brompton Cemetery, Greenwich Park and Bushey Park.

The cost of running the parks and palaces runs into more than £20 million and far exceeds income from visitors but the agency will be expected to "get the maximum revenue it can" and charge visitors "a marketable price".

A Department of Environment spokesman said: "They will still be treated as Royal buildings and parks and any developments put forward for consideration will be carefully judged so that they could not be accused of being too commercial. There is no danger of seeing Hyde Park turned into a funfair.

"It is a case of more professional expertise being applied to the running of the parks and palaces but none of those making the decisions are likely to find themselves accused of tasteless exploitation."

Londoners have frequently complained in the past about the shortage of refreshment facilities in Royal Parks and the shabby state of many of the palaces and museums.

But the extent to which restaurants and cafes in them will be improved is as yet unclear

PREACHING A PROTEST . . . Rev Beryl Morgan

Woman turns heart boy's funeral into a protest

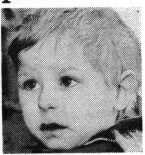

MATTHEW COLLIER . . . "Great courage."

THE funeral of hole-in-the-heart boy Matthew Collier today became as much a political event as a tragic family ceremony when Deacon Beryl Morgan preached a sermon calling for more money for the NHS.

Four-year-old Matthew died on Sunday, a month after finally having an operation which had been cancelled three times, and which his parents had tried to persuade the High Court to order West Midlands health authority to perform.

Miss Morgan told Matthew's parents at the church near his home in Willenhall:" More money is undoubtedly needed to treat people awaiting surgery."

See Page Three

Kinnock bullets protest

NEIL KINNOCK today produced two bullets from his pocket and accused Israeli soldiers of filing them down to inflict serious wounds on Palestinians.

And he revealed in Jerusalem that he had produced them as evidence of brutality during a dinner with Israel's Defence Minister, Yitzhak Rabin.

Mr. Kinnock's gesture brought his Middle East tour to a dramatic climax.

See Page Two.

Gray

Now Land Rover are going on Strike

Don't tell me — they want more money and green wellies

FORDS GO BACK

Daily  Mail

TUESDAY, APRIL 22, 1986

20p

6,000 children greet the Queen with daffodils

WHAT A BLOOMING BIRTHDAY!

THE cheering thousands said it with flowers yesterday : Happy 60th birthday, Your Majesty. The Queen, refusing to let either rain or fears of terrorist attack ruin her day, was inundated with blooms. In the afternoon (top left) daffodils cascaded into her arms after she met some of the 6,000 children who sang a royal birthday song outside the Palace. And

More pictures on Pages 2, 3, 5 and Centre Pages

last night bouquet after bouquet was pressed on her as (left) she headed for a gala show in her honour at the Royal Opera House, Covent Garden. In a walkabout, so many people gave gifts of flowers that a policewoman had to help carry them. It was a great day for the Queen. Everyone wanted to make it even more special.

DAILY Mirror

Thursday, June 2, 1988   FORWARD WITH BRITAIN   ★★★   CHANNEL ISLANDS 21p   **20p**

MENACE OF THE SLEEPY PILOTS

WEARY pilots who doze off at the controls of holiday jets are putting the lives of thousands of passengers at risk.

The charter pilots say airlines are forcing them to fly too many hours to curb costs in the cut-throat travel business.

Pilots have admitted falling asleep on the final approach to landing. In one amazing case all THREE crewmen nodded off. Ex-captain Christopher Rigby told the Daily Mirror: "It will take a Boeing 737 hitting the ground at four in the morning with a knackered pilot at the controls before something is done."

● Full story — Pages 4 and 5

ONE'S WON!

Queen's joy at Derby Day win

WITH a winning grin, the Queen raised her arms in delight at the races yesterday.

She looked as pleased as a punter who'd won a packet when 15-8 favourite Waajib triumphed in the thrilling 2.45 at Epsom.

The Queen, in a sunny yellow outfit for Derby day, was watching the Diomed Stakes with Prince and Princess Michael of Kent.

She had flapped her arms with anxiety as Waajib fell behind.

But, still holding her racecard, she flung them aloft as jockey Michael Roberts brought the horse through to win.

Later in the Derby meeting, her eye was caught by an unlisted runner.

But when she saw he was a streaker, she laughed and quickly looked away.

One simply isn't impressed by bareback racing. Even when one's had a winner!

TRIUMPH: The favourite wins a thrilling race — and the Queen flings her arms in delight.   Picture KENT GAVIN

. . And that wasn't all that streaked past the post SEE PAGES 2 and 3

THE Sun

Thursday, April 6, 1989   **20p**   Yesterday's sale 4,269,722   Thought: Whodunnit, Ma'am?

PALACE THIEF STEALS ANNE'S LETTERS

Anne . . . letters were hand-delivered and signed by the same person

● **Sun to the rescue**

● **Big security probe**

● **Fear of blackmail**

By JOHN KAY

A THIEF has stolen letters belonging to Princess Anne from INSIDE Buckingham Palace.

The four letters, all in the same black ink handwriting, were sent anonymously to The Sun.

Last night, after we handed them over to Scotland Yard, a major investigation into Palace security was launched.

The head of the Royal Protection Squad, Deputy Assistant Commissioner

SUN EXCLUSIVE

John Cracknell, took charge of the probe.

It is the worst breach of security at Buckingham Palace since intruder Michael Fagan sat on the Queen's bed in 1982.

SPIRITED

The letters had been hand-delivered to the Princess without going through the Post Office.

They were all signed by the same person.

Somehow, they were spirited out of Anne's private quarters at the Palace.

And last night horrified security chiefs were asking if the thief had:

SMUGGLED other letters or documents out of the Palace.

EXPOSED Princess Anne to the risk of blackmail, or

STOLEN itineraries or secrets which could reach the hands of terrorists.

An expert on the Royal Family said: "It is unbelievable that private letters addressed to Princess Anne

could possibly find their way to the press.

"It is among the worst Royal security breaches imaginable."

The Sun told police it would not publish or divulge the contents of the letters.

RISK

NO money was handed over by the newspaper and we do **NOT** know the identity of the person who delivered them to our offices at Wapping, East London.

Last night Mr Cracknell praised The Sun for its deci-

Continued on Page Four

£82,000 LOTTO-Numbers Page 4 ● **£31,000 BINGO-Numbers Page 26**

DAILY STAR

JUST WHAT YOU DIDN'T EXPECT!

SATURDAY, APRIL 8, 1989   20p (21p Cls)

Britain's £55m flutter on the National

By FRANK CURRAN and MARK CHRISTY

TODAY'S Grand National will be Britain's biggest-ever betting bonanza.

Punters are expected to plunge a staggering £55 million on the Royal Aintree spectacle —vitually £1-a-head for every member of the population.

And the housewives' favourite will be mud-loving Bonanza Boy which has backed from 25—1 to 10—1.

He will be ridden by record-breaking champion jockey Peter Scudamore whose father Michael won on Oxo 30 years ago.

Security

Ladbrokes spokesman Mike Dillon said: "With every drop of rain we get a flood of money for Bonanza Boy, who loves soft going.

"He has been backed down from all prices and we will lose a fortune if he wins."

And the biggest ever security operation will be mounted for the visit of the Duke and Duchess of York.

Andy and Fergie will be guarded by an army of Special Branch officers when they walk the 4½-mile course this morning.

Dozens of plainclothes officers have been told to pay special attention to thousands of Irishmen among the expected 100,000 crowd.

Upset

They fear IRA terrorists will try to slip through the huge security net.

Ladbrokes face a quarter-million-pounds pay-out if rank outsider Mr. Chris romps to victory.

For his owner Cyprus businessman Chris Liveras bet £250 at 1,000—1 in 1983—before the 10-year-old had even seen a racecourse.

Last night Mr. Chris, who is bottom of the handicap, was still a 1,000—1 chance.

Mr. Dillon said: "It would be the biggest upset in the history

Turn to Page Two, Col 2

We'll meet again...Mr. Gorbachev shakes hands with the Queen after their historic Windsor meeting

SEE YOU IN MOSCOW

● RUSSIAN leader Mikhail Gorbachev crowned his rip-roaring British visit by inviting the Queen to Moscow yesterday —and she said Yes.

● Gorby made his historic offer during a laughter-filled lunch with the Royals at Windsor Castle. And, as he left with wife Raisa, Gorby smiled and said to the Queen: "Goodbye and see you soon . . . in Moscow."

THAT WAS A GOOD LAUGH: Pages 4 & 5

Daily Mail

FRIDAY, MAY 5, 1989   22p

New twist in the stolen Royal letters row

PALACE FURY OVER MAID'S CLAIMS

By PAUL HENDERSON

THE Princess Royal's personal maid was facing possible prosecution by Buckingham Palace last night after giving an extraordinary interview about how police quizzed her over Anne's stolen letters.

Linda Joyce denies knowing anything about the letters, written to the Princess by royal equerry Commander Tim Laurence.

She also tells of her sometimes stormy relationship with Anne — and her hurt at the way the Princess and Palace insiders have cold-shouldered her since her questioning.

Socialist

The 30-year-old maid's account breaks protocol by giving an unprecedented glimpse of the workings of a royal residence, and Palace advisers are furious.

A Palace spokesman said: 'She signed a document of confidentiality three-and-a-half years ago and had a year's break in employment. We are looking into whether or not she re-signed the document.'

Miss Joyce, who says she is 'a good old-fashioned Socialist,' gave the interview to the Left-wing New Statesman and Society magazine. She reveals that in her £5,000-a-year position as Anne's dresser she had a

My life with Anne — See Page 5

close working relationship with the Princess, almost always being the first person to see her in the mornings. But it could be turbulent, and sometimes ended in the maid slamming doors. She says she made her Socialist views known and was considered an odd choice as a royal functionary.

'You do get angry with people because they do something that affects you,' she says in the interview. 'And I can't say that I am so placid that I never ever get angry with her ... I voice my opinions and don't tug my forelock.'

The four letters from Commander Laurence, which were passed to the Sun newspaper, were taken from the Princess's briefcase. Miss Joyce says she had access to the briefcase, but had never seen the letters.

She leaves her Palace job today, having given notice at the start of the year — long before the letters vanished.

The man who quizzed Miss Joyce, Detective Chief Superintendent Roy Ramm, of the Yard's Serious Crimes Branch, was at Buckingham Palace last week interviewing other household staff.

An officer involved in the inquiry said: "The investigation is continuing. We are still seeing a lot of people.'

Yard chiefs are shortly expected to send their report on the case to the Director of Public Prosecutions.

Linda Joyce: Stormy relationship with Anne
Picture: STEVE DOUGLASS

Maggie faces Labour votes shock

By GORDON GREIG and JOHN DEANS

LABOUR is set for victory today in the Vale of Glamorgan by-election.

An exit poll by the BBC last night suggests Neil Kinnock's man could win the seat by the same majority the Tories won it in 1987 — 6,000-plus.

It will be the third by-election seat they have captured from the Conservatives since Mrs Thatcher came to power in 1979.

But last night, as results from the county council elections came in — and Mrs Thatcher celebrated ten years in power — the Tories swept into a three-point opinion poll lead nationally over Labour.

And as the Premier entertained Cabinet ministers and their wives to an anniversary dinner at Downing Street, the survey also confirmed her personal backing is still way ahead of Mr Kinnock's.

Morale

The Gallup poll, in today's Daily Telegraph, shows last month's position just about reversed. Then, Labour went 2.5 per cent ahead, the first time they had been in front for over a year.

The Tories have 40.5 per cent support, Labour is on 37.5 per cent, Paddy Ashdown's Democrats are stuck at 10 per cent, and Dr David Owen's tiny SDP at 7 per cent.

The findings will boost Conservative morale at a time when the Government is facing trouble over inflation, high mortgages and NHS reform.

On a bright, warm day across most of England and Wales, an estimated nine million people turned out to vote in the 47 county council polls.

Election results —

ISLE of WIGHT

SLD 23, C 15, Ind 4, Green 1
SLD gain 1 from C and 2 from Ind. C gain 3 from SLD and 2 from Ind. Ind gain 1 from C and 2 from SLD.
No change

STAFFORDSHIRE

Lab 50, C 28, SLD 2, R 2
Lab gain 2 from SLD and 1 from C, C gain 1 from Lab and 1 from SLD, SLD gain 1 from C, R gain 2 from C.
No change

DURHAM

Lab 56, C 7, SLD 5, Ind 4
Lab gain 4 from Ind, 1 from SDP, 2 from SLD. C gain 1 from SLD. Ind gain 1 from Lab.
No change

Mark hoped they would stay together but the Princess decided to end the sham marriage

ANNE WANTED HER FREEDOM

BY RICHARD KAY, Royal Correspondent

PRINCESS ANNE chose the freedom to lead her own life instead of being trapped in a phoney marriage — against the wishes of Captain Mark Phillips.

Tired of the years of pretence, she asked her husband to release her but he wanted to stay together, if only for the sake of appearances.

But after weeks of agonising and talking to the Queen, the Princess decided that the time had come to separate. Captain Phillips reluctantly agreed.

Although Buckingham Palace stressed last night that there were no plans for divorce, it is thought inevitable that, after being separated for the legal minimum of two years, divorce will follow should either find another love.

Anne, still wearing her wedding ring, went about her duties yesterday as the British representative at an International Olympic Committee meeting in Puerto Rico. She smiled calmly and showed no sign of the tensions of the break-up.

Captain Phillips, meanwhile, was locked behind the doors of the house he must now leave.

Discreet

Under the terms of their separation, he will move from stately Gatcombe House to a pair of run-down stone cottages tucked away in a discreet corner of the huge Gloucestershire estate. From that base, he will stay in touch with children Peter, 11, and eight-year-old Zara, and run the estate and the horse trials which he set up with Anne in happier days.

Yesterday the heartache behind the broken marriage contrasted sharply with Buckingham Palace's formal, 26-word statement declaring that it was all over.

Captain Phillips's 69-year-old father confirmed that Mark believed that separation was not the ideal solution. Major Phillips, a widower, emphasised that the decision to split up had not been mutual, saying that his son would have been happy to continue the marriage.

But it was clear last night that Anne's will prevailed because she was so determined to make a fresh start.

Even though there are no immediate plans for divorce, it will pave the way for her to remarry. What remains uncertain is whether the Princess's close friendship with the

THE ROYAL BREAK-UP

Winners and losers – Pages 2,3
A father's grief – Page 5
Lynda Lee-Potter – Pages 6,7
Why it failed – Centre Pages

Queen's equerry, Commander Tim Laurence, hastened the break-up.

He spent almost two weeks with the Royal Family on holiday at Balmoral and was there when the final separation arrangements and the decision to 'go public' were made. The 35-year-old commander, who shared a riverside picnic on the royal estate with the Princess last week, kept silent last night at home in Winchester, Hampshire.

For Captain Phillips, the only indication of future plans came from his father, who insisted that any speculation about Mark's involvement with another woman was not a factor in the parting.

The official end to the marriage came in the emotionless pronouncement from the Palace.

It read: 'Her Royal Highness the Princess Royal and Captain Mark Phillips have decided to separate on terms agreed between them. There are no plans for divorce proceedings.' The statement, approved by the Queen, who is still at Balmoral, was issued at midday.

It closed years of speculation over a marriage which began in splendour in Westminster Abbey in 1973 and ended as a sham.

Senior royal aides insisted that the decision

Turn to Page 2, Col 6

Anne, calm and smiling, in Puerto Rico yesterday

£7M PAY DEAL FOR THE QUEEN

THE Queen is to receive a 55 per cent pay rise next year. It is the first instalment of a ten-year, £100million, fixed income deal announced last night by Mrs Thatcher.

Instead of having to go cap in hand to the taxpayer each spring, the Queen will have her Civil List award set at the same annual sum for the rest of the decade.

By JOHN DEANS, Political Correspondent

Opportunity

Other members of the Royal Family will also get large pay rises, then the same sum annually until the year 2000, in the package unveiled by the Prime Minister in the Commons.

As a result, Prince Edward's present annual award of £20,000 will increase five times to £100,000 next year.

The Queen Mother, who celebrates her 90th birthday next month, can look forward to her pay rising from £439,500 to £640,000 in 1991; Prince Philip will receive £360,000 next year instead of this year's £245,000; the Duke of York £250,000 instead of the current

Her 1990 payment of £5.09million — to cover staff salaries and the cost of running the royal households — will rise to £7.9million on January 1 next year. But it will be frozen at that level each year until the turn of the century.

£169,000; and the Princess Royal £230,000 rather than £154,500.

Overall, it will add up to almost £100million being provided to the Royals over the next ten years, which works out to the equivalent of an annual rise of around 7.5 per cent.

The shake-up in the Civil List was ordered by the Prime Minister and approved by the Queen in an attempt to end the annual Budget Day rumpus over royal pay.

Reverting to the system which operated for 200 years, until it was scrapped in 1975, will also give the Queen and her family the opportunity to plan their spending programmes on a more rational basis.

However, the change — approved in advance by Opposition leader Neil Kinnock — could also mean some belt-tightening at the Palace, despite the big initial leap in

Turn to Page 2, Col. 6

SISTER CATHERINE DIES WITH PCs

Sister Catherine Dunne: Dedicated her life to others

Wrecked: Sister Catherine's car lies by the roadside

Nun is killed in IRA bomb horror

By PAUL HARRIS

A NUN and three policemen were killed by a massive IRA bomb yesterday.

Sister Catherine Dunne was caught in the blast as she drove a woman social worker home.

The bomb, a landmine thought to contain 1,000lb of explosives, hurled the RUC constables' unmarked Sierra over a hedge into a field.

It left a 20ft crater across the Killylea Road on the outskirts of Armagh city.

Police said the terrorists, who triggered the device by wire from a nearby bungalow, must have seen the nun's Metro as it approached in the opposite direction from the RUC men.

Dublin-born Sister Catherine, 37, died as she was rushed to hospital by a passing ambulance. The social worker was treated for serious injuries.

Devoted

The IRA's North Armagh Brigade said it carried out the bombing, which brought a wave of revulsion and condemnation last night.

Sister Catherine, a member of the Roman Catholic Sister of St Louis order, was based at a convent in nearby Middletown, where she was assistant deputy at a girls' correctional centre. The woman with her was a staff member there.

Sister Fiona Fullam, the order's superior, said last night: 'We are heartbroken. Sister Catherine was totally devoted to the girls, who loved her and loved her work.'

Local parish priest Father Michael Toal said the nun had dedicated her life to helping others. 'She was a bright lively girl who had a long career

Turn to Page 2, Col 3

SUNDAY Mirror

October 21, 1990   LAST WEEK'S SALE: 2,929,263   ★   40p

INSIDE CHARLES AND DI'S MARRIAGE

At last, the sad truth is revealed about Royal rift

WORLD EXCLUSIVE

● **THE MOST** intimate insight into Prince Charles and Princess Diana's strained marriage is given today by the Sunday Mirror. One of their closest and most trusted confidantes lifts the public veil to show the Royal couple locked into a stale "working relationship."

● While Charles still selfishly acts like a bachelor Prince with his devoted circle of titled and showbiz friends, Diana finds herself increasingly squeezed out of his social calendar.

● In an astonishing expose of the Royal marriage rift, the confidante reveals the tensions of life inside Kensington Palace and the separate lives that the couple lead.

Full Story – Pages 4 and 5

EXCLUSIVE: Cash victory of AIDS victims –SEE PAGE 2

Army girl at war

1945

Her young play

1991

QUEEN IN CRISIS

83% disgusted by young Royals war effort

RICHARD CREASY

THE Queen is today facing the biggest royal crisis since the Abdication more than 50 years ago.

Her Majesty has watched popular support for the Monarchy slump because of the antics of young Royals during the Gulf War. A Sky TV poll yesterday showed 83 per cent of viewers were "disgusted" with the public behaviour of a privileged few.

More than 2,750 viewers took part, their opinions reflecting the concern expressed by TODAY since December over the leadership given by some members of the Royal family during the conflict in the Gulf.

British men and women are facing death in the service of their country. Yet the nearest a Royal has got to front line action is grouse shooting. Anger mounted at home while Navy pilot Prince Andrew played golf in Spain.

The Duchess of York has enjoyed slap-up meals with Sloane friends. She even squeezed in a skiing holiday on the eve of hostilities. Lord Linley flew out to the Caribbean paradise of Mustique.

The row intensified over the weekend when The Sunday Times branded their behaviour a mixture of "upper class decadence and insensitivity".

Not since the Duke of Windsor gave up the throne for divorcee Mrs Simpson in 1936 has the Royal Family faced such a severe test.

Leading royal expert Harold Brooks-Baker said: "The criticism is entirely justified. It may have come just in time to bring about the dramatic change needed.

"Some of the young Royals must learn they cannot have it both ways, an entirely private lifestyle and the responsibilities and privileges of the Monarchy."

Mr Brooks-Baker, publisher of Burkes Peerage, said: "The criticism certainly reflects the feelings of the British people at this time.

"The Queen has made it very clear what she expects. But some members of the Royal Family have got to take it more seriously.

"The situation is very dangerous. **Turn to Page 6**

I don't dress up like this as a Rula

TURN TO CENTRE PAGES

SOAP SQUAD FREES GULF OIL SLICK BIRDS TO FLY AGAIN

PAGES 4 & 5

THE Sun

Monday, May 13, 1991   **25p**   Audited daily sale for April 3,688,645   Thought: Off with his head

COSTA WILL COST US A BY-ELECTION WIN

LABOUR will lose Thursday's Monmouth by-election because of the "Costa connection," party MPs warned last night.

They fear their hopes of seizing the South Wales seat from the Tories are doomed by Neil

Kinnock's links with fugitive tycoon Charilaos Costa.

The Sun revealed exclusively last week that Mr Costa is being investigated by the Fraud Squad over a missing £10 million.

Full story – Page Two

WHAT THE BUTLER SAW

£5,000 just for dinner
EXCLUSIVE

● BUTLER Patrick Davison and wife Nicki lived in the lap of luxury working for billionaire financier George Soros and his attractive young wife Susan.

● Now the working-class couple—unfairly dismissed over an alleged feud with the new cook—have revealed how their employers blew £5,000 on small dinner parties at London's most lavish home.

PATRICK . . . worked at top home   **SEE CENTRE PAGES**

It's the arling uds of May-jor

By JOHN KAY

PREMIER John Major is arranged to catch up on TV's Larkins — ordering all six Darling Buds of May episodes on video.

Mr Major has been too busy to watch the series which ended its smash-hit run last night.

He has asked makers Yorkshire TV to send tapes of all the shows.

Last night, 18million people tuned into the last episode of the present series as Pop and the other Larkins whooped it up on holiday in France.

Taxes

Mr Major will be able to pick up all the programme's catch-phrases — including Pop's "Perfick".

The Premier said that he and wife Norma were looking forward to watching the Darling Buds.

He told The Sun: "It is a series that seems to have caught the imagination of everyone.

"I'm looking forward to watching it, probably during the Whitsun recess next month."

But when he settles down to watch it, Mr Major may be in for a shock.

Pop, played by David Jason, delights in **NOT** paying a single penny in taxes.

A Downing Street insider said: "I am not sure that Mr Major will approve."

Looking for Mr Perfick — See Page 9

SUN CUT-OUT-AND-KEEP GUIDE FOR A ROOKIE SECURITY GUARD ✂

DEAR CARL,

You refused to allow The Queen into Royal Windsor Horse Show thinking she was an 'old dear who'd got lost.' Keep this photo handy, you might bump into her again

▪ FROM ALL AT THE SUN

By JAMIE PYATT

A SECURITY guard who barred the Queen from the Royal Windsor Horse Show said last night: "I thought she was some old dear who had got lost."

So just in case clueless Carl Shimmin bumps into Her Majesty again, The Sun today prints a reminder of what she looks like for him to cut out and keep.

Carl, 45, failed to recognise the Queen driving a black Vauxhall Carlton.

The rookie guard put up his hand to stop the car and said: "Sorry, love, you can't come in without a sticker."

The Queen replied: "My husband is taking part. I think if you check, I will be allowed to come to watch him."

Carl, in his job only two weeks, said: "I

Continued on Page Two

Royal reminder . . . the Queen looks like this, Carl, in case you forget

Halt . . . bungler Carl Shimmin

The Prince of Wales tells friends: I wanted to give my wife a birthday party. She refused. It's all very embarrassing

CHARLES AND DIANA: CAUSE FOR CONCERN

Charles: Work at Highgrove and an overnight train

Diana: Lunch at Savoy and songs from Phil Collins

by NIGEL DEMPSTER

FRIENDS of the Prince of Wales are furious at reports that he refused to leave Highgrove yesterday to help Princess Diana celebrate her 30th birthday in London.

They say Charles has told them that he offered to host a party for his wife at either Kensington Palace or their country home, whichever the Princess chose. But she told him that she did not want a party at all.

He is said to have pressed the Princess on a number of occasions to let him organise a party but she said she did not want any special celebration. So nothing was organised.

This, coupled with the fact that there are no plans for the couple to spend their tenth wedding anniversary together at the end of the month, is bound to call attention to a coolness in the marriage. Royal circles are genuinely concerned at the comment this will cause.

The Princess left Charles on Sunday evening to drive to London with their younger son Prince Harry — seven in September — and took him to his Notting Hill school yesterday morning.

She lunched at the Savoy Hotel where 380 guests had paid between £400 and £1,000 each to join her in aid of Rainbow House, a children's hospice in Walsall, and was serenaded by Phil Collins.

Last evening, after working on speeches at Highgrove,

Turn to Page 3, Col. 6

DAILY Mirror

Tuesday, August 13, 1991   NEWSPAPER FOR THE NINETIES   Last month's daily sale: 3,626,550 (INCORPORATING THE DAILY RECORD)   25p

£1,000,000 LOTTERY

summer

ARE YOU A WINNER? SEE PAGE 18

WHAT A DI-FUL!

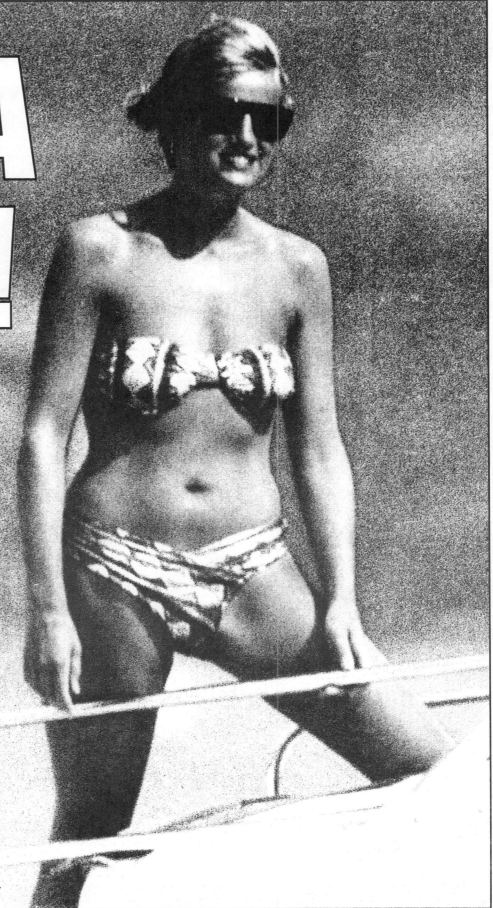

By JAMES WHITAKER

 BREATHTAKING in her bikini, the Royal Family's golden girl stands silhouetted against a sunlit sky.

Princess Diana slipped into the skimpy outfit for a speedboat trip from her Mediterranean holiday yacht.

She donned dark glasses to guard against the dazzling rays that gave her a gorgeous tan.

 And, beaming in anticipation, she got set to plunge into the cool blue sea off the Italian island of Sardinia. The yacht dropped anchor there as the princess neared the end of her cruise with Prince Charles, sons William and Harry – and a happy crowd of shipmates.

For sunshine-loving Diana, the voyage has been a dream –

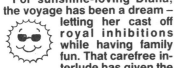 letting her cast off royal inhibitions while having family fun. That carefree interlude has given the 30-year-old princess a new glow. And there are more captivating pictures of her sizzling spree on the CENTRE PAGES.

Picture: MESSIMO SESTINI

★★

Sunday Express

2

TWIN PEAKS STAR SHOWS UP IN AN OUTLAW ROLE Page 37

CLASS APART The Tennant of Coronation Street Centre Pages

THE TOP PEOPLE'S RESTAURANT GETS SET TO REOPEN Page 44

SINGLES Shopping for a partner at the supermarket Page 38

Exhibit One

THAT REGAL POISE: From the hectic days of the Coronation, the Queen has retained all her style and all her grace throughout the tumultuous changes in Britain

by John Julius Norwich

Viscount Norwich, art historian, author and broadcaster

Her reign has lasted 40 years. Now she's really going on show

THE Queen, to mark her 40th year on the throne, is opening her wardrobes, her homes, her photo albums and her archives to help mount a unique exhibition of her reign.

When the display opens in April next year at the Victoria and Albert Museum, it will provide not just a look at her life but a view of Britain, and how we, her subjects, have changed. From the dramatic moments when she went to Africa in 1952 and returned to

Britain as Queen — a smudge of a figure stepping out of an aeroplane on to a wintry tarmac — we will be shown her ruling years set against the vivid panorama of history.

And you will be able to analyse what totally different people we are now in terms of politics, religion, sex, the arts, the clothes we wear and the food we eat. An old vacuum cleaner

will tell you much more than a great tiara. You will see household objects, Palace uniforms, and all aspects of the Queen's work.

All the major events of the Queen's early reign will be shown on old newsreels. You will be amazed by the pompous flatulence of the coverage. In 1952, Press photographers were behind barbed wire 30 yards away. That is

more telling than any single exhibit. The original message that was posted outside Buckingham Palace announcing the death of her father King George VI will herald the start of the exhibition.

Original film footage of the Coronation will be accompanied by the actual music, with commentary by Richard Dimbleby. Against this nostalgic backdrop, visitors will be able to take a close-up view of the Coronation robes. They have not been in public since 1953.

It has not been possible to obtain the original Coronation chair from Westminster Abbey, but instead we will have a 300-year-old **Turn to Page 34**

Turn to Page 34

Sunday Express

2

£4m SPLENDOUR OF GORBACHEV'S PALACE BY THE SEA **Centre Pages**

FRESHERS' WEEK Setting out at university: page 45

WHAT DID LINDA McCARTNEY SAY IN OUR FUN CAPTION CONTEST? Page 35

PEACE TEAM Who's who in the Nobel prize chase: Page 47

No abdication –it's official

Queen approves book which warns of threat to Monarchy

ANIMAL MAGIC: The Queen and Queen Mother at home in 1980. The current corgi crop — Spark, Myth, Fable, Diamond, Kelpie, Pharos and Phoenix — is the tenth generation.

Picture by gracious permission of Her Majesty The Queen

Rehabilitation for Blunt 'a much loved member of the establishment'

by John McEntee

PICTURE EXCLUSIVE

THE Queen, after nearly 40 years on the Throne, has given the clearest indication yet that she will not step aside to make way for the Prince of Wales and plans to remain as sovereign for the rest of her life.

This dramatic confirmation of her commitment to the constitutional Monarchy comes in a lengthy explanation of the implications of abdication, written by a senior member of the Royal Household.

It states: "The voluntary renunciation of the Throne strikes at the root of the Monarchy. It has, therefore, always been regarded as a particularly serious threat to the institution itself."

This section, contained in the authoritative Royal Encyclopedia, to be published later this month by Macmillan, was read in advance by the Queen. It stresses that only King Edward VIII ever stood aside.

The dissertation refers to recent suggestions that the Queen, now 65, should move over to relieve her workload and allow Prince Charles to succeed.

But it concludes: "Proposals of this kind while well meant, do not really fit into the traditions or mystique of the monarchy as it has evolved in Britain.

"They would tend to destroy some of the

Turn to Page 34

INSIDE: TV & RADIO GUIDE Pages 63 & 64 ● TWO PAGES OF BOOKS Pages 40 & 41 ● TRAVEL Pages 51 & 53 ● FILMS Page 60

NIGEL DEMPSTER was born in 1941 and educated at Sherborne. He was a broker at Lloyd's of London and in the Stock Exchange before joining the Earl of Kimberley in his Mayfair public relations firm. In 1963 he entered Fleet Street with the *Daily Express*, moving to the *Daily Mail* in 1971. After working as their American correspondent, he started his world-renowned Diary on 8 October 1973 and also became the diarist for the *Mail on Sunday* in 1986. He broadcasts regularly for BSkyB-TV, ABC-TV (America) and Canadian and Australian stations and lives in Chelsea with his wife Camilla, daughter of the Eleventh Duke of Leeds, their daughter Louise and 5 Pekinese dogs.

JOHN FROST has been collecting historic newspapers for 50 years, and his unique private library has an astonishing 50,000 editions dating back to 1630. His collection of Royalty includes the Coronation and death of every British monarch since George II, and practically every Royal event this century.

He is much in demand as a lecturer on Press history, with frequent TV and radio broadcasts, and supplies period newspapers to TV and film companies and book publishers. John Frost is married with two sons and lives in New Barnet, Hertfordshire.